MW01076999

EXPLORING THE WORLD'S
FOUNDATION IN CHRIST

EXPLORING THE WORLD'S FOUNDATION IN CHRIST

An Introduction to the Writings
and Thought of Donald J. Keefe, S.J.

Edited and with commentary
by Kevin A. McMahon

IGNATIUS PRESS   SAN FRANCISCO

With the exception of Scripture quotations found in excerpts by Donald J. Keefe, S.J., all Scripture quotations are from the Revised Standard Version of the Bible—Second Catholic Edition (Ignatius Edition), copyright © 2006 National Council of the Churches of Christ in the United States of America. Used by permission. All rights reserved worldwide.

Cover art:
Jesus Christ, Pantocrator
(Detail from the Deesis mosaic)
Hagia Sophia, Istanbul
Wikimedia Commons image

Cover design by Riz Boncan Marsella

Text by Kevin A. McMahon © 2024 Ignatius Press, San Francisco
Text by Donald J. Keefe, S.J., reprinted with permission
All rights reserved
ISBN 978-1-62164-643-3 (PB)
ISBN 978-1-64229-280-0 (eBook)
Library of Congress Control Number 2023949789
Printed in the United States of America ∞

To my treasured Mary

CONTENTS

EDITOR'S PREFACE

For all the important work produced over the years in American Catholic systematic theology, few scholars have sought to demonstrate the intrinsic connection that unites the Catholic doctrines concerning God, creation, redemption, and salvation into a comprehensive view of reality—and more, to formulate a metaphysics that can account for this view. Donald Keefe was one of the few. His distinctive contribution came from a rigorous analysis of each and every point in the Chalcedonian declaration that there is one Lord Jesus Christ, the only begotten Son of God, through whom all things were made, and his insistence that the full truth of this statement is actualized in the Eucharistic worship of the Church.

The background required for this sort of architectonic task is enormous, and the work produced is necessarily technical, as evidenced by the writings of the great European theologians, both Protestant and Catholic, like Karl Barth and Paul Tillich, Hans Urs von Balthasar and Karl Rahner. In 1975, Gerald McCool sought to make the work of Rahner, whose writing style was notoriously dense ("Somebody should translate my brother into German", the patristics scholar Hugo Rahner declared), more accessible by compiling a series of short excerpts from what were typically long and ponderous articles and supplying each with a brief introduction. He called it *A Rahner Reader*. To keep it as simple as possible, he reprinted the material, which originally had appeared in largely academic journals, without the original footnotes, some of which had gone on for more than a page.

In the case of Donald Keefe, too, a dense style, expressing what often are even more dense ideas, presuming familiarity with the long history of philosophy and theology, can overtax even a sophisticated reader. Yet consideration of any of the central problematics in Catholic doctrinal theology is that much poorer when Keefe's insights are not part of the discussion. The purpose of this book is to offer a remedy, and McCool's *Rahner Reader* has provided the model. Each of the following chapters consists of one or more selections from Keefe's work on a particular topic, with opening remarks that are intended to give some helpful background to the reader. There are three exceptions. Chapters 5 and 6 offer an overview of the theological metaphysics that Keefe develops in his seminal book, *Covenantal Theology: The Eucharistic Order of History*. There are no extended excerpts from Keefe himself; however, the content in those two chapters follows the order in Keefe's book itself, hence they can be taken as something of a reader's guide, a kind of vade mecum. The third exception is the final chapter. It is simply a reprint of the article whose title it bears, "Death as Worship".

In a further nod to *A Rahner Reader*, none of the selections chosen includes Keefe's original footnotes, despite the fact that very often, especially in the case of *Covenantal Theology*, one finds there important expansions of his argument and an astonishing body of bibliographical material. Even in the introductions to selections, notes are, for the sake of simplicity, kept to a minimum. The exception, again, is chapters 5 and 6, where the interest is to provide the reader with explanatory references to primary sources; even then, references to secondary sources are commonly limited to a single standard text. Bibliographical citations for selections are placed in unnumbered footnotes at the bottom of the page, and occasionally footnotes are also used to explain an allusion that Keefe has made in his text. Typically, however, information judged helpful to the reader is placed within brackets in the body of the selection. This includes translations of the Latin phrases with which Keefe's work is replete—a vestige of his Jesuit training.

Although some stylistic changes were made to selections for the sake of consistency, texts largely appear exactly as they were first published. This is true not only, for example, of the use of an upper or lower case "e" for the term "Eucharistic", but even of the use of feminine or neuter pronouns for "Church". The choice is quite significant, yet Keefe will employ both.

ACKNOWLEDGMENTS

Gratitude for the publication of even an introductory work on someone as challenging as Donald Keefe is due, first and foremost, to one person, Father Joseph Fessio, S.J., whose support for the idea was immediate and unflagging. I owe immeasurable thanks to my production manager, Kathy Mosier, and to the entire team, including the copyeditor, proofreader, typesetter, and others, who caught in my text a truly humbling number of misspellings, ungrammatical usages, confusing references, and pure typographical errors. Their alert eyes reading through dense material has made this a far better work than I first composed. In the same vein, very special thanks are due to William Haggerty of Gannon University. Dr. Haggerty, one of only a handful of philosophers who have grappled seriously with Keefe's thought, generously read through the drafts of several early chapters—most importantly chapters 5 and 6, which treat Keefe's effort to construct a theological metaphysics—and offered invaluable suggestions for clarification and improvement. Needless to say, with all this assistance, the flaws in writing and argument that still remain are to be attributed to me alone.

In addition to Dr. Haggerty, I would like to thank two other close friends, Dr. Daniel Hauser and Dr. Montague Brown. Dan and I were doctoral students together at Marquette University. Arriving just after Keefe himself, we were immediately drawn by his remarkable mind and his systematic interest in the Eucharist. Monte, my colleague at Saint Anselm College, had never heard of Keefe before reading his *Covenantal Theology*, but he became one of Keefe's closest students and friends. There is much I owe to the long discussions with Dan and Monte during the many drives to visit Keefe over the years, first at Dunwoodie and later at Fordham University, as we would puzzle our way through the brilliant but often arcane insights that Keefe would fire out over glasses of whiskey.

Above all, I am grateful to my son, John, and my daughter, Kara. Daily I am borne up by the gift of their devotion, by their enthusiasm for life, and by their love of the Catholic faith. But my deepest thanks are owed to my wife, Mary. She wrote to Father Keefe when *Covenantal Theology* first appeared, in hopes of buying a copy. Characteristically, he simply mailed her the two volumes, and they became her Christmas gift to me. No one followed my ruminations more closely as I read and reread those pages. Mary listened out of personal interest, yes, but chiefly out of love. And to her this book is dedicated.

INTRODUCTION

By Kevin A. McMahon

Donald J. Keefe was born at home in Poolville, New York, some forty miles southeast of Syracuse, on July 14, 1924. Bastille Day—fittingly enough, to those who knew Keefe well. He was the eldest of Donald and Frances (Balmes) Keefe's five children. It was his father's job that first brought the couple together; he was a rural mail carrier, and his route took him past Frances' house every morning and every afternoon. Keefe kept a striking portrait picture of his mother, young and beautiful, hanging on his wall. There was more than a mail route, though; the real work came in running the family's dairy farm. Tall and solidly built, even as a teenager Keefe was accustomed to grabbing hundred-pound bags of fertilizer, one under each arm. He had the large hands of a man who had grown up with hard, physical labor. Yet it would never cease to amaze how quickly those thick fingers would fly on the keys of a typewriter or, later, a computer. Keefe often spoke of that farm, 129 acres of woodland and pasture and fields, encircled by a lake and the waters of the Sangerfield River. It accounts for the deep regard he had for the diversely creative vitality of nature. The land in its entirety is now the summer home of the Fiver Foundation for Children.

Elementary education was received in a one-room schoolhouse, grades one through eight (he spoke in open admiration of his teacher, struck by how deftly she taught, going from subject to subject, age to age). From there he went to nearby Earlville High School. In May 1942, Keefe enlisted in the U.S. Naval Reserve. The acrobatics he mastered as part of his naval flight training were a vivid memory for the whole of his life. He deployed to North Africa as a navigator and completed the first of what would be two stints of active duty (the second came in 1951–1953) in August 1946. He served in the Naval

Reserve until his honorable discharge as lieutenant in June 1953. After coming home in 1946, Keefe matriculated at nearby Colgate University, receiving a B.A. with honors in political science in 1949. From Colgate, Keefe went on to Georgetown University to study law, graduating in 1951. He was admitted to the Bar of the District of Columbia in April 1951; the Bar of the Courts-Martial of the United States in June 1951; the Bar of the State of New York in May 1954; and the Bar of the Supreme Court of the United States in November 1959. By this time he had been a member of the Jesuits for six years, having entered the Society of Jesus, New York Province, on September 7, 1953.

Life in the novitiate was not easy for Keefe. He was a good ten years older than most of his peers, a war veteran, and a former practicing attorney. His very demeanor was no doubt intimidating: gravel-voiced and no-nonsense; "crusty", as his friend James Schall, S.J., would later describe him. There was no mind more organized than Keefe's, and his legal studies had trained it to be handled like a scalpel in the examination of an argument, probing for flaws. For Keefe, it was never about the person; it was about the ideas. But he could be ruthless if he came upon an argument that was not only logically defective, but whose conclusion was dangerously wrong. That is simply the adversarial method of the courts. Yet here he was in philosophy class where the sole value seemed to be passive absorption of the lecture; questions that asked for anything more than restatement were taken as acts of insubordination. Later classes in theology would prove no better. Keefe the military man was no stranger to regimented life. What goaded him was knowing that a superior of limited academic background could blithely refuse permission to read, say, Henri de Lubac's Surnaturel, despite not caring about the theology that Keefe was trying to understand, not loving theology as Keefe loved it; not being driven, as Keefe was, in his love of the intellectual life. And Keefe was driven: by his love for the mind, for the faith, for the Church, for Christ. Keefe had no interest in battling for the sake of battling. But though a deeply loyal person, generous, quick to smile, respectful of authority, he would never walk away from a battle that he believed had to be fought. Another picture hung on his wall, a reproduction of The Man with the Golden Helmet, by Rembrandt (or at least one of his students). His mother had given it to him. He liked it, he said, because of what was expressed in the face— someone who had seen a lot, but had not been corrupted.

His ordination to the priesthood on June 20, 1962, brought great peace to Keefe, and the conviction that his proper role would come as a theologian in systematics. Following his final year of seminary study at Woodstock College, Maryland, and his Tertianship at Auriesville, New York, Keefe arrived in Strasbourg, France, in 1965 to begin his post-seminary work in theology. It was apparent from the outset, however, that Strasbourg would be the wrong program for him, and he moved instead to the Gregorian University in Rome, with the encouragement of Bernard Lonergan, who was teaching there on the faculty of dogmatic theology. Two short years later, Keefe graduated with his doctorate in Sacred Theology, having defended his dissertation, entitled *The Method of Paul Tillich's Theological System*, before a committee headed by Charles Boyer, S.J. This, his first major writing, was published by E.J. Brill in 1971 under the title *Thomism and the Ontological Theology of Paul Tillich: A Comparison of Systems*. He dedicated it to "My Mother and My Father".

Already in his first book one finds the insistence on placing Christ at the center of created reality that provides the foundation for all his thought. Not that this marked a new departure. It had been an increasingly important theme among Catholic theologians since the late nineteenth century, as Hans Urs von Balthasar showed in the concluding section of *The Theology of Karl Barth*. It is only that Keefe pushed far more rigorously than had any of his predecessors the full implications of the claim.

Any effort in systematic theology to present the teaching of Catholic faith as forming a consistent and comprehensive world view must rest on a metaphysics. Yet the metaphysics in which Keefe was schooled as part of the pre-theology training at Loyola Seminary in Shrub Oak, New York, depended largely upon Aristotle. It struck him immediately that if Aristotle had developed a series of concepts to help explain what was known by sense experience and reason, then theology should do the very same for what was known by revelation. Otherwise, the theologian would be boxed into the hopeless task of fitting the teaching of a Triune God who not only created the world but redeemed it from sin into categories that presume this could not possibly be true.

The two great features of Aristotle's world are stability and change. It is filled with a complex variety of things that differ in kind and are subject to change, but in predictable ways. The principle in things that both makes them to be what they are and determines the range of changes they are able to undergo and still remain what they are is called the essence. One essence accounts for why the many different examples of a kind of thing are alike. And as making a single thing to be self-unified and separate from other things, having its own existence as a thing, it is called substance. Each individual thing, then, is a separate substance. There is a note of uniformity that belongs to substance, inasmuch as it is why distinct things can have the same qualities or behave in the same way. There is also the sense of being self-enclosed, given that a substance is all about realizing to the fullest what it means to be itself as a substance.

The world described by Aristotle, said to be encountered in experience, was referred to in the classes at Shrub Oak as the realm of nature, to which the being and action of God, spoken of in revelation, were related as supernatural. By definition, then, whatever is universally experienced would belong to nature. Yet Thomas Aquinas, whose work was a touchstone at the Scholasticate, spoke of God pulling each person to himself in an act that would clearly be a divine gift, a grace, yet a grace that is universally distributed and operative on the level of the person's existence as a substance. Karl Rahner, among those who recognized the problem, coined the phrase "supernatural existential" in his essay of 1950, "Concerning the Relationship between Nature and Grace", to speak of the human setting in which each person exists; the setting, that is, of a spiritual being open to the fullness of reality who is always being addressed and drawn by God. On the one hand, then, the person is a member of the natural order created by God, whose essence it is, as spiritual, to be open and free. On the other, God issues his call as a gift that goes beyond the created human essence. Yet the gift is offered universally, to all, and is not bestowed like other graces only on the few.

What Keefe saw is that the explanation does not go far enough. Clearly, the substances in Aristotle's physical world that are most unlike the human are those that are purely material, inanimate, reactive to other substances, and able to enter into degrees of association, but entirely immanent. What distinguishes the human is transcendence, self-transcendence, an openness that is displayed in the capacity not only to know or to choose but also to enter into a unity with

what is other, above all with another, that may be so deep that it fulfills one's own identity, even while one remains distinctly oneself. All
this is known from reflection on experience. But it is confirmed by
revelation, and the teaching that what would be, in Aristotle's reckoning, the highest substance, God, is a single being in and through
three genuine distinctions. The Father is Father precisely in giving
everything to the Son (Jn 3:35; 5:26; 13:3) including divinity identical
to the Father's, as the early writers argued (see Athanasius, *Orations
against the Arians* 3.35–36). And the Son is Son, not only in receiving
but in returning everything back to the Father. It is in this reciprocity
that their unity consists (Jn 17:10). But then the Father gives even
further, being the source, now in and with the Son, of the Spirit
(Jn 14:16, 26; 15:26; 16:7), who is Spirit in giving everything back to
the Father and Son in the relationship that the Church Fathers, East
and West, called the mutual indwelling of the three. The supreme
transcendence of the divine that belongs to God as supremely personal comes of this being rooted in what is distinctly other, a unity
of substance that, in clear contradiction to Aristotle, arises not from
uniformity but from difference.

The mutual giving and receiving that characterizes the divine being
must characterize the divine action as well. Anything other than the
One cannot simply subsist in parallel existence, as Aristotle held, but
must itself belong to what the Father gives to the Son, as a gift made
perfect in the Spirit. The world as other than God must exist as having
been created by God. And the human person, open and free, exists as
reaching beyond the self in virtue of participating beyond the self in
the being of the Son. This seems to have been insufficiently appre-
ciated by Rahner, who would speak of the human as "installed" in
the supernatural order. On the contrary, the very fact of the person's
spiritual dimension is evidence that the being of the person is shaped
by its relation to the Son.

To be created, then, is to be created in the Son, a gift made by the
Father to the Son, meant to be received back from the Son in the Spirit.
The pull to share in that offering to the Father is at work at the deepest
level of the person, and to reject being made part of that offering, in a
turn to the self, is to strike against the root of one's personhood, the
ironic employment of freedom to negate the source of one's freedom.
But to say all this is still not to describe the gift that the Father actually

created. There cannot be a personal creation that is not oriented to the Father, able to flourish as a person in any way other than by the intentional act of handing oneself over to the Father, united with the Son, in the Spirit. However, the gift the Father made was a community of persons not only related to the Son, but created to enter into his own offering to the Father; intended, in the Spirit, to be received back by the Father and, thereby, to enter into the life of the Father, becoming one with the Father as he and the Father are one (Jn 14:20; 17:21–23). This, the creation the Father actually brought about, involved a giving to the Son that was at the same time, as Keefe says, a sending of the Son; a sending of the Son to humanity in order to have one life with humanity. This is the order of grace that goes beyond the gift, the grace, of creation itself.

These are the two great categories of revelation: gift and life. And they lie at the heart of Keefe's thought as well. It is common to see Colossians 1:16 and 1 Corinthians 8:6, two passages that are frequently cited by those taking a Christocentric approach to the world, understood to mean that the world was created in view of the coming of Jesus. "Christ" is the title given to Jesus as the one sent by the Father. But if that is so, argues Keefe, then to say that all things were created "in" Christ or "through" Christ, as Scripture does, cannot mean only that the Son is destined to be born at a certain point in time. It must mean that the act of creation was simultaneously the act of the Father sending the Son. This sending involved the creation of humanity in the Son, but then also the ever-more-deeply drawing of humanity into the life of the Son: with the joining of the individual humanity of Jesus to the Son; in the transformation of the human life of Jesus in his Resurrection and Ascension; through communion with the risen Christ who remains present in the Eucharist; ultimately, with the entry of those, united with Christ, into the life of the Triune God. There is one event of the Incarnation, and only one who is the Incarnate Lord, but the one event is realized in successive stages, in the gradual coming to completion of the body of Christ (Eph 1:10, 20–23; 2:13–16; 4:12–13).

This, then, Christ come to full measure, what Augustine called the "whole Christ", must be taken as the paradigm of created substance. Accordingly, within all the diversity and multiplicity of physical creation, it is the human that is substance in the highest sense. But again, this is not the Aristotelian idea of the human, man the rational animal, where one's material separateness from others is the only thing that keeps one from collapsing into the shared essence. Here, it is each person's unique identity, as someone directly, deliberately, created, that provides the ground of one's inner unity. Distance is not required to secure individuality. On the contrary, the core of each person's identity is to be directed beyond oneself, and directed beyond oneself as male and female. For this identity, like that of Christ, is tied to an appointed mission, and all mission is tied to life. Thus, Keefe states, full human substantiality, human substantial unity, is realized only in the mutuality of one united to another. In the first instance, this means each individual united to Christ in the collaborative drawing of life into the divine. On another level, however, this same substantiality is realized in the unity that belongs to the couple, bound by a free decision, whose union is ordered to the conception of new life.

Only when one moves beyond the human to the realm of nonpersonal entities, living and non-living, the objects of Aristotle's immediate focus, may one apply the term "substance" with the derived meaning summarized in the phrase "undivided in itself and divided from all else". Of substance in the genuine sense, Keefe believes, this is inherently false. There is no clearer illustration of the contrast between Aristotle's notion of substance and what Keefe sought to work out than in Aristotle's denial that human nature as such includes sexual difference. For Keefe, the mutuality expressed in sexual difference is definitive of the human essence. And to exercise this mutuality in an unreserved, free gift of self in the differentiated union of marriage is to reflect in a distinctive way the highest order of human substantiality, the union of Christ and his Church.

The world being created in Christ, then, is not a hierarchy of natures, higher and lower, simpler and more complex, more and less real. It is an order of concrete persons, angelic and human, immaterial and bodily, the materiality of the latter making possible the further diversity and multiplicity of the physical universe. Keefe endeavored to produce a corresponding metaphysics by taking the Thomist categories and terms of his Jesuit schooling and making them equally concrete. His goal was to develop what he considered to be a historical rather than a "cosmological" metaphysics. By "cosmological", he once remarked, he meant what von Balthasar had meant in *The God Question and Modern Man*, namely, theoretical in the sense of governed by a theory, an idea, that conceives of reality as a necessary structure, whose purest representation is by mathematical equation. A historical analysis would be true to the world known by revelation. History, for Keefe, is time as united by free decision. And the central decision is that of Christ. His is not, of course, the only decision, any more than he is the sole historical figure. But it is the founding decision, the basis for Genesis' "beginning".

Christ is the Father's gift to humanity, which, in being freely received, perfects human freedom. His is the human self-offering that cannot be subject to limit, meant to be appropriated as their own by creatures who, in their deepest devotion, will only dimly comprehend the significance of what they share in. What is required is a human community, a succession of human life from which Christ may come, and the making present of his offering to the ensuing generations. Keefe took seriously the scriptural teaching of humanity having its start in a single couple, in a joint decision sufficient to determine the mode and manner of human succession. But the Father is the one creator. Humanity was to be made, and with it the world that relied on it for a center. And Christ was to come, which means that the gift offered was going to be freely, yet certainly, received. Mary is the freely absolute response to the divine offer, whose bond with Christ is the ground for the creation that Genesis says was good, indeed, "very good" (1:31).

The Church would come to speak of Christ as the Second Adam and Mary as the Second Eve, but the concern of Genesis is for the First Adam and Eve, who refused the primal gift, and how all the world was changed for the worse. Keefe takes with full seriousness, too, this doctrine of a first sin. In virtue of the Second Eve, creation is infallibly instituted, shaped by the dynamic of the Son's gift offered, received, and then handed over in fullness to the Father. But in virtue of the first sin, Christ is sent into fallenness, his union with humanity is enfleshment, his offering to the Father incurs his death, which is made present to the generations in the sacrifice of the Eucharist. Since history is history, integrated time, by the action of Christ, all of history is a reflection of Christ. There is the history of the nations before the call of Abraham. There is the history of the promise, the covenant, made to Abraham and to his descendants, that through them creation would be blessed again. The promise established a divine bond with these people, which the prophets described in marital terms, a union of masculine and feminine. For the promise concerned life, and it belongs to life to pass on life, to bring about another from the interiority of one's own identity. The principles of otherness and interiority belong even to the unity of the divine life. But among created substances, these principles exist in the separated mode of masculinity and femininity, and on this basis they are applied to Christ and creation, then to Christ and Israel.

Finally, there is the history of the promise fulfilled in Christ Jesus. Each of these distinct histories, which together compose the one history of Christ, finds its representation in the liturgy of the Eucharist: in the offertory of bread and wine, their transubstantiation into the life of Christ, and the reception of this life in a communion that constitutes the promise still at work, until the definitive blessing that is our radical acceptance by the Father. When, therefore, in 1991 Keefe published his analytical case for a uniquely theological metaphysics, he gave it the title *Covenantal Theology: The Eucharistic Order of History*. (Incidentally, it, too, was dedicated to his parents, though now "In Memory of my Father and My Mother".)

Keefe was a master of the English language. But the insight he tried to articulate—of which the preceding is only a superficial summary—was extremely dense, and his writing style gave no help to the reader, driving ahead in long sentences that are typically as involved as their thought. His second edition, which came out in 1996, therefore included an appendix that acted as a kind of "author's response to his critics", where he attempted to clarify, or at least restate, some of the points that his readers thought were most wrongheaded. Chief among these, considering that it was leveled most consistently and widely over the course of his career, was his doctrine of the preexistence of Jesus. Balthasar called the idea "gnostic" when commenting on a paper Keefe gave as part of a panel discussion of Balthasar's work (the proceedings of which were published in the journal *Communio*, Spring, 1978). It is a label that often occurs to readers, despite the fact that, seen from Keefe's side, the assertion simply amazes. There could be no viewpoint more opposed to Keefe's than the gnostic, which regards history as the sphere of existence divorced from the divine and therefore the real and treats "Jesus", "Christ", and the "Church" as terms referring to universal ideals, or to ideas in the mind of God.

Keefe always insisted that by preexistence he meant "metaphysical", not "temporal", preexistence. In other words, he was not saying that

Jesus, as born in first-century Palestine, existed before being born in first-century Palestine. Nevertheless the argument is clear, that if there is history, and there is in fact history, then the one integrating time into history, Jesus, cannot be merely the product of history. He is its source, the Alpha and the Omega (Rev 1:17). It is he who not only unites humanity to himself but guarantees that its offering will be elevated to be joined to his own. If, however, Jesus preexists in this sense, then so must Mary. If Jesus is the guarantee of humanity responding perfectly to the Father, there must also be the guaranteed response in virtue of which Jesus is actually born as a human. Without Mary, there is no certainty of the gift being complete, of the institution of the Good Creation.

For Keefe, the preexistence of Jesus and therefore Mary is an immediate implication of any Christocentric approach (Phil 2:6–8; Heb 1:2–4). Yet it cannot be denied that the manner of this preexistence is far less clear. Metaphysical existence obviously differs from the temporal lives recorded in the Gospels with the full actuality of their historical decisions. But still it is existence in the one order of persons brought about by the Father. These two, in their centricity and their relation to each other, are the structuring principles of this order. They are the basis of creation's beginning, and so Keefe will speak of their "primordiality", having in mind the idea of "beginning" as developed both in Scripture and in the writings of Pope John Paul II.

Also present in that beginning, the primal moment of the order of persons, is the first human couple. Their free bond, one to the other, the expression of their gift of self to the Father, would provide the form, the pattern, for the community that was to enter into the transformative union and gift of the ultimate couple. Their free gift to the Father was to be at the same time a deliberate entry into the absolute offering of that central couple, of Jesus and Mary, even if this central relation would not become fully actual except in the unfolding of the creation that they would perfect. What is more, by this bond, the first couple would shape themselves in their materiality as well, in their identity as embodied persons where their bodies would fully reflect the identity of the human person as created for the Father in the Christ. By this same bond, in the same free decision, the remainder of material creation would also be shaped, the panoply of physical existence and life made possible by the potentiality of created matter; for physical existence, even if not bearing the form of human identity, remains related to the human. And this means physical creation, good in itself, is made complete in being made part of the human self-offering to the Father.

Keefe referred to this central place of the human in creation as "headship", ascribing it in particular to the first man and following Saint Paul in seeing the headship of the man as analogous to the normative headship of Christ. This is the order of creation brought about in the beginning. And it was lost in the beginning. The decision of the first couple was not for each other in deciding for the Father. Rather, it was a decision for oneself. Hence, there was no bond between the two. There was no completion of themselves in the image of the divine; of their bodiliness as expressing their personhood, grounded in the divine; no inauguration of a human community deriving from a first free, human union; no material universe configured by, being made perfect by, becoming a gift delivered to God. We will never know what creation would have looked like apart from sin, Keefe declared. We will never know what humanity would have looked like, or the life of Christ united to humanity. For the only time there has ever been is fallen time. Yet the gift structure of creation, founded on Mary's response to the Son who gives unreservedly to the Father, remained intact—as has the Father's unreserved commitment to the free operation of his creation, despite its brokenness—so that even as fallen, time has proceeded as history.

The primordiality of Jesus, Mary, Adam, and Eve may well be Keefe's most perplexing position. But a conversion of these persons into a series of abstract ideas it is not.

Keefe developed his thought against the backdrop of many years spent in the classroom. The book on Tillich came out when he was on the faculty at Saint Louis University, where he taught theology from 1970 to 1978, and as an adjunct professor of law from 1972 to 1978. Prior to this, he had taught in the department of religious studies at Canisius College from 1966 to 1970. When *Covenantal Theology* was published in 1991, he was in his final year as professor of theology at Marquette University, where he had moved in 1978, teaching at the same time as an adjunct professor in Marquette's law school. From 1991 until 1994, he served as theological consultant to Archbishop James Stafford of Denver and on the faculty of the archdiocesan seminary. He returned to New York and joined the faculty of the archdiocesan Saint Joseph's Seminary as professor of dogmatic theology from 1994 to 2001. In 2002 he was the Cardinal Edmund Szoka Distinguished Visiting Professor at Sacred Heart Major Seminary in Detroit; following which he retired, after thirty-six years of teaching, to the Jesuit community at Fordham University.

During all this time, Keefe wrote prolifically, publishing a long series of articles; and the labor continued deep into retirement. To the original two volumes of *Covenantal Theology*, he added another two, massive volumes providing an exhaustive historical defense of his positions, drawn from the theological tradition. Ever the perfectionist, however, he never considered them quite finished.

The approach to the theology he termed "covenantal" is epitomized by his view of the human. Aristotle may have referred to man as an animal distinguished by the capacity to reason (*Nicomachean Ethics* 1098a 7), inclined by nature to form political societies (*Politics* 1253a 1), and anthropology might speak of humans as the tool-makers or language-crafters. But for Keefe, the defining activity of the human person is prayer: *homo venerans*, the person at worship; and the summit of human worship is the union afforded with the Son's oblation to the Father in the Eucharist.

Keefe was utterly devoted to the practice that a Jesuit priest offer Mass daily, even if privately. There can be no question that his was a theology born of the meditative recital, day in and day out, of the prayers of the Canon and of profound reflection upon the biblical readings as they wound their way through the liturgical year. The daily offering continued uninterrupted after declining health brought him to the Fordham community's Murray-Weigel Hall in 2012. When he thought it best to no longer celebrate himself, he attended Mass with his fellow Jesuits in the Hall's chapel. And in the final weeks, when he lacked the strength even for that, he watched it broadcast on television. He died quietly, shortly after midnight, on February 27, 2018. He was ninety-four. It had been a long and productive life; singularly influential, uncompromisingly faithful, supremely Eucharistic.

I

THE NATURE OF THEOLOGY

It was not Christians who gave us the term "theology". In fact, it took a very long time for Christians to assign their own distinctive meaning to what was originally a pagan word. Yves Congar, in his *A History of Theology*, attributed its first use to Plato, who in *Republic* 379a said that it belongs to the founders of a state to establish the norms of θεολογία ("theology"), meaning talk concerning the gods, where Socrates' complaint is that the fables of Homer and Hesiod not only distort the truth about God but corrupt the morals of the youth.[1] Aristotle in *Metaphysics* 6.1.1026a19 actually listed theology (θεολογική) as the highest of three theoretical forms of study or philosophies, the other two being mathematics and physics. It is the highest and the best, he added in 11.164b5, because it deals with the highest and best things, divine things, namely, eternal and immoveable causes. But this was hardly common usage. Most Greek writers followed Plato's lead and used "theology" to mean stories about the gods. Aristotle himself, a short time later in *Metaphysics* 12.1071b27, speaks more typically of the "theologians" who explain the causes of things poetically or allegorically rather than scientifically.

Clement of Alexandria (died ca. 215) was one of the earliest Christians to employ the word θεολογία, and he did so in order to contrast it not only with pagan fiction but with pagan philosophy. Even the Greek philosophers, he wrote in *Stromateis* 1.13, have torn the body of truth into pieces, just like the stories tell of the Bacchantes, the female devotees of the nature deity, Dionysus, who dismembered King Pentheus of Thebes because he denied Dionysus was a god. Except,

---

[1] Yves M.J. Congar, O.P., *A History of Theology*, trans. and ed. Hunter Guthrie, S.J. (Garden City, N.Y.: Doubleday, 1968), 26. This book is based on the entry "Théologie" by Congar that appeared in vol. 15 of *Dictionnaire de théologie Catholique* (Paris: 1946), 341–502.

Clement said, the philosophers have not torn their pieces of truth from the "mythology of Dionysus but from the theology of the eternal Word" who illumines every mind.

A century later, θεολογία is found with wider and even more nuanced expression in the work of Eusebius, bishop of Caesarea (died ca. 340), and carrying its specifically Christian sense: God's discourse about God. Writing in criticism of his fellow bishop, Marcellus of Ancyra, who apparently held that the title "son" is properly given only to the human life of Jesus conceived by Mary, Eusebius charged that Marcellus assigned "to the flesh the theology brought forward in the divine Scriptures concerning the only-begotten Son of God", having in mind such passages as Proverbs 8:22 ("The LORD created me at the beginning of his work") and Colossians 1:15 ("He is the image of the invisible God, the first-born of all creation").[2] It is Saint Paul who opens his letter to the Galatians with "the theology of the Savior" that proclaims Jesus to be the Son of God.[3] The attribution, Eusebius concedes, of a divine Son to the one God may run counter to human thinking, but here and in his other letters, the Apostle is "handing down [to us] the ineffable and mystical theology (μυστικὴν θεολογίαν)".[4]

The bulk of Eusebius' treatise had been a series of excerpts from Marcellus' work, believing that Marcellus' own words would constitute the best case against him. But soon afterward it struck Eusebius that Marcellus' copious, yet twisted, use of Scripture, if left unanswered, would threaten the very wellspring of "the true theology" of the Triune God. Since the Scripture's theology is the nourishment that "the Church of God" uses to feed her members, one may say that the true theology is the Church's theology. And in fact, this came to be the title of Eusebius' second refutation of Marcellus: *On Ecclesiastical Theology*. "I will have nothing new to say," Eusebius wrote, "nor will I relate any brilliant discovery of my own; rather, I offer the uncorrupted teaching of the Church of God." Her teaching is the teaching she received "from those who from the beginning personally saw and

---

[2] Eusebius of Caesarea, *Against Marcellus* 2.2.44, in Eusebius of Caesarea, *Against Marcellus and On Ecclesiastical Theology*, trans. and ed. Kelly Spoerl and Markus Vinzent (Washington, D.C.: The Catholic University of America Press, 2017), 134.

[3] Eusebius, *Against Marcellus* 1.1.24, in Spoerl and Vinzent, 82.

[4] Eusebius, *Against Marcellus* 1.4.57, in Spoerl and Vinzent, 114.

heard the Word from heaven".[5] Chief among these would seem to be Saint John, "the Theologian (θεολόγος)" (1.20.3, section 9), who learned "the theology concerning the Son" from the Son himself, made visible (1.20.5, sections 16–17). For distant ages before, the prophets of God had theologized about him mystically ("μυστικῶς ἐθεολόγουν") "in the prophetic spirit", "knowledge of the only-begotten Son" remaining secret, a mystery hidden from the many (1.20.29, section 89). "For the grace of the proclamation of the theology concerning him was preserved for his coming, by which his Church throughout the world, as if receiving some mystery that was long ago kept hidden in silence, is exalted."[6]

In "the very mystery of rebirth", namely, baptism, the Church teaches her children to confess belief "in one God the Father" and in the "only-begotten Son of God, Jesus Christ".[7] Which would mean that if Saint Paul, for example, may be said to "theologize" concerning Christ in Colossians 1:15–17 (called Paul's "apostolic theology" in *On Ecclesiastical Theology* 3.6.5), then the faithful, too, theologize—give voice to the truth—in reciting the liturgical prayers of the Church. In any event, Eusebius was willing to bestow the title "theologian" even upon Marcellus, albeit—to be more precise—a babbling theologian (*Against Marcellus* 1.1.6).

In the next generation after Eusebius, Augustine, bishop of Hippo, reflected the uneasiness in Western Christianity with what was still considered to be an essentially pagan term. In Books 6 and 7 of *The City of God*, for example, he took a long and critical look at the Roman Stoic philosopher Varro's tripartite division of theology (*theologia*), which Varro defined as "an account pertaining to the gods" (6.5). Varro's division, based on a Stoic analysis that recalled the thought of Aristotle, sought to distinguish mythical theology, which the educated scorn, from physical or natural, and political or civil theology. But to Augustine's mind, the entire effort was a charade. For civil theology is nothing more than the shameful myths of the gods represented in public cult; and if so-called physical theology is really a distinct interpretation of things, treating the myths as mere allegory for the natural forces that explain the

[5] Eusebius, *On Ecclesiastical Theology*, preface, 2, in Spoerl and Vinzent, 160.
[6] Eusebius, *On Ecclesiastical Theology* 1.20.29, sections 87–88, in Spoerl and Vinzent, 215–16.
[7] Eusebius, *On Ecclesiastical Theology* 1.8.1–2, in Spoerl and Vinzent, 167–68 and n. 33.

world, then what you have is a physics not a theology. On the other hand, if the stories are not allegory but fact, then this theology of nature is patently false. For according to "true theology, earth is the work of God, not the mother of God" as is had in the myths (6.8). Yet to whom among the pagans, Augustine asks at the beginning of Book 8, is one to turn for true theology, "which Greek word we understand to mean theory (*ratio*) or discourse (*sermo*) about divinity"? Even the philosophers, those lovers of wisdom, even the Platonists, who are the greatest among the philosophers, enjoin the worship of many gods, thereby proving that they do *not* think that true worship of the one unchangeable God is the source of eternal life and happiness.[8]

The approach taken by Eusebius, however, remained very much alive, as evidenced by the work of the early-sixth-century Syrian writer known only as Pseudo-Dionysius, whose treatise on unitive prayer carried the title of *On Mystical Theology* (Περὶ μυστικῆς θεολογίας). Pseudo-Dionysius has only one category of individuals in mind when at the outset of his seminal *The Divine Names* he speaks of "the theologians" (θεολόγοι): they are the biblical writers whose doctrine on God is the fruit of the Spirit; and "theology" means the teaching found in, or based on, the Scriptures. Equally important, however, as he makes clear in *The Ecclesiastical Hierarchy*, is the direction provided by the bishops, the "hierarchs", in handing on the scriptural teaching. It had been a point of emphasis in the East since the letters of Ignatius of Antioch (died ca. 107).

The practice, exemplified by Pseudo-Dionysius, of contemplative study of the Scriptures had been shaping monastic debates for centuries (assisted, it must be said, by the classical subjects of grammar and dialectic) on everything from the origin of evil to Christ's presence in the Eucharist when around 1077 Anselm of Bec, later the archbishop of Canterbury, undertook to formulate an argument that relied, not on the Scriptures, but only on reason, proving that God, the self-sufficient supreme Good, does in fact exist. To the narrative that tracked the course of his reasoning he first gave the title *Fides quaerens intellectum*, or *Faith Seeking Understanding*, which he afterward shortened to *Proslogion*. The *Proslogion* literally breathes the Scriptures, and it is as much an extended prayer as was Augustine's *Confessions*. Nevertheless, it also

---

[8] Eusebius had made a similar critique of the Stoic and Platonist theologies in Book 4 of his *Preparation of the Gospel*.

reflects the admonition in 1 Peter 3:15 (the Latin citation of which would open Anselm's *Cur Deus Homo* or *Why Did God Become Man?*) that believers should always be ready to offer a *ratio* for the hope that lies in them; which Anselm took as a call, not to reserve belief in what the Scriptures teach until it can be proven by reason, but to use reason to lay out the intellectual coherence of what is believed.

The twelfth century saw the rise in Europe of universities, and theology reached beyond the monastic enclosures and cathedral schools to join an ever-growing list of studies: Galen's medicine, Roman and Church law, Aristotle's logic, physics, metaphysics, epistemology, and zoology. Within a hundred years, the most famous work produced by the thirteenth-century scholar Thomas Aquinas bore the title *Summa theologiae*, and it was a student's introduction to the academic discipline of Christian theology.

Since ancient times, philosophy had been understood to be the activity that sought out and taught the truth concerning the highest things and the humblest things, the deepest things and the most familiar things—the truth, that is to say, concerning everything. That part of philosophy treating divine things was called theology, as far back as Aristotle. Yet, Thomas observes at the outset of his *Summa*, even the ancients knew that the deepest truth about the highest reality, God, exceeds the capacity of human reason. And the Christian knows that human perfection (*salus*) resides in a relation, whose depth exceeds reason, to God, who exceeds reason, a relation that is either fostered or violated by decision and act. Thus it was necessary that God himself teach what otherwise would be unknown. The Scriptures are the record of this teaching. They constitute a single body of knowledge, of doctrine, whose principles are held by faith, not discovered by reason. The content of this sacred doctrine is as unified as that of philosophy; and therefore, like philosophy, it is called a "science". Yet although this science may ultimately touch upon the whole of reality, it does so as centered on God. Hence it is called "theology".[9]

As an academic discipline, theology is sacred doctrine embarked on the search that characterizes all love of learning. Beyond contributing to the articulation of faith, theology, as Anselm said, is faith moved to wonder: What does this mean? Where does it lead? Why is it so? And in wondering, theology becomes part of the conversation,

[9] *Summa theologiae* Ia, q. 1, a. 7, sed contra.

of the dialogue between the many studies pursued in the university. It belongs to theology to raise questions pertaining to sacred doctrine, but then also to determine how the truths of this doctrine accord with the teachings of the other sciences. The entire structure of the *Summa* is built around this posing of questions: Does God exist? Can we be happy? Did Christ feel pain? For each major question there are subordinate questions called articles; and for each article there are proposed answers to which Thomas responds with his own replies, in a back-and-forth, dialogical style that replicated not only his classrooms at the University of Paris, but the monastic classrooms and cloisters for centuries past. Thomas composed 512 questions in the *Summa theologiae*, with 2,669 articles and 10,000 replies to others' answers, before he died in 1274 with the text still not finished.

Thomas was conscious, though, that the sacred doctrine from which theology takes its start and to which it directs its attention is not just something scriptural, it is something ecclesial. The discipline of theology is governed not only by the content of the Scriptures but by the mind of the Church. Both are the source of its questioning, and both provide the norms for its conclusions. Hence Thomas appeals to the writings of the Fathers and the decrees of Church councils as well as the Bible as he conducts his theology. Indeed, it is not as a scholar of theology, a *magister* (meaning a licensed teacher on a university faculty), that he identifies himself in the prologue to his *Summa*, but as a "*doctor* of Catholic truth". That is why, too, he speaks elsewhere not only of an academic *magisterium*, which is the office of teacher that derives from one's academic degree, but of the even more central authority of the bishop who possesses sacramentally a *magisterium* of the pastoral chair. For the bishop feeds the community of faith as the shepherd feeds his sheep.[10]

Donald Keefe shares this same concern that in a time of far greater intellectual diversity, theology retain its distinctive voice; that it make its own contribution to academic discussions on terms that belong to its unique structure. For theology is indisputably a rational inquiry. But the mind undertaking this inquiry is a mind that has already made the decision of faith. The work of theology is interrogative; but it is pursued in an attitude of prayer. And that prayer is above all Eucharistic.

---

[10] *Quaestiones quodlibetales* 3, q. 4, a. 1, ad 3. See also *Contra impugnantes Dei cultum et religionem* 2.1.

Theological Method

Theology, from the ground up, is faith seeking understanding. It is ever a quest, never an achievement; theology does not exist "out there" as a thing completed, a known edifice needing only occasional and incidental repair. It is a task pervading history, single and enormous, never to be completed and yet never to be abdicated without the correlative abdication from the faith which sustains it—which is to say, without infidelity. This quest, this *quaerens*, is an indispensable dimension of the mind's true worship. . . .

Therefore to theologize is to seek in Christ the light by and in which the beauty of our creation and the world itself is luminous with truth; it is to turn our reason toward the articulation of those unnumbered human questions that find in Christ their answer beyond all articulation, all comprehension, the Alpha and the Omega, the Word made flesh for us and for our salvation. . . .

Theology as Catholic is freed from all mere identification with its past. The historicity of theology rejects the canonization of any past *theological* achievement, regardless of its genius, in order that theology may build upon and remain in continuity with such achievement in all future inquiry. No theological achievement is perfected and thus sacrosanct; the more foundational it is, the more firm a ground it is upon which to build, but the ultimate ground of theology is never theological. The truth of the faith is actual, historical, and concrete; it is therefore capable of being mediated only by the liturgy, by the liturgical symbols which include the creeds, the doctrinal tradition, and the preaching of the bishops. Faith is not mediated, still less is it tested, by theology, and no doctrinal statement, regardless of its historical context, can be identified with the merely potential truth of

From Donald J. Keefe, S.J., *Covenantal Theology: The Eucharistic Order of History*, rev. ed. (Novato, Calif.: Presidio Press, 1996), 9–10, 12–14, 16.

the abstractions, the hypotheses, of theological systematics or with any other sort of methodologically controlled inquiry....

... The concrete norm for theology as Catholic is always the sacramental worship of the historical Church; when our theologies fail, they fail first as worship, for we worship in truth, or not at all, as we worship in freedom, or not at all....

As this worship is concrete in history, so also is the Truth which is the object of that worship concretely appropriated in history, not as though delivered in abstractions capable of neutral assimilation as information, but as mediated by the sacramental symbols integral to the worship itself. The central symbol is the Eucharist, the unique sacrifice of Jesus the Christ offered in sacramental representation in his person and by his authority....

... The responsibility for this Eucharistic worship is apostolic, borne and exercised *in persona Christi* by those who succeed to the charge given the apostles, "Do this in memory of me", and who offer the One Sacrifice in union with the successor of him to whom it was thrice said, "Feed my sheep."

The episcopal responsibility is liturgical and therefore covenantal; it does not compete with the freedom of the theologian, but sustains it. Part of this episcopal responsibility is magisterial, a responsibility for the truth of the worship—for it is a worship in truth and not otherwise. This responsibility cannot be exercised by any other authority than that charged with the responsibility for the Eucharistic worship itself, for the concrete truth of the faith is liturgically mediated, uttered in the Church's communal worship as the condition precedent of its availability for the theologian's inquiry. That it be thus available is the *sine qua non* of theology, its very condition of possibility. Absent this magisterial authority in the episcopacy, no authentically theological inquiry is possible, for it would lack a truly historical subject matter, one distinct from that of an abstract implication of method worked out by a merely secular and humanistically controlled investigation....

... Theology is thereby an experimental discipline, one whose speculation is so open upon the historically presented *Summum Verum* as to require the formal effect of that prime truth in order to continue. The historical liturgical tradition of the mystery of Christ, safeguarded and uttered by the magisterial proclamation, is the historical a priori of theology in much the same way in which the historical and intrinsic intelligibility of the physical universe is the a priori of the physical sciences. The same historical curiosity or *quaerens intellectum* prevents the reduction of the physical sciences to the abstract implication of ideal methods, ordered to the construction of cosmologies entirely dissociated from the historical order of reality in such wise that the scientist as such must profess an academic disinterest in historical reality, and at the same time equally bars theology from becoming a methodologically induced ideology similarly false to history.

An experimental discipline such as physics requires, just as does theology, an a priori inerrancy in its subject matter. The intrinsic truth of the experimentally encountered world, like the intrinsic truth of the ecclesial tradition, must be presented inerrantly, as a source of truth which, because it transcends the inquiry, is able to justify inquiry: it offers to the *quaerens* of the mind a concretely presented knowable unknown. That historical physical reality is in fact so presented cannot be proven, in the sense of being reduced to a rational necessity—for as free it is gift, not necessity—but it can be experienced continually in that existential optimism which is integral to a truly historical consciousness: "the experience of order in the present under God".[11]

This optimism is neither automatic nor spontaneous, whether for physicists or for theologians, but it is for both indispensable, and it has no sustenance but the worship of the Lord of history, by whose grace, by whose covenantal immanence, the world is good and true and beautiful, history is salvific, reality is gift, and knowledge the celebration of the gift.

It is only by entering into the freedom of this rationality that one is free to take up any experimental inquiry and thus to learn from a world whose significance one cannot control by the questions, good or bad, which one brings to it. A Faustian science is always self-defeating.

The findings of such a historical theology, whose historicity is that of the *fides quaerens intellectum*, can be stated only as hypothesis. Only as self-consciously, which is to say methodologically, hypothetical can it respect the historicity of the object of its inquiry. Only thus, as historically situated, is the theologian able to appropriate a free truth

---

[11] Eric Voegelin, *Order and History*, in *The World of the Polis*, vol. 2 (Baton Rouge: Louisiana State University Press, 1957), 16. Citation provided in Donald J. Keefe, *Covenantal Theology: The Eucharistic Order of History*, rev. ed. (Novato, Calif.: Presidio Press, 1996), 67n40.

transcendent to the logic of his method, and so able to avoid the sterile immanentization of his discipline and the idolatry that demands such immanentization, such immolation, of the mind's transcendence of all necessity....

... The task of theology is therefore at bottom metaphysical or ontological; it is the task of forming open-ended hypothetical constructs of the conversion of reality and its transcendentals (unity, truth, beauty, goodness) from the essentialist and determinist mode of monadic intellectuality, of nonhistorical consciousness, to the covenantal mode which is able to respect the transcendent truth of the Good Creation, of the New Covenant, of the Word made flesh.

2

EUCHARISTIC BEGINNING

Among the earliest words attributed to Jesus are those which Saint Paul records in 1 Corinthians as having been spoken at the Last Supper. "For I received from the Lord what I also delivered to you," he writes, "that the Lord Jesus on the night when he was betrayed took bread, and when he had given thanks, he broke it, and said, 'This is my body which is for you. Do this in remembrance of me.' In the same way also the chalice, after supper, saying, 'This chalice is the new covenant in my blood. Do this, as often as you drink it, in remembrance of me'" (1 Cor 11:23–25). These words, echoing as they do the reference in Jeremiah 31:31 to a new covenant, a new bond joining God to his people, an unbreakable bond that is rooted in the human heart, constitute the cornerstone of Keefe's thought.

Humanity was said to be the apex of creation in Genesis 1:27–28 because human beings were the only creatures in this visible world able to hear God's word and be commanded by his word. Yet the word, addressed to a free heart, came from without. It could be spurned; and having done so, the heart of humanity became a wellspring of violence in the world (Gen 6:5). God's response was to speak his word once again, in a manner parallel to his initial making of things. That is, he spoke unilaterally, giving his promise that the blessings he had conferred on the world in the beginning, now lost because of sin, would be restored; in the Hebrew text the term used when speaking of the promise is *berit*, commonly translated "covenant" (Gen 6:18; 12:2–3; 15:18). By the first century, belief in the promise was associated in much of Judaism with the idea that it would be fulfilled by a figure sent by God, his agent, an anointed one, a Messiah, in Greek, *Christos*. Yet at the center of the Christian gospel that Jesus is the Christ was the claim that Jeremiah's words pointed to something far deeper than the defeat of Israel's enemies or even a recovery of the lost Eden. If Jesus of Nazareth fulfills Jeremiah's prophecy that humanity would be inseparably united to God's word, it is because the human heart of Jesus, "born of woman" (Gal 4:4), is the human heart of the Word (Jn 1:1, 10–18).

The claim raised to new prominence a fundamental category in the Hebrew Scriptures, the category of life, and underscored the inherent openness of life. The life of Jesus is uniquely a life of union, the single life that is both born of Mary and begotten of the Father. And it is a life radically available; given unreservedly to the Father, even to the point of "death on a cross" (Phil 2:8), its presence is always the presence of a life intended to be chosen, that one may make his gift to the Father one's own. Those called to faith are called to have one life with him. This is not simply a matter of restoring human life to its state of integrity before sin, standing in the presence of God, attentive to his word. It is a matter of transforming human life by uniting it to the absolutely highest human response to God, that of Jesus, who as Son has one life with the Father. It could be concluded that the entering of human life into the divine was the very reason why God created humanity. Keefe does, following a long tradition in theology that traces back to, among other writers, Augustine and his reflection on the line in Ephesians 1:4–5 that the faithful were chosen by the Father "before the foundation of the world", intended "for adoption as his children through Jesus Christ".[1]

Taken with full seriousness, this means that the world was founded on Jesus; that the structure of the human, as well as the world, reflects the reciprocal nature of the divine life in which humanity participates, incompletely, from the beginning. And so, in addition to Paul's account in 1 Corinthians 11:23–25, Keefe has been guided by and repeatedly refers back to the statement in 1 Corinthians 8:6 that there is "one Lord, Jesus Christ, through whom are all things and through whom we exist"; the hymnic lines in Colossians 1:15–17 that Jesus the Son "is the image of the invisible God, the first-born of all creation; for in him all things were created, in heaven and on earth, visible and invisible, whether thrones or dominions or principalities or

---

[1] Augustine, *Literal Commentary on Genesis* (*De Genesi ad litteram*) 6.9.14. See also his *Confessions* 13.34.49.

authorities—all things were created through him and for him. He is before all things, and in him all things hold together"; the comment in Hebrews 1:2 that God created the world through his Son; and of course the opening declaration in John 1:3 that all things came into being through the Word.

It is in view of these passages that Keefe speaks of the preexistence, and the primordiality, of Jesus, by which he means Jesus' metaphysical preexistence; that Jesus is, metaphysically, the condition of the possibility of there being a free human creation united to God. Given that within the unity of the divine life, the Father begets the Son in giving everything to him, and the Son, having received everything from the Father, offers it back completely in return, the Father's decision to create must belong to his act of self-donation to the Son. And if what the Father creates are intelligent creatures, whose nature it is to be responsive to the Father—even more so if they are being called to enter into unity with the Father—then it must be that they are created in the Son, open and in relation to him, offering themselves with him to the Father. Keefe call this mutuality between human creation and the Son "historical", a matter of history, because it is created, human, temporal, and free. In this sense, the Word, regarded from the standpoint as the one in whom historical humanity is created, is himself historical. No absolute Word, intrinsically unrelated to the human, can either be the source of human history or unite it to himself. Thus, the human life of Jesus is the human life of the Son, the Word, perfectly received from the Father, returned to the Father, and thereby providing the inviolable basis of humanity's relation to God.

It is important to stress that Keefe speaks of the historicity of the Word in virtue of the Father's free decision to create, not in virtue of the relation as such of the Word as Son to the Father; nor is Keefe thinking of human history as we know and experience it: time as conflictual and fragmented, where change involves not only gain but loss. That is time as it has been changed for the worse by sin, the fallen human temporal and bodily condition that both Saint Paul and Saint John refer to as "flesh", in Greek, *sarx*. Hence the description of the birth of Jesus in John 1:14 as the Word becoming flesh should be taken to mean that in this event, fallen human history was drawn even more intimately to the Word, with whom history had been united since the first moment of creation.

In the mystery of the Incarnation, the Word creates himself. Jesus is the Word, the life of the Word, created. The human life of Jesus is the perfect human life because it is the life perfectly responsive to the Father; for it is the human life of the Son. In him the full meaning of being human is attained. He is the true Adam, of which the first man was but an imprint, as Saint Paul said (Rom 5:14). And the life of Jesus was conceived as the fruit of the unqualified response of Mary to the Word, the Son, and through the Son to the Father (Lk 1:38). Hence she is the true Eve, the true mother of all the living, as the Church Fathers delighted in saying.

In Keefe's reading, all this is implied in the teaching of the Council of Chalcedon, which met in 451. With Nicaea (325) having taught that Jesus is the Son of God, "true God from true God", and Ephesus (431) having both confirmed the legitimacy of calling Mary *Theotokos* (meaning the God-bearer, the human mother who bore the Son of God) and condemned the patriarch of Constantinople, Nestorius, who protested that no human being could be literally God's mother, Chalcedon sought to establish beyond further question that the one Lord, Jesus Christ, is truly divine and truly human. To be divine is to possess one set of attributes, and to be human is to possess another. Chalcedon asserted that Jesus possesses both, shares in both, which fact would later come to be expressed by the phrase "communication of idioms" (*communicatio idiomatum*). As divine he could hardly be contained within any creature's body, but as human he could be and was born of a woman. It is true, Chalcedon taught, to say simultaneously that he was not born and that he was, for Jesus and the Son are "one and the same". There is a single identity, though that identity is divine and human. There is a single "I", the perfect Son, in union with whose human perfection we ourselves may be made perfect. But, Keefe reasons, if that created identity as Son is complete, is perfect, it must be personal. Jesus must be a human person, humanly complete in his identity, born as a son to Mary, even though he is in his identity also the uncreated Son, eternally begotten of the Father.

The Primordiality of Jesus

The credal Symbol of the Council of Chalcedon, the definitive statement of the Church's faith in the full divinity, the full humanity, and
the Personal unity of Jesus the Christ, famously teaches that Jesus
the Christ, the Son of the Father, is the Son of Mary, "one and the
same". Consubstantial at once with the Father's divinity and with
Mary's humanity, Jesus is fully man, fully God, in the unity of his one
Person. A century later, the ecumenical council II of Constantinople
(553), taught that Jesus, the one Person, is the *Logos* of John 1:14.
With few exceptions, the doctrine of II Constantinople is read as a
denial that Jesus is a human Person.

Thus those theologians whose *quaerens intellectum* begins nonhis-
torically with a nonhistorical divine Son—i.e., a Son who, at the
Incarnation, "assumes" a human nature and subsists thereafter in
that intellectual nature—fail to understand that, even in this dehistoricized view of the Incarnation, in which the immanent Son, the
Word, becomes, not fallen "flesh", but simply human in a generalized,
nonhistorical sense, the Son in the "event" of the Incarnation cannot
but become a human Person, *for he is conceived by and born of a human
mother*, whose Son is the Son of God, whom Mary, the *Theotokos*,
would name "Jesus". It cannot be thought that her Son as Son—a personal name—is not human, yet the routine denial that he is a human
Person, that as Person he is human, says precisely that.

"Name" in the Old Testament and the New is always a personal
designation. One might suppose that Mary's "naming" of her Son
"Jesus"—a human name whose significance invokes the whole of the
history of the Old Testament—would be dispositive of the matter, for
he is thus named by the woman whose "Fiat mihi secundum verbum
tuum" ["Let it be done to me according to your word"] makes her to
be the Seat of Wisdom, for her "Fiat" is the form of all the worship

From Donald J. Keefe, S.J., "'The Word was made flesh and dwelt among us' (John
1:14)", *Studia Missionalia*, 51 (2002): 23–52.

of the Church, and her own doctrinal infallibility is that of the second Eve, which is to say, of the Church. Her naming of her Son has been accepted without question by all the generations of Christians who are so by their baptism and their faith in his Name: the faith that the Man whom Mary named Jesus is the Lord. The liturgical interpretation of "Son" trumps all secondary speculation: it is by the liturgy that the faith is nourished, and the criterion of its truth can only be liturgical: it is in his Name that we are baptized.

Theologians commonly agree with St. Thomas that to be a "person" is to subsist in an intellectual nature. Chalcedon teaches that Jesus is a single subsistence in two natures, this to the point of his Personal consubstantiality with both. He is at once God and man by reason of his single subsistence at once in the nature of God, as the second Person of the Trinity, the son of the Father, and in the nature of man, as the Son of Mary. The Fathers at Chalcedon seven times denied the inference that this unique subsistence by Jesus in two natures results in the personal duality of "two sons": emphatically, Jesus is "one and the same" Son....

There is an ample New Testament and particularly Pauline witness to the pre-existence of Jesus as primordial rather than as eternal, hence to his pre-existence as concrete and human. For Paul the pre-existent *Logos* is *Jesus*, whom he later describes as "the Beginning" in whom all things are created (Col. 1:15–16); it is *Jesus* who, as pre-existent and divine, emptied himself, was obedient to death, even to death on the cross (Phil. 2:5–12), and who, in 2 Tim. 1:9, is "the grace held out to us in Christ Jesus before the world began". Above all, Jesus is for Paul the second Adam, a title whose evident primordial import is taken up in the Johannine Christological title, "Alpha and Omega". The Johannine witness is equally explicit: the Prologue, where alone the *Logos* title occurs, is a borrowing from an early Christian hymn to Jesus, as also is the hymn adopted forty years earlier by Paul and inserted into Phil. 2: they anticipate and ground the piety of the early second-century Church, whose members,

> as they confessed to Pliny, were in the habit of meeting together before dawn and singing a hymn 'to Christ as to God.'[2]

[2]J.N.D. Kelly, *Early Christian Doctrines*, rev. ed. (San Francisco: HarperSanFrancisco, 1978), 143, citing Pliny, *Ep.* 96 [original footnote].

Pliny the Younger heard this "confession" in the Roman Province of Bithynia, which, for a few years after 110 A.D., he governed under Trajan: these were the years during which Ignatius Martyr, on his journey in chains from his See of Antioch to the Colosseum in Rome where he would die, wrote his famous *Letters to the Churches* of Asia Minor. Bithynia was a rural part of Asia Minor, located in what is now northwest Turkey. Its unsophisticated Christians knew nothing of a nonhistorical Son of the eternal Father. Rather they spontaneously affirmed, with the whole primitive Church, in an untutored, spontaneous "communication of idioms", the Personal unity of Jesus with God: "Jesus is the Lord." They had learned their faith in Jesus as the Lord from an apostolic tradition which Irenaeus, the quondam pupil of the martyred Polycarp of Smyrna, brought to Rome a generation later. Irenaeus refused to speculate on the generation of the Son in the manner of the Christian Stoics. Rather, his Christology had a protological focus upon the second Adam. His emphasis upon the unity of Christ, his insistence that Jesus the Christ is "one and the same", was adopted by the Fathers at Chalcedon, in whose Symbol it appears seven times.

We have no reason to suppose that the Christian community that composed the hymn which John the Evangelist wrote into the Prologue of his Gospel would have differed in the essentials of its faith from the Christian community that Pliny knew, particularly given the close links between the unitary, anti-docetic Johannine Christology and the doctrinal emphasis upon the unity of Christ and of the Church taught a dozen years later by Ignatius of Antioch and Polycarp of Smyrna.

In sum, the piety of the primitive Church of the end of the first century and the beginning of the second cannot be squared with a devotion to a nonhistorical *Logos*, a Christ, who is not the human Son of a human mother with human ancestry. All the meagre evidence we have from the dawn of the second century goes in the other direction. Quite as the authors of the hymn borrowed by Paul in Phil. 2:5–12 attributed pre-existence to Jesus, the authors of the hymn borrowed by the Evangelist can hardly be supposed to have been burdened by a Stoic reading of the *logos sarx egeneto* ["the word became flesh"]. In sum, the faith that Jesus is Lord governs the Church's reading of John 1:14. . . .

The basic Christological problem faced by theologians over the centuries since Justin [Martyr] has emerged from his false supposition that God as God is nonhistorical. This posture of Christological problematic adopts, unreflectively, the pagan notion of divinity as a monadic Absolute, incapable of relation as a matter of definition....

... It is evident under this postulate that the divine Son, *qua* absolute divinity, can have no Personal unity with any divine Person or with anything created: he can have no consubstantiality whether with the Father and the Spirit, or with Jesus's fully human nature. Thus, the man Jesus cannot be said to be the divine Son of the Father, cannot be said to be divine: neither can the Son's Personal identity with his humanity be asserted by the communication of idioms—for that communication is rendered *a priori* impossible by the dehistoricizing presuppositions under which Nestorius and his allies labored—in vain....

Once again the postulate of an abstract, monadic divinity as the subject of the *logos sarx egeneto* stood as an absolute bar to the Incarnation, for divinity so conceived must be abstract, remote from history, in order to be divine. Every rationalized paganism has known this: the alternative to the transcendence-by-absence of the *Deus otiosus* [God at leisure] is always an immanence in history that fragments the *Deus unus* into a plethora of lesser divinities.

It is enough to state the postulate to recognize the absurdity of its application to the God of the Covenant whom the Catholic tradition knows as transcending history only by his immanence within it, an immanence which cannot be rationalized according to some *a priori* notion of God as Absolute without denying either his historicity or his divinity or both. It is further evident that a humanity thus monophysitically subordinated to the divine can have no human freedom or historicity.

The abstract, impersonal humanity of Jesus is then overwhelmed by his concrete divinity, his divine Sonship, with which his humanity is presumed to compose within the unity of one nature (*mia physis*).

Against such cosmologically induced confusion, it must be insisted that the Symbol of Chalcedon, the foundational doctrinal statement of the Church's faith in Jesus the Christ, knows no non-historical "immanent" Son and can recognize as theological no question rising out of the aprioristically induced presupposition of such a Son. The Church's faith, like her worship, is historical and has for its formal object only the historical Person whom the Symbol describes so carefully, so definitively. One cannot suppose the faith of John the Evangelist, as expressed in the Prologue of his Gospel, or the faith of Paul, the missionary of missionaries, as affirmed in the second chapter of his Epistle to the Philippians, to be in some manner dissociated from the Church's mature statement of her faith in Jesus the Lord.

In brief, the Johannine "*Logos*" is a historical title of the historical Jesus, as is evident in the protological passage in Phil. 2:5–9, paralleling that of the Prologue, and in the less familiar passage in 2 John 1:7, which similarly attributes coming "in flesh" to Jesus rather than to a nonhistorical Son or *Logos*. The historical interpretation of John 1:14, compatible with Chalcedon's historical hermeneutic of the faith, understands "*Logos*" as a title of the historical Jesus, quite as "Christ" is understood. Further, with the Old Testament and in the New, it reads "flesh" historically, to refer specifically to fallen and thereby mortal, "fleshly", humanity. This historical hermeneutic extends to the pre-existence implicit in John 1:14, Phil. 2:5–9, 2 John 1:7, 2 Tim. 1:9, and many other protological statements concerning Jesus which might be cited. The pre-existence of Jesus is historical: it is to be identified with the "Beginning" of Gen. 1:1....

It follows that the Father's Mission of the Son to give the Spirit, if it is to be distinguished from and so be the revelation of the [immanent] processions, must be historical. It is so by the reference of the sending of the Son and the gift of the Spirit to the Event in which they terminate, the Good Creation, the Kingdom of God that is effectively and irrevocably signed by the sacrificial institution of the New Covenant, the One Flesh of Christ and his Church, the Father's unsurpassable gift of the Spirit through the obedience of his Son. This Event is the final term of the full exercise of the divine Trinitarian omnipotence. It is the fullness, the plenitude, the totality, of the Triune God's relation to the world, at once creative, revelatory, redemptive, and salutary. The Word does not proceed without accomplishing that for which it was sent. This, the doctrine of Dominus Jesus, was the teaching of the Old Testament before it was that of the New Testament. There is no salvation which is not absolutely dependent upon the grace of Christ, upon his restoration of all things from the cross and on the altar. There is no other Name by which we may be saved. Upon the mission of the Son all else depends.

The Event of the mission of the Son, the radical grace of God, from the Father, through the Son, in the Spirit, is clearly *ex nihilo*. Its truth is a matter of revelation, not of inference: it is evident that from the absolute freedom of God no inferences may be drawn. It must further be kept clearly in mind that from abstract, dehistoricized definitions of the divine omnipotence, omniscience, omnipresence, and so on, only abstract inferences may be drawn. Such inferences provide no ground for the gratuity of the mission of the Son. That mission in fact reveals the concrete, historical meaning of those otherwise abstract ideas, for they have no other actual meaning than that which is revealed in Christ, just as there is no other God than the One God revealed in Christ. The quest for abstract clarities of thought has no theological foundation.

This mission of the Son to give the Spirit is thus the Beginning of which Paul and John both wrote. The *terminus* of the mission of the Son to give the Spirit is the Whole Christ, the second Adam in nuptial union with his bridal Church, the Body in free covenantal union with the Head, from whom she receives her free unity with him, the freedom of their One Flesh. Theology has no other starting point than this Beginning. As the Eucharistic sacrifice is the cause of the Church, so the Eucharistic One Flesh is the foundation of the theological tradition: it is the single Mystery we seek to understand ever more fully, knowing it to be inexhaustible and always fascinating.

Christ's Pre-existence

The primordiality of the Covenant refers to the transcendent metaphysical status of the historical Jesus, the Son of God who is the Christ, the Son of Mary, in his life, his death, his Resurrection. At the same time and inseparably it refers to that created feminine reality, whether viewed as Mary or as the Church, who in covenantal and integrally free association with his Mission is the second Eve, inseparable from him because [subsisting] in the integral and primordial covenantal union with him that is their One Flesh.

"Pre-existence", then, is not a temporal nor a cosmological but a covenantal and historical notion, and therefore it has a metaphysical, covenantal, and historical meaning.

From Donald J. Keefe, S.J., *Covenantal Theology: The Eucharistic Order of History*, rev. ed. (Novato, Calif.: Presidio Press, 1996), 221.

3

CREATION IN CHRIST

Keefe, like so many theologians in recent decades, has taken note of how important in the opening lines of Genesis is the notion of gift. In stark contrast to the Babylonian account of the making of things, the *Enuma Elish*, whose copies date back to the same period, in which victorious Marduk carves the world out of the chaotic remains of slain Tiamat and, in quest of creatures to serve at the whim of the gods, forms humanity from the blood of her ally, the demon Kingu, Genesis depicts the one God, by the command of his word, bringing into existence the physical world, manifoldly varied, completely other than himself yet secure, stable, having value for its own sake, six times seen by its maker to be "good" and, at its completion, in its totality, seen to be "very good". In the Gospel of John, however, the work of the Word is far from complete. For it is the mission of the Son to bring each person to a decision for the Father who sent him; to offer those who have so decided not just life but life abundant (Jn 10:10) because united to the Son who abides with the Father; growing in this way into the fullness of Christ (Eph 4:11–16). This life, from its beginning to its final actualization in what Ephesians describes as Christ come to maturity (ἡλικία3, is what Keefe calls the Good Creation.

There is only one created reality, having spiritual members and material; indeed, Karl Rahner maintained that it is the immanence of spiritual beings in the affairs of matter that has united the physical world into a single history.[1] But whereas what Rahner had in mind was the angelic, for Keefe it is the human. The angelic may be related

[1] Karl Rahner, S.J., "The Unity of Spirit and Matter in the Christian Understanding of Faith", *Theological Investigations*, vol. 6 (London: Darton, Longman & Todd, 1969; Baltimore: Helicon Press, 1969), 153–77.

to material creation, but it belongs to the human to act collaboratively in the creation of the human and to do so precisely as material. It is this unique aspect of the human as personal that provides the ground for material creation in all its nonhuman diversity; by virtue of the human, there is additionally the vast array of the physical world said by Genesis to be meaningful and beautiful, in and of itself. As a consequence, while Rahner spoke of the angelic realm and the material world being created simultaneously,[2] Keefe includes with this the creation of the human, and the human specifically as the basis for the material.

Spiritual creatures, however, whether angelic or human, as personal, are by their nature self-transcendent. What is simply material is merely immanent, reacting to the world without ever fully engaging the world, behaving in ways that might be spontaneous or instinctive or even learned, but never self-directive and in that sense never free. Yet the limit on the capacity to transcend oneself that is characteristic of even conscious material being is the antithesis of the personal; for persons are open to what is true, good, and beautiful as they are perfected both in their commitment to these three and in the giving of themselves to other persons. What makes possible this transcendence toward the other is an existence that is rooted in the other. Created persons exist as created in the Son, who exists in the Father; the reason again why, according to Keefe, creation entails the historicity of the Word.

All of these traits of the human person—free, oriented to the other, collaborative in the generation of life—are expressed in the human as bodily, in human masculinity and femininity. For Keefe, if the order of human life was to be a created image of the divine, then it had to be founded on an unrestricted offer of self: first of all to God, but secondarily, on the basis of this primary offer, an unrestricted offer of oneself to another human person; founded, that is, on an offer made by two who are genuinely distinct, complementary but different, such that their common gift points immediately beyond itself to become the condition of possibility for another personal life. This offer between persons different even in body is a quintessentially human act, the act of the unconditional promise. However many persons God might intend to create in this order, in concert with the free collaboration of the members of this order, the order itself would be founded on

---

[2] Ibid., 158, 172.

the free pledging to each other of two, man and woman.[3] Following Pauline usage in 1 Corinthians 11:3–12 and Ephesians 5:22–33, Keefe writes that the entire created human order is structured according to the relationality of man and woman—masculinity and femininity—uniquely instantiated in the first man and first woman. That primal union, the foundation of the human order, was to arise from the "headship" of the man, meaning his role as a source of the unity made complete in the reciprocal activity of the woman, whose mutual gift of herself would underlie the "glory" (Paul's word is δόξα) that would be their shared life. It is in view of this that Keefe refers to the human order as nuptial, without thereby meaning that the ideal human state is marriage or that human perfection is reserved to marriage. He does, however, mean that marriage rests on the same free decision of two united in complementarity that first shaped human creation.

Personal freedom, of course, is not an attribute that can be created entirely from the outside. Freedom exists only in its exercise. An order of free persons that is composed, to the greatest extent possible, of individuals who exist in virtue of the free decision of unreservedly united individuals requires that it take its beginning from two. Their commitment will frame this order, in demonstration of a capacity for self-transcendence that is the effect of their having been created in the Son, who participates in the Father's decision to create as part of his self-offering to the Father. Yet their transcendence can be made complete, and completely actual, only in a response to the Father and to the Son that is a decision to join the Son in giving himself. To choose otherwise would be to stunt this transcendence, to undermine their freedom, and to diminish the free nature of the order they were to help form with their choice.

Now the Christian knows that the divine intention to create involved not simply an order of free human persons but of human persons united in one life with God himself. Thus, the order has its ultimate ground in the decision of a couple separate from the primal two: the decision of a man who, perfectly free, infallibly chooses for the Father, because his is the created identity of the Son; and the decision

---

[3] So also Karl Rahner in his early essay "Theological Reflexions on Monogenism", *Theological Investigations*, vol. 1 (London: Darton, Longman & Todd, 1961; New York: Seabury Press, 1974), 292–94.

of a woman, born of the order the first couple has shaped, who, in choosing the will of the Father which is also the will of the Son, becomes the one through whom the man is born, the one through whom he belongs to the created order in the same manner intended for every person born into that order, namely, in virtue of human femininity. It is this couple who guarantees, absolutely, the unqualified human response to God, the unreserved handing to the Father of the free human existence that was brought forth in conjunction with the first couple—even if it happens that that first couple's free decision altered for the worse humanity's condition—which, with the Father's acceptance, establishes the order of human existence in God. Notwithstanding the pivotal significance of the first couple as head and body, to use Paul's terms, in constituting the human order, those roles are fulfilled only in reliance upon this couple. And in the event of that first couple's betraying their role, it is this couple who become the exclusive Head and Body of the Good Creation, though Keefe cautions against taking these terms, which are used in Ephesians 5 to stress the depth of unity in both marriage and the Church, in any sense that would detract from the free assent on which the unity is based. Hence, according to Keefe, creation, the Good Creation, is not just nuptial in its order; it is covenantal, meaning that it is founded on a freely reciprocal yet immutable bond, the immutability of which is the basis for the divine promise in Genesis 6:18 of life's final victory over sin.

For this reason, too, Keefe considers the title "Christ" to be a primordial title for the Son, because it refers to the Son's role as the one in whom and through whom creation gives itself to the Father primordially, from the outset—a self-giving that is made complete in the Spirit, or becomes sacrificial because of sin. The New Covenant in the blood of Jesus, made present Eucharistically, is the mode of Christ's work in our own age. But Keefe is unique in taking passages such as 1 Corinthians 8:6 and Colossians 1:16 as meaning, not just that the world was created as leading up to Christ, or cognizant of the coming need for Christ, but was actually created in Christ, in the Son's free relation to the Father, belonging to the Son. And creation is made manifest as fully belonging to the Son when the Son is known to be Jesus.

The Good Creation

The *sine qua non* for the recovery of a Catholic intellectuality, for a consciousness congruent with the Catholic faith and the Catholic sacramental worship, with Catholic existence in history, is the recovery of the Trinitarian paradigm of reality, which recovery is also the recognition of the covenantal quality of the Good Creation. That is to say, we must recover the freedom and the historicity of rationality as such: this is the Catholic, the Christian birthright for which the mess of pottage now served up is no fair exchange. We must understand at a level heretofore neglected if not unplumbed the Tri-Unity of God and the covenantal unity of the created order which images God *only as covenantal*. This imaging is the actuality of the Good Creation, at once its historicity and its truth, its unity, its beauty, and its goodness. Apart from this Trinitarian imaging, which is the historical actuality of the Covenant, there remains for rational exploration only that *nihil*, that extinction of God and man long since established as the single alternative to the free historical appropriation of the Good Creation in the covenantal worship of the Church....

The reality whose truth the faith affirms, which grounds all theology and with which alone theology is concerned, is historical and free, the New Covenant. It is Covenant rather than cosmos, and this is the Good News which theology is not permitted to gainsay. This larger world of the Gospel is simply the New Creation, the primordial Good Creation to which Genesis bears witness, which Paul and John and the synoptic Gospels proclaim and which the Church celebrates in the memorial of the Sacrifice by which it is created and redeemed....

The ordered unity of history is that of the liturgy, the order of the Church's worship, whose center and source is the Eucharistic sacrifice, by which the Spirit, the Gift who enables us to turn and return to the Father of Jesus, is poured out upon the Church. Equivalently, it is

From Donald J. Keefe, S.J., *Covenantal Theology*, 6, 126, 661–63.

in and by the Spirit, through this liturgy, within this worship of the Lord of history, that we enter into the freedom that is the history of salvation, whose objectivity is free, freely to be appropriated: the free order of the Old to the New Covenant, and of the New Covenant to the Kingdom.

Within this Eucharistic liturgy we affirm, in truth—for the Spirit by which we worship the Father through the Son is the Spirit of him who is Truth incarnate—that the whole of the Old Covenant history is significant and possesses that significance, which is its historical truth, only in being objectively ordered to the New Covenant; we affirm that the New Covenant, wherein the full objective meaning of history is revealed to be immanent and salvific, is thus immanent and salvific as yet further ordered to the achieved Kingdom of God. Newman's famous observation that to be deep in history is to cease to be Protestant has here its ground.[4] ...

This historical order is Trinitarian, but not as Joachim of Fiore understood it to be, as though the Old Covenant were the time of the Father, the New Covenant the time of the Son, and the eschatological fulfillment of history the time of the Spirit. Rather, the Father's sending of the Son to give the Spirit has a single finality, the fulfilled Kingdom of God by which history is itself fulfilled, not annulled as Joachim's synthesis required—and Hegel's. It is by original sin and the fall that time itself has fallen from the nuptially ordered freedom of the primordial Beginning to the chaotic necessity of *sarx*; by the primordial fall, the obedient immanence of the Son in the Good Creation became an immanence in *sarx*, and thereby an obedience "unto death, even death on a cross", which obedience instituted the *mia sarx* [one flesh] of the New Covenant wherein the free unity, the nuptial order, of the Good Creation was restored by a grace yet more comprehensive than that offered the first Adam in "the Beginning".

The immanence of Jesus in creation, his free, creative transcendence of its freedom by that immanence, is the metaphysical prius of creation itself. The hymnic material in the New Testament is particularly eloquent of this primordiality of the Christ. His primordiality is

---

[4] John Henry Cardinal Newman, *An Essay in the Development of Doctrine*, 6th ed., foreword by Ian Kerr (Notre Dame, Ind.: University of Notre Dame Press), 8. Citation provided in Donald J. Keefe, *Covenantal Theology: The Eucharistic Order of History*, rev. ed. (Novato, Calif.: Presidio Press, 1996), 678n11.

that of Jesus, the Chalcedonian "one and the same", a primordiality which can only be Eucharistic: none other is at once human, historical, and free. His Eucharistic immanence, as thus primordial, is a historical constant, the Event transcendent to and redemptive of the fall, and is in fact itself the free condition of the free possibility of the fall. However, because immanent in the freely fallen order of creation, his transcendent immanence, his Lordship, became redemptive, the salvific reordering of fragmented time toward the Kingdom of God from which the good creation is, as fallen, alienated. This nuptial reordering, the Pauline *anakephalaiosis* [recapitulation], is his sacrificial institution by the Head of the One Flesh of the New Covenant, the Event universally redemptive of all fallen history, which within fallen history can be objective and actual only in the enigma and obscurity of its sacramental integration by the Eucharistic sacrifice.

Consequently, the Trinitarian Missions are *sacramentally* actual in fallen history, for their historical dimension would otherwise have been subordinate to *sarx* and, in common with all *sarx*, would have receded into the past, to become ever more remote, ever more inaccessible, finally forgotten. This is to say that while the terminus for whose achievement the Son was sent to give the Spirit, the fulfilled Kingdom of God, was objectively achieved in history by the life, death, and resurrection of the Son, the Head, that achievement is Trinitarian, Lordly and redemptive, and therefore transcendent to and the prius of all time....

The Christ could not be the ordering principle of history were his life, death, and resurrection merely a past event, subsumed to temporal necessity, to *sarx* merely. Therefore that fulfillment, that redemptive Lordship, is historically actual only as *mia sarx*, in the transcendent Event of the Eucharistic sacrifice, the Event of the institution of the New Covenant in history, in the One Flesh of the second Adam and the second Eve, the recapitulation of the good creation. The One Sacrifice of the Cross and the One Sacrifice offered in the Church in the person and by the authority of Christ are a single unique Event, distinct only in the manner of their offering. They cannot be thought of as in isolation or as objectively different. Each includes the other, for without the Eucharistic representation of the One Sacrifice of the Cross, that One Sacrifice could not be redemptive: it transcends history, and so redeems it, only as Eucharistically represented. The Event of the Eucharist is the Event of the Cross: they are indissociable, concretely and [numerically] identical, a single Event....

The Eucharistic immanence of Jesus the Lord is then the historical terminus of the Trinitarian Missions—of the Son by the Father, of the Spirit by the Father through the Son. It is in and by the Eucharistic sacrifice that the risen Christ is present in history, ordering it salvifically by the definitive gift of the Spirit poured out upon the Church. By this Gift, history is the effective sign of the fulfilled Kingdom of God: the past, the present, and the future have this single, ordered, and objectively efficacious significance.

It has been insisted heretofore that the event of the fall is meaningless unless it is seen to be transcended by the Event of the second Adam, the Alpha and the Omega: *only the priority of grace makes intelligible the moral freedom of the primordial fall.* But this grace can only be the grace of Christ, *gratia capitis* [the grace of the Head], the grace won on the Cross. Were it not for the Eucharistic immanence of the redemptive Event of the second Adam, the grace of Christ would not be transcendent to time and, consequently, would have receded inexorably into the historical past, subordinated to the unredeemed and unredeemable, immanent necessities which are the structure of the fallen creation.

4

ORIGINAL SIN

One of Keefe's signature concerns has been to argue against the misunderstanding that the Incarnation was God's response to sin. Yet it is hardly a unique position. Although most closely identified with John Duns Scotus (d. 1308), it may be found in the early-twelfth-century writer Rupert of Deutz and also Honorius of Autun (d. 1154), who said that Christ was incarnate in order to fulfill God's eternal plan for the "deification" of humanity.[1] Even Thomas Aquinas (d. 1274) acknowledged that one can think of many reasons why God would have undertaken the Incarnation, including that in this way the circuit of creation is made complete: for man, the last to be created, is thereby united to the beginning of all things, marking a consummation or final perfection of the universe. Nevertheless, he wrote, no one knows better what God had in mind than God himself; and what we read in the record of his revelation, the Scriptures, is that the Son became man because of sin (*propter peccatum*), in order to gain our redemption.[2]

What is unique to Keefe is the insistence that there could be no creation of a free humanity, of human individuals in full possession

[1] Honorius of Autun, *Libellus octo quaestionum* c. 2: "Causa autem Christi incarnationis fuit praedestinatio humanae deificationis: ab aeterno quippe a Deo erat praedestinatum, ut homo deificaretur, dicente Domino: 'Pater, dilexisti eos ante constitutionem mundi' (Jn 17), subaudi, per me deificandos." *Patrologia Latina*, ed. J.-P. Migne, vol. 172 (Paris, 1895), 1187.

[2] Thomas Aquinas, *III Sent.* dist. 1, q. 1, a. 3. See also *Summa theologiae* IIIa, q. 1, a. 3, c. However, Thomas conceded that the question remained a matter of opinion. In his *Compendium theologiae* c. 201, he was willing to list these many other reasons without the caveat that Scripture speaks expressly only of our redemption from sin. And in *Summa theologiae* IIa-IIae, q. 2, a. 7, c, he himself argues that the first man, Adam, knew from the start that Christ would be incarnate for the sake of the "consummation of glory" because this consummation begins with Christ's union with his Church, and the man knew that Christ's future union was already signified by his own union with the woman who had been fashioned from his side.

of their freedom in the opening moment of their existence, without the simultaneous exercise of their freedom in response to their Creator; and that the only way there could be an absolute promise, a covenantal promise, to overcome the effects of a free decision that turned away from the Creator, would be if that decision came in the context of an order of human existence founded on a human will that could not but be devoted to the Creator because it is the Creator's human will, the will of the Son who is one with the Father, in the Spirit. To Keefe's mind, this is the meaning of Genesis declaring six times the goodness of creation and, at its completion, pronouncing it very good. This creation, at whose center lies human freedom, can be injured but never lost.

The alternative would be humanity having no other intrinsic principle of unity than the primal couple whose response would shape the human existential order; and if it happened that what they imparted was the disintegrating force of their refusal to participate in the Son's self-gift to the Father, then the Incarnation would be only a single human life in a world of alienated lives, illustrating a level of human perfection available to no one else. As Keefe observed early on in his career, "the Incarnation cannot be understood as though it were an accidental incursion into natural humanity of an extraordinary God-man bearing extraordinary information, as an adventitious remedy for the Fall."[3] The Son of God coming down into the world as an outsider must remain an outsider. Certainly Aquinas does well to underscore the consistent emphasis in Scripture on Jesus Christ, encountered immediately and experientially, as our savior from sin; but not at the expense of those passages that identify him as the foundation of the created order.

It is generally held in biblical studies that Genesis 3 is a tightly constructed, symbolic narrative.[4] In fact the first three chapters as a whole are regarded as highly stylized, the stylistic differences being used to distinguish what are thought to have been originally separate literary

---

[3] Donald J. Keefe, S.J., *Thomism and the Ontological Theology of Paul Tillich* (Leiden, Netherlands: Brill, 1971), 91.

[4] The view of Joseph Coppens that the story of the first sin was intended as an indictment of the Canaanite cult of fertility was particularly influential among Catholic biblical scholars. See, for example, Joseph Coppens, *La connaissance du bien et du mal et le péché du Paradis* (Louvain: Nauwelaerts, 1948).

strands that were later joined into a single account. Yet it is understood that the intention of the authors was to make a series of objective claims; claims that, in time, were to form the heart of Judaism and of the Christian gospel. Among these claims is the teaching that there is only one God; that God, of himself, acting deliberately, systematically, and beneficently, made everything that this visible and anthropocentric world comprises. Its anthropocentrism is represented in the opening chapter by the making of humanity on the sixth and final day of creation; in the second chapter by the fact that the first living thing made is the man and the last living thing made is the woman; and in both chapters by the description of human beings as the only creatures who are able to be addressed and commanded by the divine word that, in the first chapter, brought all things into existence. Only human beings, faithful to the word, can anchor the world in the word, ensuring the continued integrity of the world the word brought about; which capacity is the source of their authority in the world.

But, Genesis 3 contends, human beings never were faithful. There is no use of unbetrayed authority. Immediately on being fashioned and united in "one flesh", the first woman and the first man reject the word they have been given. Entertaining the conceit that they would lose nothing by their act, mutual trust is the very first thing to go. And over the course of the following eight chapters, there is nothing, within themselves, between each other, and in the world around them, that is not, in the words of the Council of Trent, "changed for the worse".[5] With biting irony, the man names the woman with whom he was to collaborate with the Author of life, Eve, "because she was the mother of all the living." Yet the first instance of death is the murder by her firstborn son, Cain, of her second-born, Abel. Augustine would call the act at the beginning of things the "original sin" (*peccatum originale*)[6] both because it was committed at the origin of human history (hence the later phrase *peccatum originale originans*, meaning original sin as the first, the "originating" sin) and because its influence is present at the outset of each individual life (expressed in the phrase *peccatum originale originatum*, or original sin as "originated" meaning "present in" Adam's descendants). The turning away from God (*aversio a Deo*) and

---

[5] Council of Trent, Session 5, *Decree on Original Sin*, 1.
[6] Augustine, *To Simplician*, 1.10.

toward themselves that constituted the couple's primal sin, displayed once more in Cain's reaction when the Lord challenges his perverse idea of a gift, Augustine regards as a transmissible reflex that he refers to as concupiscence (*concupiscentia*), a term that figured prominently in the Latin translations of Saint Paul.

Keefe takes each of these claims in Genesis as foundational. In his own analysis, however, with everything having been created in Christ, and the human lying at the center of the physical world, and with the very first choice requiring a decision for the Father in Christ, original sin is located in the opening moment of human freedom, in the first instant of human existence. And that means at the very beginning of creation. It may be that Genesis represents the Fall in symbolic terms, but the meaning cannot be that the world must begin in a state of collision and conflict, only over time to grow into an integral whole, any more than to say that the world was created in and through Christ means only that it was created in view of a final union with him. The Fall, Keefe argues, was an actual event; but it was a free event that shaped space and time in their formation. It was not just another event in their continuum; not, in other words, the kind of thing to be unearthed by a Louis Leakey, conducting his digs at Olduvai Gorge. Long past decisions may be lost in the mists of history; this was a primordial decision whose stamp is in evidence everywhere.

Only in the light of Christ is there a clear understanding of the fullness of the Good Creation. The opening two chapters of Genesis are unique in placing human freedom at the center of things, but the description of the unfallen world proceeds—not so very differently from ancient accounts of a golden age—by simply inverting the features of the world as we know it. Yet there never was an Eden; no paradisal beginning of creation. There never was what would have been the initial reception of life by the man and woman, handed back to the Father in Christ. The man did not assume the role of head, did not become the source of life truly other than his own; nor did the woman become the source of life intimately rooted in her own. There was no uniting, no bond from which the nexus of human life arising from human life would take its start. The rejection of the Father was also a spurning of each other. There was literally a first moment, and literally a first couple in that moment; the structure of human creation established by the Father in and through the Son requires that. But in consequence of their sin, they remained in isolation from the world the Father brought about and that they diminished.

We will never know what the world would have looked like if there had been no sin. The openness of created being, including material being, its relationality, remained unchanged; yet everywhere it is in tension with an entropic resistance to unity. We will never know what human sexuality, masculinity and femininity, would have looked like. The persons whom God has always intended still are born from human interiority, the fruit of human union in not just otherness but difference. But it would be the physical world, created to share in the pattern of human existence, that would now govern the mode and manner of human generation; the adaptive forces at work in biological change that would determine the morphology of the human body. All of which serves to remind us that original sin is a theological, not an empirical, datum.[7] It is a doctrine founded on revelation, an insight arrived at through a very particular series of questions, questions that were very different from the questions posed, for example, by evolutionary science. And yet every formal, self-critical inquiry, whether based on faith or on reason, proceeds to the mutual benefit of the many separate human investigations into the one truth.

[7] Pope Pius XII, in his 1950 encyclical *Humani generis*, no. 37, ruled that the Catholic faithful are required to accept monogenism or the claim that all the human race has descended from a single man, despite the clear evidence of both anthropology and genetics to the contrary, only because by his own admission he could not see any other way of protecting revealed teaching, not because of some antipathy to science itself. The solution, of course, lay in a call for theologians to reexamine the way in which they were framing their questions, rather than a critique of the way natural scientists were phrasing theirs.

The Fall

The problem of understanding our factual solidarity with the sin and fall worked by the first Adam and the redemption effected by the second Adam remains very nearly where it was for Augustine. If we no longer find ourselves affirming the literal historicity of Genesis 1–3, yet we must affirm its facticity as it bears upon original sin *originans*. However reluctant we may be to admit that death entered the world by reason of a primordial sin, yet the scriptural affirmation is clear.

But since Augustine there has been a generally unnoticed development of the doctrine concerning original sin and fall, a development of late sometimes deprecated and held to be of only marginal significance, but which is of the highest importance for the doctrine of the Good Creation and, so, for the doctrine of the fall. This development is manifest in the proclamation at Ephesus of Mary's dignity as the Mother of God and, long afterward, in the papal definitions of her Immaculate Conception and of the Assumption of the woman who is the *Theotokos*, the second Eve.

These doctrines state the integrity and the eschatological fulfillment of Mary, the mother of the "one and the same" Son whose divinity and humanity are at one, unmixed and inseparable in a personal unity transcending their distinction. In her, motherhood and bridal virginity are integral: this is what the integrity of her unfallen femininity means. Like her Son, the Bridegroom, she exists primordially; she does so in utter dependence upon her Head, as the second Eve who is One Flesh with the primordial second Adam who is her source. By reason of the unique plenitude of grace which is hers, by which she is the Immaculate Conception, she alone is able freely to affirm the presence to humanity of the Lord. Apart from her unflawed and integrally free "Fiat", his presence could only be by some kind of imposition, some act of divine despotism, which would invoke all

From Donald J. Keefe, S.J., *Covenantal Theology*, 215–24, 237, 239, 242–43, 244.

the antagonism between humanity and divinity upon which pagan-ism feeds and which the cosmologies institutionalize. The covenantal immanence of God as the Son of man, the Immanuel, is comprehen-sible only on the basis of Mary's sinlessness, for her integral freedom is constitutive for the New Covenant itself.

It is evident, now as during the combat with gnosticism in the sec-ond and third centuries, that once given the fundamental doctrine of the creation *ex nihilo sui et subjecti*[8] of man in his world, the dualism which is immediately implicit in any denial of the fall or of its free-dom is barred by the Catholic tradition. Unfortunately, it has been less understood and stressed that the goodness of creation is precisely a *doctrinal* truth, a truth received in faith and available only to faith, and that therefore the created order can be understood to be good, not by commitment to a philosophical metaphysics of whatever pedigree and however time-honored, but only by the liturgical appropriation of the freedom, the covenantal and sponsal truth, of the Good Creation—which is to say, only by and in the historical worship of the Church....

Naturally enough, the theologians who have concerned themselves with the fall have done so in the context provided by the actual contro-versies which have arisen over that topic; these have concerned either the objectivity of the fall *originans* as a free moral event which stands at the beginning of fallen history, or with the solidarity of fallen human-ity with the "sin of Adam", or with our solidarity in the redemption worked by the second Adam, Jesus the Christ. Very little systematic attention has been paid to a more central datum, the free and respon-sible agency of the fall itself: viz. of original sin *originans*.

It is this primordial event, this aboriginal misuse of created freedom, that presents the central systematic problem. Given that a simple lit-eralist interpretation of the Genesis account would reduce the fall to an immanent event of fallen history and thus deprive it of its *raison d'être* by subordinating it to that which it is intended to transcend and account for, it is also true that the fall has doctrinal and therefore theological significance only as an actual event, an actual use of human freedom and, as a real moment, the primordial *terminus a quo* of that

---

[8] This Latin phrase is shorthand for the statement that God brings into existence entirely of himself, without reliance upon any other source, a creation that depends absolutely upon its creator, being derived from nothing previous, whether formal or material; a product exclu-sively of the divine intentionality.

fallen history. Its primordiality is not that of a Platonic idea extrinsic to the world, but rather is covenantal and concrete, the primordiality of the Good Creation. The theological inquiry into this primordial moment therefore must begin with an examination of that free and covenantal Event-structure which is the intrinsic meaning and intelligibility of the Good Creation itself.

The moment of the fall must be the moment of creation, the initial instant of created freedom. This is the moment in which the Covenant is both constituted and offered by the covenantal freedom of the last Adam and the last Eve. In this connection it must be remembered that the last or second Eve, as unfallen, as created in covenantal integrity, is as essential to the constitution of the Covenant as is the free obedience of the second Adam to the Father. Without her free affirmation of her Lord, the primordial creation in Christ which is the New Covenant, which is the term of the Mission of the Son to give the Spirit, would not be actual, for it would not be free and therefore not historical in the sense of morally responsible. In such a hypothesis, creation could not be good for it would not be covenantal or nuptial in its order.

But this is only the primordial condition of possibility of the freedom of the fall: the offer of a covenantal integrity whose refusal is effective, *ex opere operato*,[9] in fallenness. Thus, in some manner yet to be accounted for, the Good Creation is at once constituted in the only way in which it can be constituted, *in Christo* and, in the same instant, is rejected in the only way it can be rejected, by a single act of moral responsibility which in some manner infects us all with sin and death. Yet the Good Creation is not wholly rejected, because the free refusal of the offer of created existence *in Christo* issues not in annihilation but in the substantial diminution of being that is fallenness, the loss of created integrity, the loss then of that free order of existence which is pure gift, supernatural then in the usual meaning of the term.

[9] The expression *ex opere operato*, translated as "by virtue of the work having been worked" or "the action having been performed", is taken from Catholic sacramental theology, where it refers to the teaching that a sacrament makes grace available simply in virtue of the sacramental act being performed according to the manner that the Church teaches it must be performed. Keefe uses the expression here to say that creation fell in the very rejection by the first couple of the unity that is structured by the free response of Mary and Jesus, the Son, to the Father in the Spirit.

The biblical data underlying the doctrine of the fall are therefore baffling: the fact of the Good Creation, a reality and an Event antecedent in being—i.e., metaphysically, which is to say, metaempirically—to the fall; the fact of the fall itself of the first Adam whose responsibility is that of a "representative personality", a "head" in Pauline terms, whose act therefore involves all humanity; the fact of the primordial marital imaging of God by the primordial Christ, the Head who is the last, the second Adam, the Christ, in covenantal union with the primordial and integral second Eve; and the fact of our solidarity with the fallen Adam to the point of a universal but indeliberate participation in his guilt.

By their moral and historically significant (viz., effective) refusal of the integral goodness of their creation, the first Adam and Eve cause the creation to exist as *sarx*, as fallen and so as dying. Their bequest, "propagated" to all those in solidarity with them, for whom their refusal is effective, is of sin and death to a humanity by that "inheritance" alienated, averted, diminished and dying, a humanity deprived henceforth of the fruit of the Tree of Life, existentially acquainted with evil, ashamed, submitted now to the immanent necessities of a fallen world. Thus enslaved, they are no longer able to affirm and to appropriate in covenantal freedom the primordial plenitude which is proper to their own humanity, but which has been irrevocably alienated and disowned in their own name by the first Adam.

Yet with all this, there remains to them the promise of a redemption from this servitude through the seed of the woman henceforth at enmity with her seducer.

The fall as described in Genesis is not then merely moral in the simplistic nominal or juridical sense of an extrinsic punishment for disobedience which leaves creation substantially intact. It is a loss on the level of being, for in the fall the intrinsic free unity, the integrity, of every fallen person and of the fallen community is broken, and no historical reassociation of the fragments can restore that integral unity: it is no longer possible to represent its free unity and plurality. Fallen man comes to the end of all his devices as he began them, fragmented. Original sin is not merely a refusal to obey, a refusal to act in a morally good way; because the freedom of covenanted existence is intrinsic to creation, the fall is first of all *a refusal to be* which is effective at the level of each of the transcendentals, hence a refusal of human and personal unity, goodness, and truth—which is to say, a refusal of the plenitude of covenantal existence that is life in Christ, *plena gratia*.

But in the mystery of iniquity to which we have referred, the freedom of the prospective first "head", the first Adam to whom the offer of integrally covenanted existence was made, is actual only in his refusal as "head" to be thus covenantally integral: i.e., to be free, to be integrated in the One Flesh of the Covenant.

Only by the revelation of this fallenness may we learn that the free creation of a free humanity entails the possibility of its refusal. The *negative* possibility of the fall is actualized only in concrete conjunction with the covenantal condition of that same possibility, the New Covenant in its integrity, for of itself the fall is only negativity, only nothingness. . . .

Personal acquaintance with this mystery is the "knowledge of good and evil" forbidden to the first Adam and the first Eve. It is forbidden because it has within itself, even as actual, no intelligibility, no truth. In this the mystery of iniquity is contrasted with the mystery of Christ, the fullness of being and of truth, whose free plenitude transcends all thought, all possibility.

While original sin in the first Adam does not escape the providence of the Lord of history, the fall, the usurped knowledge of good and evil, is actual only by sin. It is not hidden away in the foreknowledge of God as in a *principium quo*; still less is it rooted in the finitude of our freedom, as is so often supposed; that way lies only a dualist cosmology, requiring finally the negation of moral freedom. But by reason of our creation in Christ we are morally free. To be created in him is to be created in that image and likeness of the Triune God which the fall has refused but not undone, the covenantal image of the second Adam in marital union with the second Eve. The covenanted creation that is in Christ thus imports the offer of covenantal life, a life of integral freedom, which must be freely taken up to be lived, to be actual, for it is impossible, even for God, to create a free creature who is not freely free.

To repeat, the offer of that integral covenantal freedom cannot be delayed to some subsequent moment of creation, for it is constitutive of creation itself, of the Covenant itself. It is then clear that the refusal of creation cannot but also be effective on the level of creation. It is deconstitutive, a metaphysical refusal on the level which is possible to creatureliness primordially constituted in grace—for only a humanity so constituted can be fallen. A people, a humanity, so situated and so created in grace, *in Christo*, cannot annihilate itself, but such a created freedom can choose ever to be less: it is thus that the pit, the obstinate descent into ever more profound depths of nonbeing, is the classic image of damnation.

The initiation of such a refusal is therefore possible only in the primordial moment of creation, for the creation is single, providing but a single moment for the single Event *in Christo*. At any subsequent moment, creation is by supposition already constituted in integral freedom or in fallenness. The actual creation is thus freely fallen, with the unfallen second Adam and second Eve as the covenantal actuality and norm by which fallenness is measured and is real. . . .

It must be remembered that an appropriate demythologization of the biblical accounts of the primordiality of the first Adam cannot rest content merely with a rejection of a naive literalism, and the substitution for it of an equally naive subordination of the theological question to the findings of, e.g., paleontology. Theologians must also respect the explanatory role of such a primordiality and cannot refuse its metaphysical character. This is to say that the mythic statement of a primordial temporal beginning is properly interpreted or demythologized as announcing a *metaphysical* priority.

The lingering suspicion that talk of a primordial moment of a primordial Covenant, and of the primordial actuality and *causal* priority of that Covenant, places the second Adam and the second Eve in some local relation to an aboriginal utopia should firmly be laid to rest. A localization of the pre-fall "paradise", whether in fallen time or fallen space, can make no contribution to our understanding of our solidarity in the first Adam. The primordiality of the Covenant refers to the transcendent metaphysical status of the historical Jesus, the Son of God who is the Christ, the Son of Mary, in his life, his death, his Resurrection. At the same time and inseparably it refers to that created feminine reality, whether viewed as Mary or as the Church, who in covenantal and integrally free association with his Mission is the second Eve, inseparable from him because in the integral and primordial covenantal union with him that is their One Flesh.

"Pre-existence", then, is not a temporal [or] a cosmological but a covenantal and historical notion, and therefore it has a metaphysical,

covenantal, and historical meaning. Only when this is clearly understood is it possible to approach the systematic inquiry as a historical
project rather than a cosmological one, and so to avoid the dualist traps
which have surrounded the discussion of the fall in much of contemporary as well as of classic theology.

To resume the argument, the interest of this question is metaphysical in the sense which we have indicated, and is not at all paleontolog-
ical. Original sin is such a radical refusal as to be possible only in the
moment of creation, the moment of Covenant. In that moment of its
constitution, the Good Creation is constituted as freely integral or as
freely fallen: as freely constituted then whether in integrity or in fallenness in and from its inception: viz., "in the beginning". In this event,
this "beginning", by reason of the sin of the first Adam and the first
Eve, the Good Creation was constituted in fallenness rather than in the
nuptial free unity which was offered. Creation thus has had no unfallen
history [or] prehistory: paleontology, like all other science, deals with
the fallen world, and cannot reach that moment of beginning which,
as the transcendent moral cause of the fall, stands outside fallenness.

Further, the sin, the free refusal of integral creation, is single, an
act of the projected "head" of mankind, the first Adam; it consists in
his refusal of headship. All human beings, save the two whose integral
union [constitutes] its metaphysical prius, the primordial Covenant of
the second Adam and the second Eve, are comprehended and entailed
in a single broken involuntary solidarity with the sin of that "head"
and with the loss of free unity it entails. This is to say that by reason
of the fall there is a sundering in and of the human community on the
level of substance: human freedom and human unity are now at odds.
Between the primordial first Adam and first Eve, whose primordial
refusal of Covenant is the prius of our fallenness, as well as between all
their descendants, a gulf is fixed, a fragmentation of creation which only
the Creator can repair by an act of re-creation, by a gift of the *Spiritus
Creator* poured out by the Father's sending of the Son. This reparation
is recapitulation, the work of the life, death, and Resurrection of the
Christ. It is emphatically not the work of theological speculation....

Inevitably, there is recognized to be something bizarre in the notion
of a primordially fallen couple who, concretely actual in our fallen
history, are uniquely responsible for its fallenness. For in this view, the
first Adam and first Eve would be members of the historical human

community, perhaps our neighbors, but at any rate, certainly some-one's neighbors at some period in history. At the same time they are understood to be *ex hypothesi* the sole causes and responsible agents of that fall, in that, although they have themselves never known an instant of integral existence, they alone in history are freely fallen and freely responsible for the fallenness of all human existence throughout all of history....

... That it [the first couple's sin] has not been stated as a properly *theological* metaphysical problem, and thus has been largely burked by the *theological* tradition, is yet another unhappy consequence of the mistaken cosmological, pseudo-theological postulates under which the theological tradition has long labored, not the least consequence of which is the notion that the discoveries at such sites as the Olduvai Gorge are significant for the doctrine of the fall.

Specifically, we shall show that the free, moral, primordial event of the fall—"in the beginning"—is beyond any theological or systematic reconstitution. We know of it only by faith in the revelation of its effects in us, which are a diminution in our reality, a negation of our being. Consequently, any attempt at its reconstitution by theological speculation will be nonhistorical, thus cosmological. We cannot by speculative *ratio* transcend our beginning; fallen *ab initio* ["from the beginning"], we cannot by taking thought reconstitute from histor-ical material the primordial, prelapsarian *status quo ante*, for it has no historical ground. Otherwise put, there is in fallen history no ratio-nal theological prius by reference to which we might reconstruct the unfallen "original situation" prior to the fall. The fall, whether *originans* or *passive spectatum*, is radically *ex nihilo*, the mystery of iniquity. The reparation of the degradation of the Good Creation by original sin is for God alone, who alone creates *ex nihilo sui et subjecti*. For the theo-logian to attempt this re-establishment of a primordial *status quo ante* is to re-enter systematically into the original insolence.

Because the Good Creation (*creatio*) is constituted by the free, cov-enantal, Spirit-giving immanence of the Son in humanity, redemption (*recreatio*) is implicit in the primordial freedom, the primordial gratuity of the New Covenant in which the Mission of the Son terminates. The love of God for his creation is not undone by sin, and original sin is not the undoing of the Mission of the Son, nor of his covenantal fidelity, which is irrevocable. As we learn from Luke's Gospel, it was *necessary* that Christ should suffer, and the necessity includes the suffering of Our Lady, as second Eve, who in our fallen world is by the same necessity the *Mater dolorosa*.

Therefore the cosmological imagination's spontaneous *quaerens* into the nonhistorical *prius* of the fall is not to be pursued. The attempt to reconstruct the *rejected* headship of the first Adam and the integral humanity, the integral community of those for whose creation in perfection the Son was sent, is futile, for it is with the refusal of this headship and of the integrity it connotes in head and body that the fall is actual in history. Any attempt at its theological reconstruction cannot but be a nonhistorical concession to a cosmological and not a theological *quaerens*, for as has been seen, there is no historical ground for such a reconstruction. The problem of the responsibility for the fall in the first Adam can be dealt with only historically, only in the context of a covenantal metaphysics. Only by a rigorous adherence to its historical method can theology, without distorting it, inquire into the meaning, the intelligibility, of our moral and historical solidarity in the fallen first Adam and in the risen second Adam. Only when freed as a matter of method from the cosmological presuppositions which obscure the systematic inquiry into the doctrinal tradition can the theological task proceed with its properly historical *quaerens*.

Therefore the theological *quaerens* and the metaphysical task which that *quaerens* sets [are] historical in the sense that we are methodologically forbidden to seek a theological understanding of history from outside history. If, conceding this, we seek in fallen history the responsible "head", the first Adam, with whom fallen humanity, as fallen, is in solidarity, we will find only a pure negation of that offered and rejected headship, and a consequent refusal of the Good Creation which implicates us in the free refusal to be free by the diminution of our created humanity from integrity to fallenness, to *sarx*. By our participation in this diminished creation we participate involuntarily in the moral negation of the Covenant, for that refusal signed creation with a *substantial* fallenness, whose spontaneous personal dynamic is the unfree *aversio a Deo* by which we all are analogously sinners by the fact of our creation as *sarx*....

... As sin, the fall is the deed of a free and responsible human agency whose responsibility is covenantal and so is for us all, but without the suppression of our free and personal responsibility. The sin of Adam, original sin *originans*, is the refusal of this covenantal responsibility as "head" freely to unite the "body" of which he is to be the "head". Original sin *originatum*, in us, subordinate to and solidary with that "head" who refused rather than appropriated his proper covenantal headship, means that his sin as "head", by which he refuses headship, issues in our loss of our free covenantal reality, our free unity as body to that head. This loss entails our unfreedom, our disunity, our involuntary loss of our own covenantal substance, our involuntary loss of free covenantal integrity, rather than the free covenantal appropriation of our substantial covenantal integrity....

It is only by its ground in this primordial event of moral evil that the dynamic aversion from God that is innate in us can be named sin: the analogy of sin is fundamental to the doctrine of the Good Creation. Original sin in us is sin only as *originatum*, which is to say, only by its intrinsic causal dependence upon and therefore by analogy with a prime analogate of sin. The analogy demands, if it is to be more than an extrinsic metaphor without any theological signification, that it be grounded causally in an actual personal sin in which we share. This requirement does not rest on the definition of analogy, over which we might delay indefinitely. Rather it rests upon the long since dogmatically established unacceptability of the gnostic alternative to the doctrine of original sin: viz., a nonmoral origin of evil in the world and in ourselves. It is not enough to speak of our moral immaturity, of the burdens of finitude, of the "sin of the world", or of the inherently tragic condition of man, unless this unhappy state is also affirmed to be a *moral* evil, irreducible to any psychological, sociological, physical or whatever other human flaw that is in principle susceptible to human remedy, or to any explanation reducible to a prior possibility necessarily inherent in humanity as such.

When scholars find it necessary to dismiss the Pauline and the Augustinian contribution to this tradition in order to save a modern humanism, their *quaerens* would appear to be fed by cosmology rather than by the historical faith of the Church. The doctrinal tradition requires a fallen moral solidarity in a moral event of sin. To refuse the tradition is to refuse the historicity of the problem of evil, and so to fall back once again upon cosmological rationalization of evil....

... The metaphysical (again, not temporal) prius of the refusal of the New Covenant is the substantially diminished humanity which is fallenness, because an integral human being cannot sin. To affirm this is only to assert the priority, within their correlation, of substance to operation. The actually operative sinful choice, the refusal to be integral, is metaphysically correlative to a concupiscent nonintegral human existence, that of a substantially damaged humanity whose damage finds its spontaneous expression in an *actus secundus* of *aversio a Deo*. Even with the sacramental restoration by baptism of the lost substantial integrity, that restoration is not manifest, not consciously experienced. Thus, after baptism, the experience of fallenness still prevails, not as *aversio a Deo*, but as a divided consciousness, *simul justus et peccator* ["at once righteous and sinner"], anxious by reason of the tension between the two loves, concupiscence *ex peccato ad peccatum*, that marks fallen existence in history whether individual or communal. Concupiscence, therefore, is the experience at once of the loss of freedom which is the solidarity of the fallen creation with the first Adam, and of the gift of freedom which is free solidarity with the risen Christ. Throughout our personal and communal history, each of these polarities of the divided self seeks expression. By baptism we are freed from the original sin *originatum* by which we are spontaneously alienated from God. By that sacrament our lost integrity has been restored *in sacramento*, and it seeks the sacramental expression and the sustenance that is the Eucharistic worship of the Church. At the same time, our solidarity with the sin of Adam, concupiscence, is experienced as a continuing ever-present temptation. But of itself, it is not sin; it is only an emptiness not susceptible of clinical description. It is the condition of possibility of sin, the divided heart freely and responsibly appropriated in the sin of the first Adam and the first Eve; and, until the Parousia, apart from the Eucharistic immanence of the integral second Adam and the second Eve in the One Flesh of the New Covenant, achieved by the life, death, and Resurrection of the Christ, there is no other integral human existence than the sacramental integrity given in baptism. . . .

We must conclude to the primordial immanence of the Son in the covenanted people, in the Good Creation, as the immediate effect of his obedience to his Father's will. The nature of this primordiality we have examined. It is metaphysical or creative, and it requires that the Covenant be immanent in creation also as fallen, for the lack of that immanence would connote annihilation, the severance of the intrinsic relation of God to creation and thus of the covenantal relation of creation to God, by which Covenant it subsists as created and as good. Once more it must be stressed that this conclusion—the primordiality of the Christ of the Covenant—is systematic, theological rather than doctrinal; it relates to doctrine as does question to answer, as intrinsically necessary hypothesis to the transcendent freedom of the historical reality.

5

COVENANTAL THOMISM

Pope John Paul II in his encyclical *Fides et ratio* urged our generation to turn its mind once more to the quintessentially human questions; to pursue with renewed confidence the question of meaning, of being, of human existence, of ultimate destiny. These are questions that have belonged uniquely to the work of philosophy and in particular to the discipline called metaphysics, which studies the whole of reality, absolute and contingent, immanent and transcendent, in all its fullness and its depth. For the person of faith, however, there is something more. The living God, the one source of reality, has made available truth that transcends human experience and exceeds our comprehension. Hence speculative theology, which draws the first principles of its inquiry from revelation, begins with knowledge that could never have been discovered by reason on its own. Yet theology does not find in revelation either the terminology or the conceptual categories necessary to articulate this knowledge. And for this very reason, Pope John Paul argued, if theology is to perform its proper function of providing an *intellectus fidei*, an integrated and universal understanding that is founded on revelation, it must rely upon the assistance of metaphysics.

But there is a problem. Plato and Aristotle, historically theology's most important source for technical language and conceptual frameworks, developed their systems to account for a very different view of reality than the one proposed by the gospel. Aristotle's world is a highly complex interrelation of all kinds of entities, earthly and celestial, material and immaterial, inanimate and animate, reacting and acting according to the capacities and functions appropriate to the kinds of things they are. It is a world in constant motion; and common experience teaches that the things we perceive are always changing, sometimes in small ways and sometimes completely; coming to be and passing away. There must be a being, Aristotle reasoned, that possesses of itself every possible perfection and so exists beyond change, the origin of the motion at work in every other, imperfect thing. Yet it also made sense to say that the entire structure of beings, from the perfect, unchanging source to the buzzing plenitude surrounding us, is itself eternal, having no beginning and no end.

Compare this to the doctrine summarized by the early Christian writer Justin Martyr (ca. 100–ca. 165), in his *First Apology*.[1] Plato spoke of the One, and Aristotle of the First, Unmoved Mover. Justin, however, speaks of God the Father who, although entirely self-sufficient and in need of nothing, created everything that exists, working with unformed matter to fashion a world for the sake of humanity. Yet creation is only the first part of his plan. The intention is that people, with life led in imitation of the divine beneficence, will dwell with him after death in bodies reunited with their souls, for all eternity. Not that it requires special revelation to know that righteousness ought always to be sought, despite the conflict and temptations of this world; for God's Son, his Word, illuminates the reason of every person. But to break the hold on us exerted by evil desire and the forces of darkness, God's Son, the Word, was born a man, born of a virgin, and named Jesus. He is the Teacher who healed the sick, even raised the dead, changing and recalling humanity back from its servitude to vice. It did indeed lead to his crucifixion by Pontius Pilate. Still, by the power of God he rose again and ascended into heaven, all of which had been prophesied generations before through the inspiration of the divine Spirit. Men and women who have been persuaded by his teaching and have made the decision to convert their lives come to the community of believers who will take them to water and wash them in the name of God the Father, and of the Savior Jesus Christ, and of the Holy Spirit, cleansing them from their past sins. This washing is a new birth. One who has been washed in this way is then led to the community of brethren where prayers are offered, a kiss exchanged, and then bread, water,

---

[1] The following is based on the text of *The First Apology* found in St. Justin Martyr, *The First and Second Apologies*, trans. Leslie William Barnard, Ancient Christian Writers, no. 56 (New York and Mahwah, N.J.: Paulist Press, 1997); Greek text in *Justin: Apologie pour les Chrétiens*, introduction, critical text, translation and notes by Charles Munier, *Sources chrétiennes*, no. 507 (Paris: Éditions du Cerf, 2006).

and wine mixed with water are brought to the "head" of the brethren, who offers praise and glory to the Father through the Son and the Holy Spirit and recites a prayer of thanksgiving. This thanks-blessed (in Greek, "eucharistized") bread and wine and water are distributed to the assembled, and portions brought by deacons to absent brethren.

The blessed food, Justin continues, is called by Christians "Eucharist", and no one is permitted to receive it who has not accepted the community's teaching, undergone the washing for the forgiveness of sins and rebirth, and does not live in imitation of the life of Christ. For this is not ordinary bread and wine. Rather, just as Jesus became incarnate by the Word, taking both flesh and blood for our salvation, so this food that is eucharistized by the words he handed down to us is made his own flesh and blood; and hence, in receiving it, our blood and flesh are fed by a transformation (μεταβολὴν). The Apostles, in their memoirs or Gospels, record that Jesus took bread, gave thanks, and said, "Do this in remembrance of me, this is my body." Similarly, he took the chalice, gave thanks, and said, "This is my blood." This is why, on what is called "the day of the sun", Sunday, when all have come together in the same place, from city and village, first the memoirs of the Apostles or the prophets are read, an exhortation is given by the Head, and prayers are offered by the assembly; then bread and wine are brought forward and eucharistized by the Head, and each partakes of the eucharistized food with, again, portions being taken to the absent. For Sunday is the first day, on which God changed darkness and matter into the Cosmos and on which Jesus Christ rose from the dead.

Justin's younger contemporary, Theophilus, bishop of Antioch, would soon speak of God not requiring matter or anything else that already exists in order to make the Cosmos, as would Irenaeus, bishop of Lyons (d. ca. 200).[2] By the fourth century, the predominant view of the Church, both East and West, was that the soul of each individual person is immediately created by God when it is united to the body.[3] In other words, Christianity described a telos in the world, with the purposeful activity of God in the world, that had never even been imagined by Aristotle, for whom the definitive change undergone by a human individual is the total cessation of the individual at death, or

---

[2] Theophilus of Antioch, Ad Autolycum 2.4.10; Irenaeus of Lyons, Against Heresies 1.22.1.
[3] J. N. D. Kelly, Early Christian Doctrines, rev. ed. (San Francisco: Harper & Row, 1978), 345.

by Plato, whose *Phaedrus* proposes that we are so many souls in an eternally recurring cycle, faltering in our contemplation of the distant One, descending into this physical world, and then struggling to make our way back up, before falling away once again.

And the problem is not restricted to Plato or Aristotle, Zeno or Plotinus. No metaphysics formulated to undergird an exclusively rational world view can possibly do the work required of it by the Christian search for understanding; and no series of accommodating adjustments will suffice to fill in the gaps. Naturally, many of the same concepts can still be employed. After all, unbeliever and believer alike are born into, and wonder about, the same world. But, Keefe insists, mere borrowing will not do. Use the same words, include the same concepts, but not without redefining them. Christianity must produce its own metaphysics, one proceeding from the gospel and responsible to the gospel, despite the fact that it will always be in need of the more wide-ranging questioning of philosophical metaphysics. And the core datum that is the starting point for a Christian metaphysics is the central act of Christian prayer, the Eucharist.

For Keefe, as it had been for Justin, the Eucharist is the point in the world where the believer encounters created reality in its revealed fullness. The Eucharist is an event, an action. It is a shared event, a communal action. It is a sacrament, a sign, signifying the ongoing work of the primary event, the creation of the world by the Father in his Son in order that a plenitude of persons might be united to him in his Spirit. The Father sends his Son, and the Son becomes incarnate by the free assent of a woman, Mary. This is life truly given and finally perfected in being offered back to the Father; life given as individual and distinct by virtue of the Son, and as present through the interiority of a life in virtue of the woman. The community of human persons entering into the life of the Father through the Son and thereby undergoing a transformation, indeed what the Church Fathers called a "divinization": this is the fulfillment of the promise forecasted for generations in the law and the prophets, the New Covenant. Having been made possible by the united action of the Son and of Mary, it has a complementary structure; it rests on the self-giving of a man and a woman, named the Second Adam and the Second Eve. For the human life that the Son, Jesus, and Mary offered to the Father without reserve was at the outset of life seized with a proprietary grip by the First Adam and First Eve. Hence for Jesus and for Mary, their gift became a sacrifice, a complete relinquishing. The Synoptic Gospels record that the last meal Jesus took with his disciples, before his dedication to the Father won him betrayal, was the Passover meal that commemorated the liberation of Israel from slavery in Egypt. They also record, as Saint Paul had earlier (1 Cor 11:23–25), that Jesus identified the bread and wine of the meal as being his body and blood; and he enjoined them to repeat his action "in memory of me" (Lk 22:19). This lived body and blood, a lifelong offering to the Father made definitive on the cross, was received by the Father, in the Spirit, through the Resurrection. So that now, made perfect in obedience (Heb 5:8–9) and joined with the Father, this life—Christ's body and blood—becomes present at the Eucharist in the change of bread and wine that the Council of Trent declared is "aptly and properly named" transubstantiation.[4] And with his Real Presence, the faithful are able to offer their lives as a gift to the Father through Christ's. These, Keefe writes, are the "dogmatic facts" that must control any genuinely Christian metaphysics. It is why, as Bonaventure observed, metaphysics is Christology.[5]

A Conversion of Metaphysics

With Pope Leo XIII's promulgation of *Aeterni Patris* (1879), the study of Thomas Aquinas was raised to a position of primacy in Catholic education that lasted well into the middle part of the twentieth century. By 1960, if one could speak of a received, standard Catholic metaphysics, it was the metaphysical thought of Thomas Aquinas. Aquinas, of course, relied heavily on the writings and terminology of Aristotle in his articulation of the *intellectus fidei*; and largely because of Aquinas, terms like act and potency, matter and form, and substance and accident became the common vocabulary of Catholic philosophy and theology. One concept, though, of central importance in Thomism is really more the inheritance of Christian Neoplatonism.

---

[4] Council of Trent, *Decree on the Sacrament of the Eucharist*, chap. 4; cf. Denzinger, 43rd ed., no. 1642.

[5] Donald J. Keefe, *Covenantal Theology: The Eucharistic Order of History*, rev. ed. (Novato, Calif.: Presidio Press, 1996), 386, citing Bonaventure, *Hexaemeron* 1.12–13 (V 331ab).

It is analogy. Analogy had long been used, perhaps most famously by Pseudo-Dionysius in his *The Divine Names*, to explain how Scripture could speak of both God and human beings as "just" or "good" or "loving". The answer was that the terms were used legitimately, correctly, but analogously: Genesis teaches that everything God made he proclaimed to be good; nevertheless, only God is perfectly good, good without limit, good so fully that it transcends human comprehension. In the language of analogy, God was said to be the "prime analogate" of the term "good", meaning that it is used most properly of God alone, and of his creatures only by comparison, who are said to be "secondary analogates" of what it means to be "good".

It is this Thomist language that Keefe enlists in his construction of a theological metaphysics. As a metaphysics, its purpose is to present a systematic view of reality as intrinsically knowable. As theological, its focus falls most immediately on this world, taken as a first premise to have been created, whose most enigmatic element is the human, that is, the human as free, in virtue of whose free decisions mere temporal sequence becomes a history. Accordingly, Keefe himself talks of a prime analogate, and the prime analogate of existence in this world is the New Covenant. This is the paradigm that must guide the analysis of each particular entity, for only the dynamic union of the human with the divine, founded on the human response to the divine self-offer, the beginning of which union marked the creation of the world and the fulfillment of which will mark its consummation, can account for what above all in this physical world is in need of accounting, and that is the fact of human freedom.

It is often said that the questions that first occupied Aristotle's attention concerned change in the world, especially the development of living things from immaturity to maturity. The acorn may actually be only an acorn; but as a living thing, nestled in the ground, it also has the possibility of being something else, and it actualizes this possibility in the process of becoming an oak tree. Aristotle used the ideas of act, potency, and becoming to describe a variety of changes in the world, from the growth of a tree to the erosion of granite into clay, to the shaping by a potter of clay into a bowl and then the reshaping of it into a cup, to the difference between a person knowing how to use a potter's wheel and that person actually sitting down to use it. Following Aristotle, Keefe writes, Thomism used the act/potency distinction on three separate levels corresponding to three separate descriptions that can be made of a physical thing: that typically it is only one example of many instances of the same kind of thing (matter/form); that it is open to temporal change (substance/accident); and thirdly—a description missing in Aristotle, who took the world as simply there and so eternal—that the thing, like the world, is utterly contingent, because it is created (esse/essence). This distinction between what a thing is, which is determined by its essence, and that it is, or the claim that to exist (Latin verb *esse*) does not belong to the essence of anything in the world (otherwise it would exist by necessity, since it necessarily is some kind of thing), was a critical point in Aquinas, and he owed it to Christianity, not Aristotle. Nevertheless, Keefe states, just as Aristotle posited a Prime Mover to be the highest instance of being, so Aquinas looked to God described merely as one, *Deus Unus*, and not the Trinity, certainly not God immanent in his creation as the Son, in whom the Father made all things, received back through the Spirit.[6]

Yet the Father and the Spirit revealed by the Son are precisely what constitute the theological prime analogate. And so Keefe embarks on the project of redefining the fundamental terminology of Thomist metaphysics, in order that the Thomist analysis may bear upon a covenantal understanding of the world. He begins with "*esse*" and "essence".

Esse

As noted before, in Aristotle's reckoning the things of this world may be said to be contingent because they come and they go, are born and die, but the world itself, like the kinds of things in the world, is eternal and unchanging; it always has been exactly as it is. Individuals are contingent. The world and species in the world are not. There is no doctrine of a freely enacted divine creation in Aristotle's thought. It is one of Keefe's principal assertions, however, that there is in fact no place for one. The principles of act and potency that constitute everything in the world form a necessary relation; and necessity cannot be created. The matter, though, runs deeper than that. Aristotle's approach provides the relation between act and potency as the

---

[6] Ibid., 440.

intrinsic cause of existence in the world. A corresponding Christian explanation would have to provide an intrinsic cause of free existence in a freely existing world; for the doctrine of creation claims not only that God freely brought into existence a world that otherwise would not be, but that the object of God's creation was free persons who freely subsist and freely choose. Nor is this merely to affirm that these persons are self-directing; rather, it affirms that in full self-transcendence they are capable of choosing to act in a way that contradicts the very ground of their freedom, which ground is the person's subsistence beyond the self, in Being.

Given that the fundamental description of the world is that its existence, its being, is received, Aquinas describes the Creator as the fullness of being, the being who cannot not exist, the being who exists of himself, *Ipsum Esse Subsistens*.[7] Yet once again, a description of the prime analogate of being that begins by referring to it simply as the full actualization of being runs the risk of reducing the creation of the person, for example, to causing a possible individual actually to exist. But the defining feature of the person is not the range of one's capacities and the degree to which they are in act. It is freedom. The Father who exists with the Son through the Spirit is the meaning of *Esse*; the free person is created in the Son who is the free response to the Father, created to be rooted in that response, rooted in the response that as incarnate is the created response transformed. For Christ's response is the perfect fulfillment of human freedom.

Thus, in Keefe's usage, *esse* refers in the first instance to the immanent "eternal Son, by participation in whose actuality all created reality is created".[8] And the Son's immanence in a free reality has the character of an event: "Any intrinsic 'cause' of a novel and free (i.e., historical) subsistence must itself be free, and therefore must be a free Event immanent in that substance, for only a free Event can be the immanent cause of created freedom."[9]

The principle that is correlative to immanent *Esse*, the order that belongs to existing reality, is the New Covenant. Just as this *Esse* is the personal existence only of Jesus, so its immediate correlative is the

---

[7] *Summa theologiae* Ia, q. 4, a. 2, c.; Ia, q. 3, a. 4, c.; *Summa contra gentiles* 1.22.
[8] Keefe, *Covenantal Theology*, 442.
[9] Ibid., 441.

humanity of Jesus. But to this humanity all of creation is related. As Keefe puts it, the "subject" of the immanence of the Son is his Incarnation, "the full or integral personal humanity, 'one and the same', which alone can be the transcendental correlative of the personal freedom of his immanence and therefore can support this immanence as its correlative within the personal unity of the incarnate Son". The "object" of the Son's immanence is the society of free persons who have devoted themselves to one life with him.

> The consequence or term of the Son's mission by the Father, his free immanence in creation, is therefore the *sancta societas* of which Augustine spoke; it is not simply the Christ, conceived in terms of the static analysis of the Incarnation of the Son, viz., of a "hypostatic union" understood in disjunction from the New Covenant, as by the classic Thomist analysis.

The Incarnation, he continues,

> is of course primarily proper to and constitutive of the second Adam of the primordial Good Creation which is the New Covenant, but it is also constitutive of the One Flesh of his covenantal union with the second Eve, and [at] the same time is constitutive of historical humanity at large, in which he is freely immanent. The *terminus* or object of the divine creative act of the sending of the Son is only thus free and historical: not simply as the Son incarnate in a "human nature", but as the Son freely, covenantally incarnate in historical humanity which is created in and by his mission from the Father.
>
> It must be insisted that it is the Covenant, not simply the Christ, that is created by the Trinitarian mission of the Son.... Nonetheless, it is by the free personal immanence of the Son that this creation is actual. The Son's immanence *is* the actualization of creation, for creation *passive spectata* has no other relation to the Triune God than that which is actual in the Christ, and in ensuring that this relation is understood to be the mission of the Son, we also ensure that the free *and covenantal* immanence of the Son in creation is understood as the formal cause of creation as such: creation in its totality subsists in and by the Son, and not otherwise. It does so, however, as covenanted, in the free appropriation of a *free* relation to the historical Son, the Christ, in such wise that the *Esse Christi* is personal to him alone. The appropriation of creation by every creature is by participation

in that Esse, but it is a participation that is historically and humanly mediated: mediated then by Christ as One and the Same. We have no relation to existence except in the Christ, in whom humanity and divinity are so joined that of him it must be said that One and the Same is the eternal Son of the eternal Father, the human Son of the Virgin, the second Adam joined in One Flesh to the second Eve.

... The New Covenant is the free immanence of God in man and includes in its reality the whole of humanity, the whole of the created universe: all that is exists uniquely by reason of the Father's sending of the Son to give the Spirit. We cannot isolate the metaphysics of the Incarnation from the metaphysics of creation: they are mutually implicatory in their contingency. Only when this is realized is Esse understood historically, in the context of a theological metaphysics.[10]

Keefe's covenantal ontology emphasizes the dynamism of being, understood not so much as the intensity of the act of existence as the distinctiveness of each act of being, yet the openness of being to integrative union, because of its nature as free.

It is not then at all anomalous that each snowflake should be an utterly unique and even unrepeatable expression of the hexagonal crystalline order of the H^2O molecule, or that each gannet should so easily recognize its mate out of a dozen myriads of such waterfowl at a nesting site, for reality is of this free, unrepeatable, historical order. Despite the spontaneous monadism of our fallen minds, no duplicates exist in reality, for whatever exists does so by participating in a Covenant whose meaning is not monadic but Trinitarian, and whose existence is responsive, not to the working-out of a blind necessity, but to the magnanimity of an infinite freedom.[11]

Essence

The ordering principle of created reality, the New Covenant, which is the intrinsic correlative to immanent *Esse*, is the prime analogate of essence. Yet if Keefe makes use of the notion of essence, he is quick to add that he does not mean by it what medieval Aristotelianism meant

[10] Ibid., 442–43.
[11] Ibid., 451.

by "species". The New Covenant is not a class concept. It is not a universal, an unchanging, defining pattern that is the full expression of the qualities that particular individuals only partly possess. Understood as a species, the essence of the human being is said to be rational animality. But then what becomes of human masculinity and femininity? One can hardly say that uniform human essence, transcending the differences between concrete individuals, encompasses the fullness of both, for that would be to negate a quality whose entire meaning is founded on distinction.[12] Aristotle, who explained differences between members of a species as the falling short of essential perfection, solved the problem by describing the female as a defective male.[13]

The New Covenant, however, functions as an essential principle in virtue of the identities of the persons created in the Son, and their relations to one another, organizing the responsiveness and novelty inherent in the being even of nonpersonal entities, as the Son makes of everything a gift to the Father.

Angelic essence would refer to the pattern formed by the identities and interrelations of persons who are immaterial, immediately created, constituting a subordinate order in the New Covenant; intended to be a cooperative order, drawing each other and also human persons into the Son's gift of self to the Father. In the same way, humanity, human essence, would refer to the defining identities of the persons mediately created, that is, of persons created in and through the self-offering of one to another; created, therefore, in temporal succession. Hence, the essence of the human is material personhood, responsive to the angelic, and collaborative with the divine both in bringing forth human life and in joining it to the Son; collaborative, too, in the perfection of physical creation that could be made an offering to God only in and through the self-offering of the human. The essence of physical creation would be diverse and associative multiplicity expressed in spatial and temporal extension.

These are proposed as examples of what Keefe calls secondary analogates of essence, or secondary analogates of the New Covenant. Secondary analogates, he writes, "are themselves historical and covenantal, and are therefore secondary images of the Trinity"; hence they are free

[12] Ibid., 444–45.
[13] Aristotle, *On the Generation of Animals* 2.3.

in their intelligibility, their being, and their historicity.[14] This is true also of the physical universe and even of inanimate things, analogously.

> Their unity, truth, beauty, and goodness are covenantal, but they are so on a level of participation which underwrites their dignity but not their responsibility. The scientific understanding of their essential potentiality, i.e., their materiality or spatial and temporal extension, has in the past century escaped the determinism both of the Newtonian mechanics and the Euclidean geometry, but has found no other determinism to replace these, and the prospects of discovering yet another conceptualist cage in which to imprison the physical universe are at least remote. Perhaps it is not too much to suggest that each material entity by its materiality is historical *per se;* its materiality, as historical and therefore free, is the continuing invocation of novelty from the covenantal unity, goodness, and truth of its being....[15]

Nevertheless, Keefe is adamant: in the covenantal view, an essence is not a "possible". It is not a divine idea "realified", as it were, by an act of existence, any more than creation was God's decision to make actual a particular range of essences he had chosen from a gallery of possibilities.[16] An essence is not the complete reality of which multiple individuals are but separate and limited specimens. Although Keefe does make use of the notion of participation, it is participation in the sense of communion, the Pauline κοινωνία, rather than the Platonic appeal to the quantifiable degree to which different individuals share in the same, transcendent quality in order to account for their similarities. For Keefe, the stable though not unchanging kinds of entities that have arisen in the physical universe, from particles and forces to compounds and organisms, are witness to the diverse complementarity of physical being, responsive to the pervasive action of the Covenant.

Matter/Form

In the Aristotelian view, everything in the physical world both exists as a certain kind of thing in a certain kind of way and has

[14] Keefe, *Covenantal Theology*, 451.
[15] Ibid.
[16] Ibid., 443–44.

the possibility of being different. Each thing, then, is a composite of two principles: a principle of potentiality called matter and a principle of actuality called form. This view is summarized by the word "hylemorphism" (from the Greek ὕλη or "matter" and μορφή or "form"). Since it is the essence of a thing that accounts for its being the sort of thing that it is, the principle that makes something to be what it is may be called its essential form. In Aristotelianism, forms only exist as actually informing things, and they always exist in composition with matter. Similarly, matter is always the principle of possibility belonging to some particular thing. Nevertheless, one can extrapolate from the possibilities of this thing or that thing and speak of the principle by which possibility belongs to the whole of the physical world in the most basic way. For at the bare minimum, in Aristotle's mind, what will characterize everything in the physical world is location and duration (remembering that for Aristotle the world is eternal, and its existence is simply a given). And the term traditionally used for this most basic state of possibility is prime or primary matter.

Thinking theologically, however, the primary datum is not the world as a plurality of objects subject to the forces of causation, but rather the world as creation, that is, the world as created, as freely brought into existence by God. It is the world having been created by the Father in the Son, for the purpose of being united with the Father as belonging to the self-offering of the Son. It is the world freely joining in the Son's offering, freely responding to him in and through the created persons who lie at the heart of creation; and also the world as having rejected the Son from the start. Hence it is as the Christ that the Son has united creation to himself in a gift to the Father that is sacrificial. Christ, then, is the prime analogate of form; the Son in his free relinquishing that makes possible the fulfillment of the Father's purpose. And the prime analogate of matter is the correlatively free assent to Christ of Mary and of the members of the society that she inaugurates, the Church. It is her active, not passive, potentiality for union that Christ realizes. This is what it means to think theologically, Keefe states. This represents "the historical transformation of the meaning" of the categories of form and matter.[17]

---

[17] Ibid., 454.

Substance

The "entire subject matter" of metaphysics, Keefe writes, "is concerned with substance."[18] Certainly that is true of Aristotelian metaphysics. In the *Categories*, where he takes language as expressive of the structure of the world, Aristotle speaks of substance (οὐσία) as the individual object about which things may be said, whether properties attributed or a situation described. An example would be a squirrel—small, gray, four-footed, bushy-tailed—which I can tell a friend I saw scampering across the grass the previous day, in hot if playful pursuit of a second squirrel that seemed twice its size, chasing it up a tree. On the other hand, Aristotle notes, what in talking to my friend I called a squirrel a biologist would categorize as a rodent, and anyone could identify as an animal. For that reason, although only an individual thing, like a squirrel, is a substance in the primary sense, Aristotle says that the squirrel's species and its genus are also substances in a secondary sense, inasmuch as the squirrel is what it is and can be called small and gray and fast-moving only because it belongs to a particular genus and species.

Later, in his treatise on metaphysics called *Metaphysics*, Aristotle turned from an analysis of our speech about things to an analysis of things themselves and introduced into his discussion the concepts of act and potency, form and matter. Now the focus was on the individual object understood as a composite of the substantial form that makes the object to be what it is and the matter or material of which it is made, like the marble of a statue or the living cells of a squirrel or a tree. As in the *Categories*, the primary mark of being a substance is existence as a distinct thing rather than being only a quality or property, what Aristotle in the *Metaphysics* calls an "accident", of a thing. And just as in the *Categories* a squirrel's species has a kind of priority as substance over the squirrel itself, since it is the squirrel that belongs to the species, so in the *Metaphysics* substantial form has a priority over the individual whose form it is, since any tree or squirrel will eventually perish, but the form that makes a squirrel to be a squirrel and not a tree never disappears; there will always be other squirrels and other trees.[19]

---

[18] Ibid., 385.
[19] Aristotle, *Metaphysics* 7.15.

In Aristotle's philosophical metaphysics, composition with matter makes possible multiple instances of a substance, of a specific kind of thing, and therefore multiple, derivative substances, each of them striving to express the kind of thing that it is as fully as its material conditions will allow, while acting upon and being acted upon by other substances. Even further, the activity by which a thing endeavors to express what it is can be described as an effort to imitate the transcendent One, the Good that is possessed of every possible property and capability in the highest degree and that is eternally engaged in the most sublime activity of all, namely, contemplation of its own perfection.[20] But one will have noted what is most important about substantial being in saying that a substance is what exists as self-subsistent and as self-identical, distinct from every other substance. It is otherwise in the theological metaphysics proposed by Keefe.

The defining activity in Aristotle's system is represented by the perfect act that is the One, mirrored imperfectly and fragmentarily by the aggregate of forms and the things that instantiate them. This is substantial being as unitary independence. For Keefe, the defining activity is the reciprocity that constitutes the divine unity of Father, Son, and Holy Spirit; and out of this reciprocity comes the further gift of creation. This is substantial being as inherently mutual. Hence, just as the New Covenant, regarded as the principle that provides order to created reality, is the prime analogate of essence, so the concrete actuality of the New Covenant is the prime analogate of substance, the fullness of created substantial being. It is "the free *plenum* which is the Father's sending of the Son to give the Spirit, a fullness of being which is at once Trinitarian and covenantal".[21] This, in fact, is what it means to say that the human was created in the image of God. For the true *imago* lies in the Son, Christ, born of the free response of Mary, having united humanity to his perfect self-offering to the Father, definitively received by the Father in his resurrection, a reception by the Father made complete in the Spirit, so that with the Son and in the Spirit, the believer undertakes to enter into the one life of God. The human community created in Christ is the complete image of God. "In concrete created dependence upon and by free participation in

[20] *Metaphysics* 12.7, 9.
[21] Keefe, *Covenantal Theology*, 456.

this prime," writes Keefe, "each human being possesses, *suo modo*, the fullness of humanity, of human substantiality." He adds,

> individuals are irreducible in the quasi-qualitative personal uniqueness of their interrelations, and their irreducibility is extended to the point of their each being intelligibly unique as an individually subsisting person, nor is this unique particularity of the "material individual" restricted to the human level: it is true of the full range of created reality, which knows no mere replication of entities.[22]

Nevertheless, it is the person qua person who shares in the image, bears the image, either to embrace it or to reject it. As covenantal, the human substance is differentiated; and it is differentiated, since concerned with life, as masculine and feminine, founded on the free union of the Second Adam and the Second Eve. Thus Keefe speaks of the nuptial or marital character of the human substance. And since this substance is constituted by the entry of humanity into the Son's offering to the Father, its constitution is liturgical.

Accident

As noted above, "accidents" in Aristotelianism refer to the properties of a thing, without which thing there would be no properties to refer to; so there is the greenness of an oak leaf, its shape, etc., only because there is the oak leaf. If a substance is what subsists of itself, accidents subsist only as the accidents of some substance. By the same token, the oak leaf expresses what it is only in and through its particular properties. There is an interrelatedness between a substance and its accidents such that, to put it in terms of the act-potency distinction, it is the accidents that actualize or realize the possibility of what their substance can be; and this is the meaning of "accident" that is of greatest use to Keefe. The paradigmatic created substance is the community of human persons. And the primary accident of this substance is the activity of their worship, their offering to the Father whereby they exercise their unity with the Son, their conformity

---

[22] Ibid., 388–89.

to him whom the Gospels portray as praying unceasingly. Since it is this activity, as accident, that actualizes the human substance, the accident-substance relation on this primary level may be said to entail "the personal appropriation in worship of one's objective reality".[23]

Of course, the human substance, the human community is historical. It had a beginning, and its sojourn in the present order will have an end. At its beginning, human history was fractured by sin. Yet it was created in the Son, to be drawn by him and with him into his life with the Father. Therefore, all of history proceeds in the Son, oriented by the Spirit as the Son's gift to the Father. In every age, the openness of each person is addressed by the Son in the Spirit, called to fulfill the truth of all created personhood and the specific truth of one's own identity by turning in worship to the Son and, with him, to the Father, as clearly as one is able, always animated by the Spirit. Hence, there is no society and no culture that has been ignorant of religion. Granted, the varieties of religion, reflecting the varieties of religious experience, also reflect the existential alienation wrought by the first sin and, so, the distortion of thought and perspective that is the fruit of that sin's conversion to self. A clear illustration is had in the religions of the ancient Middle East. As human affairs are governed by struggle and the drive for domination, so the same is attributed to the divine. Authority is understood to mean license to control. The weak are invariably subject to the strong; their only recourse is cunning and manipulation. Sacrifices may be offered to honor the gods, but more immediately to placate them and, perhaps, gain advantage with them. Among men and gods, multiplicity means conflict. It is uniformity that brings peace, and perfection lies, if anywhere, in an absolute One.[24]

Together with the sense of what lies beyond the self, there is an intuition of the significance of masculinity and femininity as principles of life. This relation, too, is ascribed to the divine (except in the instance of an ultimate, transpersonal reality), and it is ascribed in just the manner in which it is understood to be true of the human. The masculine, as superior, has controlling authority over the feminine; the feminine, as inferior, is passive, though not entirely without resistance, to the

---

[23] Ibid., 458.
[24] See H. and H. A. Frankfort, John A. Wilson, Thorkild Jacobsen, *Before Philosophy: The Intellectual Adventure of Ancient Man* (Baltimore, Md.: Penguin Books, 1973).

masculine. With the emergence of philosophy from this liturgical soil, a vestige may be seen to linger in the femininity of matter. This is the mode of human praying, public and typically civic, that Christ united—though not unconverted—to his own life of unremitting prayer, made perfect in his Passion and present in the Eucharist.

The Eucharistic Order of History

The French theologian Henri de Lubac, whose work had such an influence on Keefe, demonstrated in his historical studies the unified view of history that prevailed among Christian writers, from the Church Fathers through the medieval scholastics. History was the great unfolding of God's eternal plan, from creation and paradise to the scattering of the race after sin, to the call of Abraham, the Law given to Israel, and finally the coming of the Messiah, with the promise of life in his Kingdom. Keefe's move, however, has been to argue that the unity does not derive from the plan as an immanent idea but as a free reality, an event, the sending of the Son by the Father to give the Spirit, the event of the Incarnation. This event is the prime analogate of created being and, so, of created substance. Its unfolding is equally free; hence the possibility of sin. Therefore substance, like its existence in time, has the inner unity "of a free Trinitarian and covenantal *ordo*" rather than of an immanent formal structure, a defined potentiality that is actualized in change.[25]

The event of the Son's Incarnation has proceeded in the sequence of Old Covenant, New Covenant, Kingdom, and Keefe points to a number of analogues to the free, Trinitarian order of the event's unity. For example, the individual existent is analyzed as potency (matter), act (form), and substance. The human condition has seen our fleshly solidarity (*sarx*) in the First Adam become a "one flesh" (*mia sarx*) union with the Second Adam, to be perfected as spirit (*pneuma*) by the "Life-giving spirit" of Christ. A third example is the unity of Scripture.

Beryl Smalley opens *The Study of the Bible in the Middle Ages* with a quotation from Origen's *Homily on Leviticus* in which Origen draws a parallel, common in the patristic period, between the Incarnation

---

[25] Keefe, *Covenantal Theology*, 391, 457.

and Scripture. Just as the body taken from Mary, that everyone could see, clothed the divinity that was visible to only a few, so Moses and the prophets clothed the Word in letters for all to read, but it is the spiritual sense lying within their letters that reveals the divinity.[26] The divinity Origen is referring to is, of course, Christ, whose coming is foreshadowed in the law and the prophets. Yet it is not just Christ who is revealed in the spiritual sense, but also the Church, her sacraments, the coming of the Kingdom, and the relation between God and the soul.[27] For Origen and the entire tradition that he both inherited and passed on, as the body of the Word is one, so Scripture is one, and the Old and New Testaments constitute a single revelation and a single text in which a literal sense is integrally united with a spiritual sense in all its dimensions. Writing some twenty years after Smalley, De Lubac in his *Medieval Exegesis* undertook an exhaustive review of the medieval commentators in order to illustrate just how deep the supposition ran that the Word is always teaching in Scripture on multiple levels, in multiple ways; and that it is within the life of the Church that the intricacy of this teaching is understood.[28] The medievals subdivided the spiritual sense into often two, occasionally six, but typically three further senses for a total of four: the literal; the allegorical, which identifies types or figures in Scripture of Christ, the Church and our salvation; the tropological, which trains the soul in morality; and the anagogical, which teaches of last things and of the promised end. Keefe links the allegorical and tropological in his third analogous unity: the literal, allegorical-tropological, and anagogical senses of Scripture.

Because of sin, it is a broken humanity to which the Son is united; his Incarnation is an event, Keefe writes, in fallen history. Hence it continues to be present and proceeds in time only in sign, and that sign is the sacrament of the Eucharist. The Eucharist is the analogue Keefe calls radical, for it lies at the root of, and indeed brings to realization, the covenantal reality to which the other analogies refer. It is

[26] Beryl Smalley, *The Study of the Bible in the Middle Ages* (Notre Dame, Ind.: University of Notre Dame Press, 1978), 1, quoting Origen, *Hom. in Lev.* 1.1.

[27] Ibid., 7.

[28] Henri de Lubac, S.J., *Exégèse médiéval*, 4 vols. (Paris: Aubier, 1959–1964). *Medieval Exegesis*, vol. 1, trans. Marc Sebanc (Grand Rapids, Mich.: Eerdmans, 1998); vol. 2, trans. E. M. Macierowski (Grand Rapids, Mich.: Eerdmans, 2000); vol. 3, trans. E. M. Macierowski (Grand Rapids, Mich.: Eerdmans, 2009).

the integrating life by "which the fallenness of the historical order is unified". This sacramental worship, "the Eucharistic Sacrifice, the New Covenant accomplished in history as the One Flesh of Christ and his Church, [is] the center, the source, and the unity of history."[29]

Henri de Lubac in *Corpus Mysticum* wrote that the tradition spoke in three ways of the body of Christ: his physical body now risen in glory; this same body, sacramentally present in the Eucharist; and his ecclesial body, meaning the Church, which the Eucharistic body feeds and joins together in charity.[30] So Augustine admonished the newly baptized of Hippo who were about to receive the Eucharist for the first time: "Be what you can see, and receive what you are."[31] From the very beginning, the Church insisted that after Consecration, what is seen on the altar, although unchanged in their qualities, are no longer bread and wine. It is Christ himself, his body and his blood. During the early medieval period, however, writers spoke of Consecration, which was assigned to the liturgy's entire Eucharistic Prayer, as bringing together all three senses of Christ's body. Through the Consecration, Christ's Eucharistic Body, which re-presents his sacrificial death, is elevated to the state he possesses in glory at the Father's right hand; and through Consecration, all those gathered for the liturgy are united to Christ, entering by their prayer into his offering.[32]

It may be that the tradition insisted that the consecrated bread and wine are Christ's body and blood, but critiques were easy to make. Ambrose (d. 397) clearly taught that the Eucharist is the flesh of Christ, the very body that was born of Mary.[33] But he also called the Eucharist a "figure" (*figura*) of Christ's body and blood.[34] The Benedictine monk Ratramnus (d. 868) reasoned that if the Eucharist was a figure, then Christ's reference to the bread and wine being his body and blood had

---

[29] Keefe, *Covenantal Theology*, 391.

[30] Henri de Lubac, S.J., *Corpus Mysticum: The Eucharist and the Church in the Middle Ages*, trans. Gemma Simmonds, C.J., Richard Price, and Christopher Stephens, ed. Laurence Paul Hemming and Susan Frank Parsons (Notre Dame, Ind.: University of Notre Dame Press, 2007).

[31] Augustine, Sermon 272, *The Works of Saint Augustine*, ed. John E. Rotelle, O.S.A., pt. 3, vol. 7, *Sermons 230–72B*, trans. and notes by Edmund Hill, O.P. (New Rochelle, N.Y.: New City Press, 1993), 301.

[32] Edward J. Kilmartin, S.J., *The Eucharist in the West: History and Theology*, ed. Robert J. Daly, S.J. (Collegeville, Minn.: Liturgical Press, 1998), 61–67, 117–26.

[33] Ambrose, *De mysteriis* 8.53–54.

[34] *De sacramentis* 4.5.21.

to be a figure of speech. And since Christ sits now at the right hand of the Father, it must be that the Eucharist is the image of that body and the means whereby its divine power is received by the faithful.[35] When two hundred years later, Berengarius of Tours, Archdeacon of Angers, wrote approvingly of Ratramnus' treatise on the Eucharist (which, like everyone else at the time, he mistakenly attributed to another ninth-century writer, John Scotus Erigena), he contended that if the Eucharist is a sacrament, then it must be a sign, and if a sign, then it cannot simultaneously be the very thing it is signifying.[36]

During the preceding two hundred years, however, Church reflection had sharpened; and through the course of seven synods, Berengarius found his position repeatedly condemned, until he agreed in 1079 to retire from teaching and abandon the lists of debate. Yet the simple logic of his thought was enormously persuasive. Indisputably the Eucharist was something real (a *res*), but it was also a sign (*sacramentum*); Augustine himself had used both terms to describe it. What was necessary was a standardized language that would stress that the Eucharist is itself literally the body of Christ, even if a sign. The result was the formulation of three phrases that came to be most closely associated with Peter Lombard (d. 1160): *sacramentum tantum, res et sacramentum, res tantum.*[37] *Sacramentum tantum* or "sign only" referred to the rite whereby the bread and wine are consecrated. It also described the qualities of bread and wine that remain after Consecration. These things are only signs. *Res et sacramentum*, "reality and sign", referred to the compound nature of the Eucharist. On the one hand, the Eucharist really is the body and blood of Christ. On the other, this Eucharistic body, even though unseen, signifies spiritual food and, furthermore, points to what receiving this food brings about, namely, incorporation into Christ's ecclesial body, which in the twelfth century was coming to be called his "mystical" body. Finally, *res tantum*, "the reality only", referred to Christ's ecclesial body come to full maturity through his Spirit.

Keefe values these three phrases because they express the Eucharist as an integrating unity, the prime integrating unity. There is no denying,

[35] Ratramnus, *De corpore et sanguine Domini* 7, 19, 30, 49, 72, 74, 77, 89.

[36] James T. O'Connor, *The Hidden Manna: A Theology of the Eucharist*, 2nd ed. (San Francisco: Ignatius Press, 2005), 97–112.

[37] Bernard Leeming, S.J., *Principles of Sacramental Theology* (Westminster, Md.: Newman Press, 1956), 255–56.

though, that they lack something of the earlier, more broadly liturgical understanding of the Eucharist that obtained before the Berengarian controversy forced a narrowing upon the consecrated elements. To recover, then, that richer understanding, he aligns the phrases with a threefold division of the liturgy that dates back to the fourth century: Offertory, Canon, and Communion. The Offertory, when bread and wine are brought forward as gifts, corresponds to the *sacramentum tantum*. The Canon, also called the Anaphora, which includes the Eucharistic Prayer with Jesus' consecratory words, corresponds to the *res et sacramentum*. And Communion, the reception of the Eucharist, effects the believer's entry into the Son's perfect response to the Father. This unity with the Son is the fullness of the event of the Son's mission, completing creation; it is the *plenum*, the *res tantum*. Not a sign of anything, it is only the reality itself, whose consummation belongs to the end of time but that the Eucharist is making a reality in our midst.

Transubstantiation

The Church had persistently insisted that the Eucharistic bread and wine are changed. Not just that Christ really is present in the Eucharist together with the bread and wine, nor that the bread and wine are changed only in terms of their meaning, having now a significance greater than ordinary food. Rather, after Consecration, what is seen on the altar, despite every quality being unchanged, is no longer bread and no longer wine. It is Christ himself, his body and blood, his risen life. At the seventh synod called to examine Berengarius, at Rome in 1079, he signed a profession of faith that stated that the bread and wine placed on the altar are "substantially changed" (*substantialiter converti*) by the Holy Prayer and Jesus' own words into the body and blood that were born of Mary and ascended to the right hand of the Father.[38] By the middle of the twelfth century, the term "transubstantiation" was being used to refer to the Eucharistic change, and in 1215 the Fourth Lateran Council declared that the bread and wine are "transubstantiated" into Christ's body and blood.[39]

[38] Aidan Nichols, O.P., *The Holy Eucharist: From the New Testament to Pope John Paul II* (Dublin: Veritas Publications, 1991), 64.

[39] O'Connor, *Hidden Manna*, 116–18. The word comes in the Council's opening creed, *Firmiter*.

No doubt nothing more was intended by this usage than to reaffirm that the Eucharist literally involves a change from one reality to another. "Substance" had been used in this context for centuries. At the time of the Berengarian dispute, the word "accidents" began to be used as well. In his critique of Berengarius entitled *On the Truth of the Body and Blood of Christ in the Eucharist,* Guitmund, the Benedictine bishop of Aversa (d. ca. 1090), noted that the Eucharistic change is something unique, unlike the simple change of an *accidentia,* or of one substance into another, say a seed into a plant, or like the body's conversion of food and drink into flesh and blood.[40] Nevertheless, with the entry of a growing number of Aristotle's works into the schools, including his *Physics* and *Metaphysics,* during the latter decades of the twelfth century, it was his understanding of these terms that came to govern their meaning, at least in academic circles. And in Aristotle's terms, the whole notion of transubstantiation is absurd. Accidents or qualities inhere in the substances whose natures they express. You can change the qualities of a substance; Aristotle calls this accidental change. Go far enough when changing something's qualities, and you can change the thing itself; Aristotle calls this substantial change. But it makes no sense to speak of changing the substance while retaining the qualities. Changing its qualities is the very way a substance is changed. Now the Christian can certainly appeal to divine omnipotence in explaining how one thing can be changed into an entirely different thing without its qualities being touched. But with the former thing having gone, its qualities must now be left hanging with nothing for them to qualify. All the qualities of bread and wine exist even though the bread and wine no longer exist. That was the position even Aquinas was forced to adopt.[41] Martin Luther was hardly the first theologian to conclude that it is a great deal simpler and more reasonable to say that Christ really is present in the Eucharist, along with bread and wine.[42] John Duns Scotus (d. 1308) had said the same thing two hundred years before. The difference is Scotus noted the Church taught otherwise, and for him that was decisive.[43]

---

[40] Ibid., 105–9.

[41] *Summa theologiae* IIIa, q. 77, a. 1 corpus and ad 3.

[42] See, for example, Luther's argument in *The Pagan Servitude of the Church* (1520) that the teaching on transubstantiation constitutes the second of three "shackles" the pope and Romanists have clamped on the Eucharist. *Martin Luther: Selections from His Writings,* ed. with an intro. by John Dillenberger (Garden City, N.Y.: Anchor Books, 1961), 264–70.

[43] O'Connor, *Hidden Manna,* 121–22.

Guitmund was able to avoid being boxed in this way because in his use, "substance" and "accident" did not yet have the technical Aristotelian meaning of two principles existing in a necessary relation: every accident is the accident of some substance, and every substance is qualified by its accidents. When he spoke of the Eucharistic change, he identified accidents more generally with something's appearance and therefore could speak of their role shifting rather than simply being reduced to a logical contradiction. Before Consecration, they were the "species" or outward appearances that belong to bread and wine. After Consecration, they are the "species of the Lord", the means whereby the Lord appears to his faithful, as he appeared in different ways to his disciples after the Resurrection.[44] Guitmund keeps his account of the Eucharist within the setting of salvation history, rather than subject it to the categories of necessary relations, what Keefe calls the "cosmological" understanding of the real. It is the understanding characteristic of human thought apart from revelation. In the mythic mind-set, it is evidenced by a depreciation of the temporal, seen as being a mere shadow of the eternal ideal.[45] Greek mythology, on the threshold of abstract inquiry, asserted that even the gods were subject to the necessity of fate, personified as the goddess Moira. In Greek philosophy, where the cosmological understanding is raised to the level of intellectual system, it is the universal, whether transcendent or immanent, that controls the particular.

Cosmos, from the Greek κόσμος, means "order". But it is order as restricted and determined. Naturally things in this material realm are ordered only imperfectly. Yet that, too, belongs to the larger cosmic structure. Hence, for the classical reader, the paradox in the name given to Jesus by the Gospel of John: "the Lamb of God, who takes away the sin of the world" (1:29), where "world" is translating the word κόσμος and "sin" translates ἁμαρτία, meaning "error" or "failure". But how can there be a flaw or failure in the cosmos, whose order embraces everything that can be? The principles of the order that is given in revelation are Trinitarian and personal, concrete and deliberative, decisive and free. In short, Keefe writes, historical. And the work of the Son,

---

[44] Ibid., 109.

[45] See the studies by Mircea Eliade, *Cosmos and History: The Myth of the Eternal Return*, trans. Willard R. Trask (New York: Harper & Row, 1959), and *The Sacred and the Profane: The Nature of Religion*, trans. Willard R. Trask (New York: Harcourt, Brace & World, 1959).

in virtue of whom the order exists, progresses Eucharistically, in the liturgy taken as a whole. For it is not just the Canon, but also the Offertory and Communion that are "integral to the Eucharistic celebration, and therefore to the efficacious sign-character of the sacrament itself, whose efficacy", in making present the body of Christ in each of its senses, "is more than consecration, as the Mass is more than Canon."[46]

Going back at least to Justin, the *metabolē*, or change of the Eucharistic bread and wine, was taken as analogous to the conception of Jesus by Mary with which the Incarnation begins. And it is the fullness of this event that the Eucharist signifies. Hence Keefe writes that

> the historical unity of the Eucharistic worship integrates the Incarnation, from Mary's "Fiat" to the death of Christ on the Cross, and his Resurrection ... in the complex density of a single order of a historically effective symbol, in which the death of Christ on the Cross is sacramentally (therefore really, actually, in the actuality of a historical Event) represented as the unsurpassable fulfillment of the Paschal promises and the Messianic prophecies of the Old Covenant, as the uniquely pure Sacrifice of the unblemished Paschal Lamb that alone establishes the New Covenant, and at the same time as the eschatological consummation of the Old Covenant and the New.[47]

The Offertory is the Eucharistic liturgy as *sacramentum tantum*. The bread and wine that are brought forward are not some "value-neutral" food. As offerings of praise, they signify "the manna that sustained the Israelites during their desert wandering" and the celebratory wine of thanksgiving to God.[48] It was by a free decision that Abram turned from the life and worship he had known in Haran to embrace the word spoken by the Lord, promising that through him and his offspring all the peoples of the earth would be blessed (Gen 12:1–3). And the perfect expression of the converted praise that began with Abram was Mary in her immaculate, meaning unvitiated, freedom, speaking her "Fiat mihi". She is the Daughter of Zion, the embodiment of the attentive fidelity that was the fruit of the Old Covenant. And she is the antetype of the Church. Thus, the bread and wine of the Offertory are

---

[46] Keefe, *Covenantal Theology*, 422–23.
[47] Ibid., 424.
[48] Ibid., 437.

signs of the praise given by the Church, who, as Marian, is herself the Daughter of Zion and the New Eve. This offering, Keefe says, represents "all that the New Eve has to give her Lord, all that she has received from the Old Covenant as the Daughter of Zion: concretely, this is her historicity, her free offer of her free humanity as radicated in the Old Covenant people of God."[49] It is given to her Lord "as to him in whom she has her source", freely obedient to his command; and by his act, the act of "the risen Christ", it becomes one offering, one oblation, joined to his "One Sacrifice", effecting their union in "One Flesh".[50] This is the event of transubstantiation.

But as substance, and also accident, are to be understood historically, so, too, is this particular kind of change that is completely unknown in an Aristotelian system. It is not that the bread and wine themselves become something different, as bronze does when, molded into a statue, it gains a form, or when, being melted back down, it loses one. The bread and wine no longer exist. Yet they are not destroyed. As Ambrose and the tradition following him had it, from (*ex*) the bread comes the body of Christ, just as he was born from (*ex*) the body of Mary.[51] There is in this change an element of continuity, something the bread and the body have in common, even though they are utterly different. Thomas is pointing toward a solution when he states that the something is "being" (*ens*). The entire substance of the one is changed into the entire substance of the other by the action of the "Author of being", who finds in the being of the bread a point of contact with the being of Christ's body.[52] Yet the openness of even nonpersonal being means that more is at work here than mere facticity, however dynamic.

The complete self-offering of Mary—body, soul, and spirit—is received by Christ and changed into his body, the flesh of his created Sonship, but in a moment of genuine novelty. There was nothing in her that of itself can account for the conception of Christ. His Incarnation is pure gift. Similarly, nothing in the Old Covenant promise of the restoration of creation after sin accounts for the gift of the New: the transformation of creation through the entry of humanity into the

---

[49] Ibid., 428.
[50] Ibid., 436.
[51] Ambrose, *De sacramentis* 4.4.14; *De mysteriis* 9.53.
[52] *Summa theologiae* IIIa, q. 75, a. 4 corpus and ad 3.

life of God. The change from Old to New, a change on the level of substance that marks discontinuity in the midst of continuity, goes beyond the actualization of an antecedent potentiality. Equivalently, there is no prior possibility in the bread and wine of the Offertory that is merely realized in consecration. They are changed from a *sacramentum* to being a *res et sacramentum*. They are, as Keefe says, "the historical, sacrificed and risen personal reality of the Christ; they are the physical Body and Blood, soul and divinity, of Jesus the Christ."[53] It is not just that the reception in Communion of the sacramental reality of Christ points to the final union, the *res*, which is the Kingdom having come. Bread and wine remain as intrinsic to the sacramental reality of Christ himself, manifesting his presence; they do so, not as substances, but nevertheless in the reality of their qualities, their accidents. It is by virtue of the spoken words of institution and also of the sign-function of bread and wine that Christ is sacramentally present. The bread and wine, before signifying the manna given to Israel, now signify the Bread of Life, as Jesus identifies himself in John 6, and the Cup of Eternal Salvation.[54] They are changed in their substantial reality, but it is only because their accidents remain that the Eucharist is efficacious as a sacrament.

Since the New Covenant is the prime analogate of substantial being, it might be said that the substantial change that occurs in the Eucharist exemplifies the ongoing, integrative work of the Son, carried out now in union with his Church, through the Spirit. In the Eucharist, the Son joins the bread and the wine definitively to himself. Their nonpersonal and in that sense immanent being is fulfilled in the Son's in such a way that, unlike in the case of each person who is created in the Son for the Father, his becomes the one act of being. The accidents exist with their created being as accidents, but only through the substantial being of the Son. Initially these accidents had arisen as qualifiers with the production of bread and wine; thus, Christ's sacramental presence can be said to be taken from (*ex*) those two substances. But with the Eucharistic change, it is Christ's substantial being that sustains the continued actuality of the accidents in terms of which he is sacramentally present. It is his presence that accounts for the accidents retaining their

---

[53] Keefe, *Covenantal Theology*, 428.
[54] Ibid, 422–24.

proper organization, acting and reacting as the qualities of bread and wine do until, ultimately, they break down and are taken up into other substantial unities.

The conversion of the bread and wine is an efficacious sign, too, of the conversion that takes place when the self-offering of the worshippers is joined to the offering of Christ. There appears to be no difference. There is the same attitude of prayer displayed from the opening processional to the Canon's end. It is one liturgy. Yet the change is real on the level of substance. There is a union in intentionality, joined with Christ who is really present; and in Communion, at least in seed, there is an entering into a single life. By virtue of the historical truth of the Eucharist, there is universally a building up of the corporate substance that is the New Covenant, the drawing into Christ of each person with each person's individual identity, coming thereby to be perfected, even as each is free to reject that identity. For Keefe, then, Eucharistic transubstantiation is anything but "an exception to metaphysical intelligibility arbitrarily inserted into reality as a requirement of faith". On the contrary, it is "the very criterion of metaphysical intelligibility". It constitutes a norm for metaphysics, an a priori for metaphysics; because the New Covenant, "the prime analogate of substantial being", is the key to understanding the nature of the real.[55]

Pierre Teilhard de Chardin did not escape the cosmological consciousness of which Keefe is so critical. But in an unpublished lecture from 1923 entitled "Pantheism and Christianity", which explores the common human intuition of a unity, a whole, lying behind the multiple that is everywhere in evidence, his tendency to the cosmological is checked by a deep attachment to the teaching of Saint Paul. In consequence, he ends the essay with a view of the Eucharist that closely parallels Keefe's. Speaking of the transformation begun by Christ's Incarnation, the source of wholenesss, he observes in a passage worth quoting in full:

> The greatest change, however, comes with mass and communion, when we realize the full depth and universality of their mystery. We now understand that when Christ descends sacramentally into each one of his faithful it is not simply in order to commune with him;

[55] Ibid., 429.

it is in order to join him, physically, a little more closely to himself and to all the rest of the faithful in the growing unity of the world. When, through the priest, Christ says, '*Hoc est corpus meum*', 'This is my body', the words reach out infinitely far beyond the morsel of bread over which they are pronounced: they bring the entire mystical body into being. The priestly act extends beyond the transubstantiated Host to the cosmos itself, which, century after century, is gradually being transformed by the Incarnation, itself never complete. From age to age, there is but one single mass in the world: the true Host, the total Host, is the universe which is continually being more intimately penetrated and vivified by Christ. From the most distant origin of things until their unforeseeable consummation, through the countless convulsions of boundless space, the whole of nature is slowly and irresistibly undergoing the supreme consecration. Fundamentally—since all time and for ever—but one single thing is being made in creation: the body of Christ.[56]

---

[56] Pierre Teilhard de Chardin, *Christianity and Evolution*, trans. René Hague (New York: Harcourt Brace Jovanovich, 1971), 73–74.

6

COVENANTAL AUGUSTINIANISM

Thomas Aquinas endeavored to provide a systematic description of the world as an integrated whole, an intrinsically intelligible unity; hence to offer a rational account of things, aided by the teaching of revelation. Augustine, too, regarded the world as endowed with order, beauty, harmony, and purpose. But that was not his primary interest. His primary interest was in making sense of himself, raising the question that Socrates had posed in Plato's *Phaedrus*, the question of identity: Who am I? "Am I a beast", wondered Socrates, "more complicated and savage than Typho, or am I a tamer, simpler animal with a share in a divine and gentle nature?"[1]

Among the very first books Augustine wrote after deciding to become a Christian was a dialogue he had with his own reason, a conversation he called *Soliloquies*, about the two things he wanted most to know, God and the soul. He wanted to understand the nature of the soul, how it differs from the body, in what sense it is subject to change, and whether it is immortal. He wanted to know what his good as a soul consists in and what he should avoid. His reason suggests that he should begin the effort with a prayer. So pray Augustine does, to God who has made all things, God who has made man to his image and likeness—a fact, Augustine says, anyone who knows himself recognizes.[2] Yet he is a fugitive from God, a slave who has run away, fleeing to the embrace of deceit and delusion, to the "weak and destitute elements" spoken of in Galatians 4:9.[3] Only God can turn him, can

[1] Plato, *Phaedrus* 229E–230A, trans., with introduction and notes, by Alexander Nehamas and Paul Woodruff (Indianapolis and Cambridge: Hackett, 1995), 5–6.

[2] "Quod qui se ipse novit, agnoscit." Latin text in *Saint Augustine: Soliloquies and Immortality of the Soul*, intro., trans. and commentary by Gerard Watson (Warminster, England: Aris & Phillips, 1990), 28.

[3] "Infirmis et egenis elementis", which repeats the Vulgate. Ibid., 26.

remind him who his true master is, can heal him, free him, and lead him back to his father, back again to life.[4]

In other words, Augustine's investigation was never going to be a detached, clinical study of the nature of soul or body or the divine. It was not intellectual curiosity that lay behind the question, Who am I? It was more a matter of self-indictment: How can I be the sort of person I am? or What kind of person runs from God, who gave him life, to become the slave of forces that deal in death? It makes virtually no sense. Nevertheless, the very posing of the question means he was not abandoned. God has turned him, recalled him. It is Augustine the convert who sees how absurd he is, and also how absurd his situation continues to be. For there is no denying the lure of vassalage, even though he knows he was made to be free.

If the Thomist approach, looking to explain the world and individual things in the world with their changes and processes, may be called analytic, Keefe writes, the Augustinian approach may be called phenomenological, which for Keefe means observation and description as a method of inquiry; in particular, the observation and description of self-consciousness. It is an experiential method; and Augustine's foundational experience of himself is of someone at once changed, made right, and still a sinner.[5] But if this is the Augustinian starting point, it was equally that of Saint Paul, who declared, "I do not understand my own actions. For I do not do what I want, but I do the very thing I hate" (Rom 7:15). The lament was classical as well, illustrated by the familiar line of Medea in Ovid's *Metamorphoses*: "I see and approve what is better, but I follow what is worse."[6]

For the pagan Roman, however, the irony was simply a fact of the human condition. For Plato, the irony had a deeper source. In the *Phaedrus* he explains the cause with one of his mythic accounts, a so-called "likely story". Each human soul is immortal and properly dwells in the celestial realm above, the abode of the gods, steady and unchanging, illuminated by eternal Knowledge and Justice. Yet one

---

[4] *Soliloquies* 1.1–7.

[5] Donald J. Keefe, *Covenantal Theology: The Eucharistic Order of History*, rev. ed. (Novato, Calif.: Presidio Press, 1996), 479. Keefe takes as a label for the Augustinian experience the phrase *simul justus et peccator*, which, although generally associated with Martin Luther and the Lutheran tradition, he uses to express a very different understanding of Augustine.

[6] "Video meliora proboque, deteriora sequor." Ovid, *Metamorphoses*, bk. 7, line 20.

after another, each soul turns away from its contemplation of divine things, falling down into the physical realm, becoming attached to a body and thereby subject to the shifting, tossing vagaries of this world below. It is possible for every soul to return to its place among the gods through the pursuit of wisdom and the practice of philosophy. But the return can never be secure because the instability lies within the soul itself. The soul is like a chariot, Plato writes, drawn by two horses. One is disciplined and obedient to the charioteer. The other is not, rearing, lunging, looking to drag the chariot downward. And eventually, inevitably, it succeeds.[7]

Augustine, like Paul, attributed the irony to neither human circumstance nor soul but to human will. It was, in fact, during the course of commenting on the same passage from Paul quoted above that Augustine formulated the expression "original sin" (*peccatum originale*) in his treatise *To Simplician*. There is indeed a divide running through the human heart, but that is not how the heart was made. Its division is a malady, introduced by an act of human freedom. And as a malady it has a cure, for those who by the act of faith are united to the heart of the incarnate Son. This Augustine knows; which is why his experience of the irony cuts in a way unimagined by Ovid or Plato. It is Augustine the believer who observes in himself the attraction to sin. He knows that he has been freed, redeemed; and he knows at what price he was bought (1 Cor 7:23). He knows that everything has been changed; he knows that he has been changed. Changed; and yet, irrefutably, not quite. Hence the paradox.

There was a fundamental contrast between Augustine's intuited sense of himself as renewed in Christ, integrated in his true self, and his conscious experience of being fragmented, still splintered by the desires that, he recorded in the *Confessions*, had nearly unmade him. The experience, Keefe writes, of oneself as a unity-in-tension is what identifies Augustinianism as dialectical.[8] The tension is characteristic of Platonism, too. At least in the *Phaedrus*, it seems to define the soul. Certainly it defines the relation of the soul to the body. For the native realm of the body, where things are only imperfectly shaped and ordered by the influence of distant divine forms, is an alien, repressive

---

[7] Plato, *Phaedrus* 245C–250C.
[8] Keefe, *Covenantal Theology*, 477.

place to the soul, which yearns to return to its homeland. As nothing in the physical world has intrinsic worth, neither does life in the world, including the history of human life. This was not Augustine's view, however, versed though he was in Platonism. Christ, who turned him from his former life and in whom Augustine knows himself to be whole despite the fracture of sin, has united history by his Incarnation; and this presence of Christ in history, this process of Christ uniting history to himself, is continued in the Eucharist, where believers who receive the body of Christ are themselves made the one body of Christ.

It was only eight years after his baptism by Ambrose that Augustine was consecrated coadjutor bishop of Hippo Regius, in modern-day Algeria. Within a year he was Hippo's sole bishop; and he presided over the community for the next thirty-four years. So Augustine composed the great bulk of his writings as a bishop; and much of what he has to say concerning the Eucharist was actually preached. Thus, it was at the outset of a homily he delivered to the newly baptized on Easter that he observed:

> I haven't forgotten my promise. I had promised those of you who have just been baptized a sermon to explain the sacrament of the Lord's table, which you can see right now, and which you shared in last night. You ought to know what you have received, what you are about to receive, what you ought to receive every day. That bread which you can see on the altar, sanctified by the word of God, is the body of Christ. That cup, or rather what the cup contains, sanctified by the word of God, is the blood of Christ. It was by means of these things that the Lord Christ wished to present us with his body and blood, which he shed for our sake for the forgiveness of sins. If you receive them well, you are yourselves what you receive. You see, the apostle says, *We, being many, are one loaf, one body* (1 Cor. 10:17). That's how he explained the sacrament of the Lord's table; one loaf, one body, is what we all are, many though we be.[9]

Just how seriously Augustine took the claim that the consecrated bread and wine are the body and blood of Christ is evident in the

---

[9] Augustine, Sermon 227, *The Works of Saint Augustine*, ed. John E. Rotelle, O.S.A., pt. 3, vol. 6, *Sermons 184–229Z*, trans. and notes by Edmund Hill, O.P. (New Rochelle, N.Y.: New City Press, 1993), 254. Hill dates the sermon to 414–415.

interpretation he offered for Psalm 34 (in Augustine's Psalter, Psalm 33). The title of the psalm, "Of David, when he feigned madness", refers to the time in 1 Samuel 21:12–15 when David fell into the hands of King Achish of Gath. Augustine's Latin text has it that David "carried himself in his own hands" (1 Sam 21:13), which he has to admit to his listeners is an undeniably odd phrase.

> How on earth are we to understand this, my brothers and sisters, how is it humanly possible? How can someone be carried in his own hands? A person can be carried in the hands of others, but not in his own. Well, we have no way of knowing what it literally means in David's case; but we can make sense of it with regard to Christ. Christ was being carried in his own hands when he handed over his body, saying, *This is my body* (Mt 26:26); for he was holding that very body in his hands as he spoke.[10]

Augustine was less concerned with explaining how this Eucharistic change took place. It was enough for him to point out to his congregation that they were examples of the same thing. For while they had been made new creatures in Christ through their baptism, outwardly there was nothing to see.

> You who are reborn to a new life, above all you who see this thing for the first time, hear the explanation which we have promised you— and you too of the faithful who are used to the sight, hear me, for it is good to be reminded, lest you fall into forgetfulness. What you behold upon the table of the Lord is that which, so far as its outward appearance is concerned, you see upon your own tables; yet only the appearance is the same, not the power. Similarly, you yourselves have remained what you were; you did not return to us with new faces when you returned from the baptismal pool. Yet you have been made anew; your fleshly form is the old one, but you are new through the grace of holiness. In exactly this way this is something new; for what you see, what stands here, is bread and wine, but once the

---

[10] Augustine, Exposition 1 of Psalm 33, *The Works of Saint Augustine*, ed. John E. Rotelle, O.S.A., pt. 3, vol. 16, *Expositions of the Psalms 33–50*, trans. and notes by Maria Boulding, O.S.B. (Hyde Park, N.Y.: New City Press, 2000), 21. In his general introduction to the *Expositions*, vol. 15, p. 17, Michael Fiedrowicz notes that although it is difficult to determine the particular setting for each exposition, few were delivered as homilies in a Eucharistic celebration. More often the occasion was Vespers or Matins.

consecration has taken place, the bread becomes the body of Christ and the wine his blood.[11]

On the other hand, Keefe writes, in terms of his phenomenology, there was no further explanation Augustine could give.[12] The presence of Christ in the Eucharist, although known with certainty, is not what is experienced. On the contrary, it is what renders unified the paradoxical consciousness of oneself that *is* experienced. It is an experience that is ecclesial and liturgical; the experience of oneself as engaged in a public, communal event of worship.

According to Keefe, Augustinianism's dialectical explication of this experience relies upon a single relation between two principles: form and matter. In Aristotelianism, form and matter are one instance of the act/potency correlation; and as correlates, they evidence a kind of, as Keefe puts it, "continuity" as they compose their substance. In Augustinianism, however, it is differentiation that characterizes form and matter. They are distinct principles—taken as the components of physical things, oppositional principles—even as they are mutually related. And in fallen human consciousness, they are conflictual principles, accounting for the simultaneous unity and disintegration we sense in ourselves.[13]

A covenantal Augustinianism, like a covenantal Thomism, in order to explain the feature of novelty in the physical world and freedom in the human, takes concepts like form, matter, and substance as concrete and personal rather than abstract and general. Augustine's point of departure, though, namely, the self-experience of the believer whose faith is fully expressed in the act of Eucharistic prayer, means that in many respects, Keefe's project can be said merely to develop what is already latent in Augustine's thought, being guided by Augustine's own insights.

Form

As in covenantal Thomism, the prime analogate of form becomes Christ. That is, it is Jesus as the Christ, the one who in establishing

---

[11] *Codex Guelferbytanus 4096* 7, 1. Quoted in F. Van der Meer, *Augustine the Bishop: The Life and Work of a Father of the Church*, trans. Brian Battershaw and G. R. Lamb (London: Sheed and Ward, 1961), 374.

[12] Keefe, *Covenantal Theology*, 544.

[13] Ibid., 545.

the New Covenant fulfills the promise given to Abraham and, what is more, unites our human life with God. Further, in Augustinianism the meaning is dialectical; form is understood in terms of a differentiated complementarity. Thus, Jesus is the groom who is one flesh with his bridal Church. Augustine will in fact stress the depth of the union to the point of referring to a single, nuptial person, though of course the power of the image presumes retaining the distinctive identity of the two and not a reduction of one to the other.

> So out of two people one single person comes to be, the single person that is Head and body, Bridegroom and bride. The wonderful, surpassing unity of this person is celebrated also by the prophet Isaiah, for Christ speaks prophetically in him, too: *The Lord has arrayed me like a bridegroom adorned with his wreath, or a bride decked with her jewels* (Is 61:10). He calls himself bridegroom and he calls himself bride: how can he say he is both bridegroom and bride, except because they will be two in one flesh?[14]

And, following the Letter to the Hebrews, Augustine says that Jesus is the High Priest. He is priest because the offering he made to the Father was sacrificial. It was a sacrifice because the gift he offered meant a loss; an absolute sacrifice because an absolute loss. For the gift Jesus offered was his life; and there was nothing that was not stripped away on the Cross. His passion was a perfect reversal of the egoism that characterizes every sin; a perfect illustration of the turning away from self, of the relinquishing of whatever good the self might lay claim to, in turning unreservedly back to God. It is through free forfeiture that the converted sinner does some specific thing in recognition of what is good, as sin had involved its violation. It makes of self-accusation the beginning of a return to dignity rather than a descent into the black hole of self-hatred. We are the ones who have deserted our dignity, however. It is we who are in need of some act to declare our conversion to the Father, imperfect as it always will be; not the Son whose will is inseparable from the Father's. The perfect sacrifice of Jesus was offered that we might, to some degree, unite to it our own. And there is no more immediate way of entering into this sacrifice than through the Eucharist.

---

[14] Augustine, Exposition 2 of Psalm 30, *The Works of Saint Augustine*, ed. John E. Rotelle, O.S.A., pt. 3, vol. 15, *Expositions of the Psalms 1–32*, intro. Michael Fiedrowicz, trans. and notes by Maria Boulding, O.S.B. (Hyde Park, N.Y.: New City Press, 2000), 324.

Any true sacrifice, writes Augustine in *The City of God*, is a work done, directed to God, in order that we might cling to God by means of a holy companionship ("sancta societate inhaereamus Deo"), a line often quoted by Keefe, who emphasizes its clearly marital association. Hence, the self-offering of Christians, body and soul, is a sacrifice made and fulfilled, definitively, in Christ; made and fulfilled definitively as Eucharistic, in such a way that Christians themselves become Eucharistic. For,

> the whole redeemed city, that is, the congregation and fellowship of the saints [*congregatio societasque sanctorum*], is offered to God as a universal sacrifice through the great priest who, in his passion, offered himself for us in the form of a servant, to the end that we might be the body of so great a head.... This is the sacrifice of Christians: *although many, one body in Christ.* And this is the sacrifice that the Church continually celebrates in the sacrament of the altar (which is well known to the faithful), where it is made plain to her that, in the offering she makes, she herself is offered.[15]

Matter

As Jesus is the dialectical meaning of form, so Mary is the dialectical meaning of matter. Unlike the hylemorphism of Thomas' act/potency analysis, where one principle is the necessary actualization of the other, the Augustinian hylemorphism concerns a composition of two; it is a union between matter understood concretely to be the Second Eve, informed concretely by the Second Adam.[16] Her identity is rooted in her free relation to the Second Adam, that is, in her free consent by which she becomes the mother of the Son. The Incarnation, then, is at once the prime analogate and the prime event of history. And the historical order that is constituted by this event, an event made continually present until it comes to final fulfillment, provides the paradigm of the Augustinian matter/form relation. This is

---

[15] Augustine, *The City of God* 10.6, *The Works of Saint Augustine*, ed. John E. Rotelle, O.S.A., pt. 1, vol. 6, intro. and trans. by William Babcock, notes by Boniface Ramsey (Hyde Park, N.Y.: New City Press, 2012), 310–12.

[16] Keefe, *Covenantal Theology*, 563.

the order of the New Covenant, liturgically at work in the order of *sacramentum tantum, res et sacramentum,* and *res tantum.* Mary, the material principle of this order, is understood at the stage of *sacramentum tantum* to be

> the "daughter Zion", within the moment of the Offertory; this is the created, free, historical, feminine personal correlation that is her "Fiat mihi", her unqualified because immaculate assent, to the nuptial One Flesh of the New Covenant. As *res et sacramentum* she is understood noumenally (spiritually) as the Church, constituting with Jesus the One Flesh, the *res et sacramentum* of the Eucharist, represented sacramentally in the eschatologically consummated fulfillment of her "Fiat mihi" by which she is the *Theotokos.* As *res tantum* she is understood eschatologically (anagogically) as assumed into the risen Kingdom to constitute with him the eschatologically fulfilled and consummated New Covenant, the pleroma of the New Creation, that is sacramentally manifest with him, as the sign which is the Church, in the *mia sarx* of the Eucharistic worship.[17]

Substance

In a covenantal Augustinianism and Thomism alike, the New Covenant is the prime analogate of substance. Therefore substance, Keefe writes, "is the inclusive object of the divine creation". It is "the deed of the Trinity: of the Father, in sending the Son; of the Son, in historical obedience to the Father; of the Spirit, poured out by the Father, through the mission and obedience of the Son, in the creation of the New Covenant".[18] Substantial being is free because the New Covenant is free; meaning that the Son is freely present in a creation freely brought about. It is a historical presence, not cosmic; a presence made possible by the change, the transubstantiation by the Son—in a continuation of his handing everything back to the Father—of the Second Eve's gift of herself. The event of the Incarnation, of that sacrificial life, is present Eucharistically by an identical change, the "transubstantiation of the Church's offering, the

[17] Ibid.
[18] Ibid., 568.

bread and wine which are the symbols of her sacrifice of praise".[19] Nevertheless, the liturgical offering by the faithful is not immaculate as was the Second Eve's. It is not unconditioned, not unqualified. Although shaped by the decision of faith, there remains the keen awareness not only of having fallen short in the past but of continuing to fall short of an absolute turn to the Father. The praise symbolized by the bread and wine is penitential. It is the praise of a people who know that their contrition would remain impotent if not for the self-denial of the Son who had never departed from the Father. There is, then, another change effected in the liturgy, the moral change. It is, Keefe says, a "moment of *metanoia*, of the lifting up of the mind and heart to God, which is indeed rooted in the Eucharistic *metabole*" though entirely distinct from it.[20]

This *metanoia* is one dimension of the process of entering, on the level of intentionality, into the sacrificial and risen life of Christ received in the Eucharist. It is the process of undergoing the integration of common human consciousness, the experience of which is the proper object of Augustinian phenomenology. Only in the act of Eucharistic worship is this universal human predicament—"of anxiety, of guilt, of alienation from God and man"—known to be freely caused and known to be freely healed by the action of Christ.[21] Just as only in and through Eucharistic worship is history itself known to be unified within the free *ordo* of Old Covenant, New Covenant, and Kingdom of God.

Since metaphysics is a probe into being as substance, and phenomenology is concerned with the phenomena of experience, an Augustinian metaphysics can deal with substance only experientially. That is, it is through reflection upon the experience of the unification of one's divided self that substantial existence can be known. And this unification is experienced as freely undergone, without suppression of the ambiguity that nevertheless continues to characterize the human condition, in the liturgy of the Church.

Consequently, it is in this worship that the Augustinian theologian, whose fundamental experience is of the fragmentation of experiential knowledge and whose phenomenological inquiry can have no

---

[19] Ibid., 557.
[20] Ibid., 559.
[21] Ibid. 566.

concretely different subject matter, encounters in the freedom of the Church's Eucharistic worship a free event which does not annul that radical datum, the fragmentation of existence, but transforms it, integrating it into the ordered free unity of historical being which, as has been said, is radically Eucharistic, at once the memorial, the Sacrifice, the Communion and the celebration of our creation in Christ.[22]

The substantial reality of the New Covenant is present sacramentally in the *ordo* of *sacramentum tantum, res et sacramentum, res tantum*. Our personal substantiality is a participation in this prior reality, made evident to us as integrated consciousness, as unified subjectivity, born of the liturgy's prayer. Again, the prime analogate of substance, as transcending the realm of phenomena, cannot itself be an object of experience. It is known directly only in an act of intuition; and that under the light that illuminates all consciousness, the light of Christ.

Trahi a Deo

Keefe writes that one point where Thomas clearly became aware of the inadequacy of his Aristotelianism to account for the Christian view of the person came when he considered Christian conversion. His reliance upon an act/potency analysis initially led him to regard the act of faith as a matter of the will, which naturally desires the good, making a decision for the obviously desirable gospel of Christ, after its content has been tested by the faculty of reason, which naturally seeks what is true. Citing the work of Robert Aubert and Max Seckler, Keefe notes that it was Church doctrine that caused a change in Thomas' thinking.[23] Seckler dated the change to sometime between 1259 and 1260, when Thomas, residing then in Italy,

---

[22] Ibid., 568.

[23] The particular works cited are Roger Aubert, *Le Problème de l'acte de foi: Données traditionnelles et controverses récentes*, 3rd ed. (Louvain: E. Warny, 1958), and Max Seckler, *Instinkt und Glaubenswille nach Thomas von Aquin* (Mainz: Matthias-Grünewald-Verlag, 1961). This was Max Seckler's doctoral dissertation, and Keefe's reference is to the extended review of the book by Edward Schillebeeckx, O.P., in his *Revelation and Theology*, vol. 2, trans. N.D. Smith (New York: Sheed and Ward, 1968), chapter 2. Schillebeeckx points out that Seckler was himself building on the research of, among others, Henri Bouillard in *Conversion et grâce chez saint Thomas* (Paris, 1944).

apparently came across the documents, or at least the substance of the documents, of the Second Council of Orange (held in southern France in 529). What they contained was a formal condemnation of the teaching known as Semi-Pelagianism, whose distinguishing principle is that the decision of faith is to be credited entirely to the choice of the believer. If the quality of faith is a grace, a divine gift, it is a gift the believer accepts of himself. Before his discovery, in the early commentary on the *Sentences* of Peter Lombard, one finds Thomas remarking: "from free will alone a person can prepare himself to have sanctifying grace; for by doing what is in himself, he attains to grace from God."[24] But some seven years later, in the third book of his *Summa contra gentiles*, he argues the very opposite. Just as we need supernatural help to attain our ultimate end, which consists in knowledge of a truth that exceeds the capacity of our nature—God himself, the First Truth—so we need divine help, God's grace, even to accept this help. For how can anything we do according to the ability of our nature be sufficient preparation for what lies above our nature? And since no one can will what is not known, how can anyone of himself choose to accept a gift that exceeds everything we know? All of which proves the error of the Pelagians, and he quotes, in addition to a series of lines from the letters of Paul, Lamentations 5:21 (in Thomas' Latin), "Convert us to yourself, O Lord, and we will be converted."[25]

The reference to Lamentations points to another important reason for Thomas' change: his return while in Italy to the study of Scripture, marked in particular by the request of Pope Urban IV that he produce a nearly verse by verse commentary on the Gospels, composed of excerpts taken from the Fathers of the Church. The result, entitled *Catena Aurea* (*The Golden Chain*), was compiled between 1263 and 1267, while he was at work on the *Summa contra gentiles*. It draws on the writings of more than fifty authors, from the Greek and Latin Fathers down to Anselm of Canterbury. But in his commentary on the fourth Gospel, Thomas relies especially on Augustine and Augustine's *Tractates on the Gospel of John*. The words of Jesus in John 6:44, "No

---

[24] 2 *Sent.* 28.1.4. sol.

[25] *Summa contra gentiles* 3.147, 149. The chronology of St. Thomas' life and works is that argued for by James A. Weisheipl, O.P., in *Friar Thomas D'Aquino: His Life, Thought, and Works* (Washington, D.C.: Catholic University of America Press, 1983), 351–405.

one can come to me unless the Father who sent me draws him", had been cited in Canon 8 of the Second Council of Orange; and Thomas himself had referred to the saying in book three of *Summa contra gentiles*, chapter 147. Here in the *Catena Aurea*, however, and due to the influence of Augustine, they play an even more direct role in Thomas' developing reflection on the antecedent action of God.

"This is the great commendation of grace: no one comes unless drawn", Augustine remarks concerning John 6:44 in the excerpt that Thomas quotes from *Tractate* 26.2. And soon afterward he strings together two lines from Augustine's *On the Predestination of the Saints*, 8.15 and 16.33: "If God does not make willing people out of the unwilling, why does the Church, according to the precept of the Lord, pray for her persecutors? . . . For no one can say, I believed, therefore I was called. Certainly it is the mercy of God that comes first, so that one is called in order that he might believe." To ensure, however, that God's mercy not be taken as a display of coercion or power, Thomas immediately adds the (somewhat conflated) line from *Tractate* 26.7: "Behold, therefore, how the Father draws by teaching the truth, not by imposing necessity. For it belongs to God to draw."[26] This idea of God's drawing, which will appear with increasing frequency in Thomas, is summarized by the phrase *trahi a Deo*, "to be drawn by God". To it Thomas will add a range of ways in which God acts, as he specifies more fully the statement in *Summa contra gentiles* 3.149.1 that man does not move himself so he may obtain divine help, for that help lies above him. Rather, it is God who moves man.

After returning to Paris from Italy, Thomas continued not only to write and lecture on Scripture, but to work on his magisterial *Summa theologiae*, that sweeping examination of Christian faith that he divided into three parts, the first of which he had finished and the second just begun before leaving Italy for Paris in 1268. As would be expected, the relevant passages in the first part of the *Summa*, like his other work from that period in Italy, focus on the teaching that even one's readiness to receive grace must be attributed to God. So, for example, in answering whether God bestows his grace on those

---

[26] *In Joannis Evangelium* (*Super Johannem*) 6.6, in *Opera Omnia*, vol. 17 (Paris: Vivès, 1889), 499–501. For an English translation, see St. Thomas Aquinas, *Catena Aurea*, vol. 4, pt. 1 (Albany, N.Y: Preserving Christian Publications, 2000), 234–37, first published by John Henry Parker, London, 1842.

whom he foreknows will be worthy of grace, Thomas responds without hesitation: No, that was the opinion of the Pelagians, who held that "the beginning of doing well is from us"; and he cites Saint Paul (Titus 3:5; Romans 9:11–12; 2 Corinthians 3:5) and Lamentations 5:21.[27] It had not been that long, however, since Thomas himself had thought it made sense to say that God will turn to the person who turns to him. Since every person as rational has a capacity to know what is true, and therefore every person simply as a person will seek what is true, one could hardly imagine God coldly ignoring this highest quest, which he himself created. It may be somewhat in his own defense, then, that Thomas observes in the second part of the *Summa* that Augustine, too, as he conceded in the *Retractions*, had initially thought that whereas the good works of the believer are the fruit of grace, faith is of our own choosing.[28] In actuality, however, it is always a matter of the grace of God, of God creating, God revealing, God drawing the person to himself that the person might cling to God as God, not just as the Good.

It was this scriptural vision, which he met both in the biblical text and in the work of Augustine, that prodded Thomas' thought at Paris. He spoke now of God's drawing, his attracting, as something that operates both from within and from without. A person draws another through persuasion, he stated in the Paris lectures he gave on John, "and this is the manner in which the Father draws people to the Son, by clearly showing that he is his Son; and he does this in two ways: either by an inner revelation (Mt 16:17: 'Blessed are you, Simon bar Jonah, for flesh and blood has not revealed this to you,' namely, that Christ is the Son of the living God, 'but my Father') or through the working of miracles, which are done in virtue of the Father."[29] Further, since as John teaches whatever the Father does the Son does as well (Jn 6:19), Thomas in these lectures described Christ, too, as working to attract from within and without: "for the voice of the Son of God, which moves the hearts of the faithful inwardly through inspiration or outwardly through his own preaching and that of others,

[27] *Summa theologiae* Ia, q. 23, a. 5, c. See also Ia, q. 62, a. 2, ad 3.

[28] Ia-IIae, q. 114, a. 5, ad 1, referring to Augustine's admission in *Retractions* 1.23.2 that in his early *Expositio* of some themes in the letter to the Romans (written ca. 394), he had misunderstood St. Paul's point in Romans 9:10–13.

[29] *Comm. In Ioan.* 6.5.3. *Opera Omnia*, vol. 20, 41, cols. 1–2.

has life-giving force."[30] And similarly, during the Advent disputation of 1269, he noted: "To those works which Christ performed among people must also be added the inner call (*vocatio interior*) by which he attracted certain of them."[31]

More than the idea of God's attraction, however, Seckler argued that Thomas brought back from Italy the concept of a divine impulse, an *instinctus*, that he had also found in the documents of Second Orange. It occurs repeatedly in his writings at Paris. "It is not only exterior or objective revelation that has the power of attracting," he remarks in the lectures on John, "but there is also an interior instinct impelling and moving one to believe; thus the Father draws many to the Son through this divinely operating instinct, moving more inwardly the heart of a person to belief."[32] Inasmuch as belief is a matter of assenting to the teaching of Christ, Thomas speaks of the intellectual effect of the *instinctus*: "The inner instinct, by which Christ was able to manifest himself without exterior miracles, pertains to the power of the First Truth, which illuminates and teaches a person interiorly."[33] But also, more broadly, he calls the instinct simply God's invitation: "It must be said that the person who believes has sufficient cause for believing, for he is induced by the authority of the divine teaching, confirmed by miracles, and, what is more, by the interior instinct of God inviting."[34] The divine action, then, has many facets and works on many levels: "It must be noted that Christ attracted by his word, with visible signs, and also by invisible signs, namely, by moving and inciting hearts inwardly. 'The heart of the king is in the hand of God' (Proverbs 21:1). Therefore, the interior instinct to acting well is the work of God; and they who resist it, sin."[35]

The inner work of God, as entirely distinct from outward signs, miracles, or preaching, can operate as a preparation for the preacher's word; and the prime example of this is the case of the Roman centurion, Cornelius, found in Acts 10. It may be that, as Saint Paul said,

[30] *Comm. In Ioan.* 5.4. *Opera Omnia*, vol. 20, 10, col. 2. See also Ia-IIae, q. 109, a. 6, c. and ad 1, 2; and the remark in part two of the second part of the *Summa* that the assent of faith is due to "God moving interiorly through grace" (IIa-IIae, q. 6, a. 1, c.).

[31] *Quodl.*, 2, q. 4, a. 1, ad 1 (Marietti, 1956, p. 29).

[32] *Comm. In Ioan.* 6.5.3. *Opera Omnia*, vol. 20, 41, col. 2.

[33] *Quodl.* 2. q. 4, a. 1, ad 3 (Marietti, 1956, p. 29).

[34] IIa-IIae, q. 2, a. 9, ad 3.

[35] *Comm. Ioan.* 15.5.4. *Opera Omnia*, vol. 20, 270, col. 1.

faith comes from hearing, Thomas notes in his commentary on the letter to the Romans, but what is heard only specifies what is believed; also required is "the inclination (*inclinatio*) of the heart to believing, and this is not from hearing but is a gift of grace." Thus, it was necessary that Cornelius' heart be so inclined, or there would have been no point in God sending Peter to instruct him.[36] Earlier in the same commentary Thomas had written: "The call of a person is indeed twofold. One call is exterior, coming from the mouth of the preacher.... The other call, which is interior, is nothing other than a kind of instinct of the mind, by which the heart of the person is moved by God to assent to those things that are of faith or virtue."[37] In fact, in the case of the first man, there was only this interior work; there was no outer word to be heard, only "God inspiring inwardly".[38] Given, then, that, as Thomas writes, at all times and in all places it has always been necessary that one have faith—implicit or explicit—that Jesus is the Christ, it must be supposed that it was by interior instruction that the first man knew, as Thomas says he did, of the future Incarnation in knowing that his relation with the woman was a sign of Christ's union with the Church.[39]

Thomas may have begun to speak of an interior instinct or an inclination to faith only during his second period teaching at Paris, but it was anticipated by what he had already said concerning the will. God, he stated in the *Summa contra gentiles*, is the author and sustainer of our nature and of all the powers of our nature, including the power of willing. Nor does God only sustain the will. It is he who is the driver of its activity, for "nothing can act by its own power unless it also acts through his power", just as the movement of the brush in painting is an extension of the principal action of the painter. Therefore, Thomas writes, it must be said that "God is the cause in us, not only of the will, but also of our willing."[40] And what the intellectual creature wills, above all, is to know the highest Truth. Hence, it is from Aristotelian premises that Thomas argues, God is "the first object of desire and the first agent of willing", the one desired and the cause

[36] *In Ep. ad Rom.* 10.2 (Marietti, 1929, vol. 1, 150).
[37] *In Ep. ad Rom.* 8.6 (Marietti, 1929, vol. 1, 122–23).
[38] IIa-IIae, q. 5, a. 1, ad 3.
[39] IIa-IIae, q. 2, a. 7, c.
[40] *Summa contra gentiles* 3.89.5.

of our desiring him.[41] If, as the Gospel teaches, we are called to seek the Father himself, for his own sake, then desiring of another order is required; and so is the inclination that will urge us to that level of desiring.

It is clear in Thomas' work that humanity was endowed with grace from the beginning, which would include the divine *instinctus*. And the human will originally consented to this grace; so that humanity, in that "first moment of creation", possessed both faith and charity.[42] And even if subsequently it was the choice of the will to turn away from grace, with the result that all humanity is born into a state of sin rather than rectitude, it was Thomas' position that that same primal choice presents itself anew in every life. Because of sin, come the first exercise of reason, whenever that may be, it is oneself that each of us immediately thinks of, how to direct all things to oneself, regarding them in terms of oneself. This is the moment for the person to turn to God; to turn away from the self.[43] And it is as contrary to the nature of the will to resist the divine help to moral conversion as it is to the nature of the human mind to resist the *instinctus* that, it must be presumed, is at work even in this inchoate stage of belief.[44]

With this, as Keefe points out, there arises a problem for his approach that Thomas failed to recognize. He maintains that the grace of conversion operates universally; that is why the sin of unbelief can be charged to any person who does not have faith, at least implicitly and at least in rudimentary form. It is distributed on the level of human nature, moving the individual toward the one ultimate end of our nature—even though, paradoxically, that end lies beyond the capacity of our nature, apart from grace.[45] Nevertheless, in Thomas' substance/accident analysis, grace in any sense, and not only in the sense of a virtue—like faith—that admittedly a person may lose and then later recover, has to be treated as an extrinsic accident.

---

[41] *Summa contra gentiles* 3.67.4.

[42] Ia, q. 95, a. 1, c. and ad 5; a. 3, c. See also *De malo* q. 5, a. 1 and ad 13; *2 Sent.* d. 30, q. 1, a. 1, sol.

[43] Ia–IIae, q. 89, a. 6, c. and ad 3. If the person is unbaptized, then the very act of turning to God brings, through grace, the remission of original sin. If, however, the person turns to himself, then he is said, though acting only at this first awakening of reason, to sin mortally. See also *De malo* q. 5, a. 2, ad 8; q. 7, a. 10, ad 8.

[44] IIa–IIae, q. 10, a. 1, ad 1.

[45] Ia–IIae, q. 5, a. 5; q. 62, a. 1; *De veritate*, q. 14, a. 2.

For substance, Thomas says, is equivalent to nature, and grace, of course, is supernatural.[46] That is the dilemma Keefe avoids in positing the New Covenant as the prime analogate of substance. It allows him to speak of grace as something substantial, meaning that it operates, first and foremost, on the level of substance. For human nature understood covenantally must be understood relationally: the human by definition having a relation to the divine; created in the Son for the Father. This relation is constitutive of the human, not extrinsic to the human or superadded to the human. It is by speaking of grace as substantial that Keefe is able to account for our subsistence in God that is so central to Thomas.[47] And the interiority of grace, which Thomas describes as both urging and drawing us, for Keefe is our participation in the Son's response to the Father; our gift of self being guided by the Son's gift to the Father.

Illumination and the *Imago Dei*

From the time of his earliest writings, one finds in Augustine, doubtless under the influence of Platonism, the theory that our minds are able to apprehend incorporeal and immutable truth, like the truths of mathematics, thanks to the illumination of God, whose light makes them visible to reason, as the sun makes the objects of the world visible to our eyes.[48] Later he associated this idea of divine illumination with the doctrine of the human person as an *imago Dei*, as being an image of God.

Often, by "image" Augustine meant that the human person provides an illustration of God, or, more exactly, a demonstration on behalf of the Christian teaching about God, namely, that God is a Trinity. It is perfectly reasonable, he said, to claim that the one God is a unity of three distinct persons whose distinction, one from the other, in no way divides the divinity; and the proof lies in the person. Consider, he argues in the treatise *De Trinitate*, a human mind seeking to know itself as mind. It exercises simultaneously three distinct capacities:

---

[46] Ia–IIae, q. 110, a. 2, c. and ad 2.

[47] *Summa contra gentiles* 3.68, 88–89.

[48] See *Soliloquies* 1.6.12, 8.15; *Confessions* 4.15.25. Plato, in *Republic* 508c–509a, says it is the idea of the Good that illuminates the truths known by reason.

memory (*memoria*), since one must remember and retain what is gathered as one conducts the inquiry; understanding (*intellectus*), which is the very activity of leading the inquiry; and love (*amor*) or will, the source of the desire to continue inquiring until one has arrived at full self-knowledge. It is one person, whose one mind is expressed rather than split by the operation of three activities. "And so you have a certain image of the trinity, the mind itself and its knowledge, which is its offspring and its word about itself, and love as the third element, and these three are one and are one substance."[49] This is not to lose sight of the ways in which the mind does not even approximate to God. The three activities of remembering, understanding, and willing belong to a human person without being human nature, because human nature is not simply mind. Furthermore, each human being is a unity because each is a single person. But the unity of God is predicated on a trinity of persons, three persons who coinhere and whose action is one and undivided, unlike the separate operation of our memory, understanding, and will.[50] Nevertheless, the parallel afforded by the mind, though limited, is real.

In fact, it is this use of "image" to mean likeness that occurs most widely in Augustine. It is, of course, the literal meaning of *imago*; and his first reference to the person as God's image, in *On Genesis against the Manichees* (begun in 388), comes as a commentary on Genesis 1:26, where the biblical author seems to use "image" and "likeness" interchangeably. Hence, to say that we image God, Augustine writes, is to mean that we are like him. And we are like him in virtue of reason.[51] A short time later, in *On Eighty-Three Different Questions* (which he worked on from 388 to 395), Augustine states that everything in creation may be said to be like God in at least some sense, even if that sense is mere existence. But a living thing is more like God than something nonliving, and an animal is more like God than a plant; and human beings are more like God than any other creature in this

---

[49] *De Trinitate* 9.18, *The Works of Saint Augustine*, ed. John E. Rotelle, O.S.A., pt. 1, vol. 5, *The Trinity*, intro., trans., and notes by Edmund Hill, O.P. (Brooklyn, N.Y.: New City Press, 1991), 282. See also *Confessions* 13.11.12. Augustine was anticipated in his argument—and, in part, his illustration—by Tertullian (d. ca. 230), who, in *Against Praxeas* 2.4, wrote that God possesses a threefold *unitas* that he termed a *trinitas*.

[50] *De Trinitate* 14.11; 15.43.

[51] *De Genesi contra manichaeos* 1.17.28.

world, because again, human beings have reason. Thinking is a partic-ipation in God's wisdom, and it reflects a kind of union with him.[52] However, Augustine adds that there are those commentators who say that "image" and "likeness" should not be treated as simply equivalent. Why would the author have used two words to say one thing? Rather, because we are living bodies we are like God; but it is our mind or spirit that is called image. For the mind is made by Truth to know Truth. This is the meaning of the line in Genesis 1:26 (in Augustine's Latin) that humanity was made to the image of God. The Son, Augus-tine writes, is the image and likeness of God. We were made "to" the image, meaning, as these commentators say, made to adhere to the Son, to the Truth.[53]

He returns to the same point in *On Genesis according to the Letter* (begun in 401). Human beings were created "to" the image of God since, as intellectual, they were made "participating in the eternal and immutable wisdom of God".[54] More, they were created as ordered to Wisdom, to the Word, knowing him in the sense of acknowledging (*agnitio*) him. The first sin had consisted in our falling away from this *agnitio*, and our salvation rests upon returning to it, as it is written (according to Augustine's Latin) in Colossians 3:10: the believer "is being renewed in the recognition (*agnitio*) of God according to the image of him who created him".[55] The life of faith marks the begin-ning of our reunion with God, in his Image and through that part of our nature by which we ourselves are most aptly said to image, to resemble, him.

Interestingly enough, in Sermon 52 (which he delivered sometime between 410 and 412), Augustine so stresses the qualification of calling the person an image of God that he treats the ideas of "image" and "likeness" as opposites. If you want to see a likeness of yourself, he says, go look in the mirror. If you want to see a genuine image, that is, to see a living expression—not manufactured reflection—of yourself, look at your child. The child is a parent's actual image because the

---

[52] *De diversis quaestionibus octoginta tribus* 51.2.

[53] Ibid., 51.4.

[54] *De Genesi ad litteram* 3.20.31.

[55] *De Genesi ad litteram* 3.20.32; *The Literal Meaning of Genesis*, trans. Edmund Hill, O.P., in *The Works of Saint Augustine*, ed. John E. Rotelle, O.S.A., pt. 1, vol. 13 (Hyde Park, N.Y.: New City Press, 2002), 235.

two are identical in substance, having the same nature, even though they are different in person. That is why the Son is the one true image of the Father. Even so, Augustine concedes, one speaks legitimately when one refers analogously to us as God's image.[56]

Over time, it was the moral, rather than a purely cognitional, understanding of image on which Augustine built. In book 14, the second to last book of *De Trinitate* (which he finished by 420), he qualifies the statement he had made in book 9 that the memory and understanding and love exercised by the mind of a person engaged in self-knowing constitutes an image of the Trinity. It does, but being nothing more, it is a deficient image. It is deficient inasmuch as it abstracts from the existential fact that, first and foremost, each of us is a creature made by God, for God. It is deficient if the knowing mind is not also taking into account its awareness of its own lack, indeed, of its loss. What the mind does not have, and what lies beyond its reach, is happiness. No mind exists independently of the omnipresent God in whom each mind lives and moves and by whose light each mind sees eternal truth and unchanging justice—and sees, too, its own injustice. For a mind, then, to exercise memory in the full sense is for it to be mindful of this light, of the Lord, and to be incited to turn to him, aware of the distance separating one from God and heeding the admonition of the Gospel to conversion. It is the believer, having received the Spirit of the Lord, who genuinely remembers the Lord and who has learned through a most intimate guiding (*intimum magisterium*)—confirmed by the Scriptures—that one's unhappiness is a fall, due to a voluntary failing, as one's rise can be possible only as the result of grace. Similarly, it is the mind of the believer that truly exercises understanding in its effort to know the Lord, as it exercises love in holding fast to the Lord. An image of God ought to conduct itself as an image, Augustine declares, and worship its Creator. "Those", he writes, "who do, on being reminded, turn to the Lord from the deformity which had conformed them by worldly lusts to this world are reformed by him; they listen to the apostle saying, *Do not conform to this world, but be reformed in the newness*

---

[56] Sermon 52.17, *The Works of Saint Augustine*, ed. John E. Rotelle, O.S.A., pt. 3, vol. 3, *Sermons 51–94*, trans. and notes by Edmund Hill, O.P. (Brooklyn, N.Y.: New City Press, 1991), 58.

of your minds (Rom. 12:2). And thus the image begins to be reformed by him who formed it in the first place."[57]

As close a student of Saint Paul as he was, however, it seems to have escaped Augustine's notice that the Son whom Saint Paul calls the image of God in Romans 8:29 and 2 Corinthians 4:4 and Colossians 1:15 is the incarnate Son, Jesus Christ, the head of the Church who is his body. It is not the eternal Word or Wisdom. So even as his adherence to Saint Paul delivered him from a purely individualistic, self-enclosed understanding, where the human person was said to image God when in remembering itself and desiring to know itself it acted from itself and within itself, Augustine was constantly pulled away from the diverse multiplicity of life into the unity and simplicity of the inner person. The body has nothing to do with the person as image, except inasmuch as the human capacity to stand erect symbolizes our power to know higher things.[58] Sexual distinction is equally irrelevant to us as image; except that femininity represents the side of reason that has to be bracketed off—the practical side, meaning reason as concerned with getting things done—when discussing the person, since it is in virtue of reason's capacity for contemplation that reason provides an image of God.[59] And when Augustine writes that we most fully image God when we worship him, it is private devotion that he has in mind, not the public act that forms the summit of prayer: the Eucharist. Yet the Eucharist was the summit of prayer for Augustine, too. So the covenantal, hence Eucharistic, explanation of the *imago Dei* with which Keefe ends *Covenantal Theology* is for him an authentic development and strengthening of Augustine's insight.

Memoria, Intellectus, and Amor

In *Covenantal Theology*, Keefe regards the concept in Thomas of the *trahi a Deo* as parallel to the Augustinian notion of illumination. The *trahi*, he writes, is "the noetic aspect or dimension of our existential participation, by reason of our creation in Christ, in the *Lumen* who

---

[57] *De Trinitate* 14.22, trans., ibid., 388. See also *De Trinitate* 7.12.
[58] *De Genesi contra manichaeos* 1.17.28; *De Genesi ad litteram, imperfectus liber* 16.61.
[59] *De Trinitate* 12.12.

is the historical Christ of the historical New Covenant.... At bottom, the *trahi* is for the Thomist the universally distributed substantial grace that makes us free to worship—or to refuse to worship, as Thomas saw."[60] The difference is that while the focus here is on the conversion to God that the illumining grace makes possible, the focus with Augustine is on the consciousness of one who has converted. It is on the contradiction-in-unity that is seen in this light: one's awareness of oneself as a unique "I", inclining to what is condemned by a universal sense of justice, yet ever drawn to life by absolute Justice. *Memoria, intellectus,* and *amor* are for Keefe three "modes of fallen consciousness", of "fallen subjectivity",[61] describing the person as developing only in fits and starts, freely seeking to understand, or choosing not to. The free prime analogate, freely immanent in history, is affirmed by a free act, the act of faith; and in this affirmation, one has knowledge of oneself in knowing the prime by which one is sustained. The prime analogate, the New Covenant, is immanent in history as an event, the actual life, death, and Resurrection of Christ. It is an event, however, that unites history into the one history of salvation. Christ himself instituted the historical sign through which the believer has access to this prime analogate that, although immanent, is also transcendent and, so, cannot be the object of direct experience. The sign is a memorial, or a remembrance—in Greek, *anamnesis*— but not as a memorial that recalls in time something that has drifted into the past. Rather, it is a sacramental anamnesis that joins time to its source. This sacramental anamnesis, the Eucharist, lies at the center of the liturgical life of the Church, whose life is one with Christ and who, in teaching of Christ—the Son sent by the Father to give the Spirit—teaches of the self.

Existence informed by faith, Keefe states,

is of course itself liturgical: it begins with the sacramental entry by baptism into the death of Christ, as the preliminary essential to Eucharistic Communion in the medicine of immortality, the antidote for death that is the Eucharist. But basic to the ordered sacramental worship of the Church is the single affirmation of the faith: Jesus is the Lord. The

---

[60] Keefe, *Covenantal Theology,* 571–72.
[61] Ibid., 567, 577.

recognition that this lordship is Eucharistic grounds the Augustinian phenomenology, which has no other object than the Eucharistic worship, in which all sacramental worship is resumed and consummated.[62]

Again, true knowledge of the self must wait upon knowledge of God,

> whom Augustine describes as more intimately present to the self than the self is to itself.... This self-knowledge is of a guilty self, whose guilt is indissociable from the self's own awareness of the self; it is an existential awareness of standing in the presence of the Judge who as the Truth incarnate neither abandons one to one's guilt nor condones it, but rather redeems it by the One Sacrifice of the Christ, which is historically actual and effective by its representation in the Church's Eucharistic worship. But however existential this awareness may be, it is always dogmatically informed by the historical concreteness of the liturgical tradition.[63]

The person, Keefe writes, is fully realized as image of God through participation in the Eucharistic liturgy, *memoria, intellectus,* and *amor* coming to be united in a single subjectivity, where *memoria* corresponds to *sacramentum tantum, intellectus* to *res et sacramentum,* and *amor* to *res tantum.* He refers to Augustine's treatment of *memoria* in book 10 of the *Confessions,* where the talk is of a vast space "illumined by the obscure presence of the Christ, the 'Beauty ancient yet forever new.' "[64] It is not, however, a multiplicity of things that occupies this space but of moments; a string of what, considered exclusively in terms of themselves, are disconnected and meaningless events that for the Platonist effect a nullifying distention of the soul. Such is true of time for the world, too, apart from Christ. It was sin that made time into an absurdity, just as sin makes of one's personal time a duration leading nowhere. The New Covenant, founded on the sacrifice of Christ, provides the integrating center, at once immanent and transcendent; and we the worshippers, fully cognizant of our sin, by entering the liturgy, enter into the efficacious cause of "the unity of the history of salvation and of our own historical consciousness".[65] Thus is *memoria*

[62] Ibid., 574.
[63] Ibid., 576.
[64] Ibid., 578.
[65] Ibid., 579.

the *sacramentum tantum*, life that is brought forward as gift. For this reason also does the Eucharistic liturgy open with a Penitential Rite, preparing us "to join in the Church's Offertory, her sacrifice of praise".[66]

We know the full impact and significance of sin only in knowing of the crucifixion, as Paul declared in Romans 1:16–18. There is, then, a kind of circumincession of *memoria* with *intellectus*, with understanding taught by faith. Through faith one has certain and universal knowledge of oneself and the world, but knowledge that is free rather than determined by ideal necessities, because it is knowledge of the free prime analogate of being, really present in the Eucharist and personally encountered in the liturgical worship of the Church. *Intellectus* therefore bears the same relation to *memoria* as *res et sacramentum* to *sacramentum*: it is the true self-knowledge that has come from illumined experience in an act that is the deliberate uniting of oneself to the sacrifice of Christ.

Amor, love, denotes for Keefe not only desire or attraction but the capacity to make a settled commitment and, at its highest, a free gift of oneself, an unreserved dedication to another for the other's sake. In truth there can be no genuine love of anyone or anything that does not proceed from love of God. Yet according to our divided consciousness that regards all goods as competing goods, even the worship of God is a diminishment of oneself. Augustine took the pagan reaction to the sacking of one city, Rome, by the Visigoths in 410, as an illustration of rival loves in the monumental treatise he named for another, *The City of God*. Nevertheless, only one city is real, the other is fabricated; in the Fall, the human heart was split, not doubled. "The paradoxical quality of *amor*", Keefe says,

> underlies the Augustinian theology of history: two loves have built two cities—not in the sense of two clearly distinct communities, but rather as the disjunct finalities of two mutually exclusive loves, the one selfish, the other sacrificial, which are innate in all human beings. All of us, throughout our lives, are marked by this personal schism: one so profound as to leave us incapable of an unwavering and single-hearted commitment to God, incapable of an unambiguous love of the supreme Unity, Truth, Good, and Beauty. In consequence we find ourselves equally incapable of a comparably unambiguous

[66] Ibid., 580.

commitment to each other; of ourselves we are simply incapable of doing good.

Our historical commitments at their most profound, i.e., to repentance, to Christ in his Church, to marriage, and to the priesthood, are therefore historically actual only as sacramental; their objectivity is liturgical, realized only insofar as assimilated and ordered to the Eucharistic worship of the Church and thus to her sacrifice of praise. It is only by Eucharistic union of the Church's sacrifice with the Sacrifice of the Christ, represented in his Person in the Mass, that our free historical commitments are then made capable, in and by that union, of causing the truth they signify.[67]

The worshipper, conscious of sinfulness, approaching as a penitent, knows that redemption has come by the gift of Christ. The knowledge is intuited, of course, possessed sacramentally; one still experiences oneself as divided. But with the Consecration, the Redeemer himself is present, and the worshipper joins in the Church's responsive sacrifice, her sacrifice of praise whereby she becomes one with Christ in sacrifice as she is one in flesh. It is that one-flesh life with Christ that the worshipper receives and actualizes in Communion, a building up of the holy society, the communion of saints, whose fullness is the *res tantum*, the good creation come to completion. In this Communion, *amor* has its integration with *intellectus* and *memoria*, the believer turning in love to God as Creator and Redeemer—despite the requirement that this conversion be repeated in continual re-conversion—in accordance with the fundamental truth of each person's identity. The liturgical unity of Offertory-Consecration-Communion becomes the locus, too, where the rift running through the heart begins to close and the restoration to single-heartedness is begun, and the competing proclivities of the heart are overcome in the fashioning of an integral freedom that can be grounded nowhere else but in Christ. The worshipper, whose freedom arises from and is strengthened in Eucharistic prayer, is made free for the commitments that are a source of life and free for the service that fosters life.

With his emphasis always on this freedom, Keefe will stress again and again that the order of the liturgy re-presents the order of history—Old Covenant, New Covenant, Kingdom—as the order of the liturgy

[67] Ibid., 583.

effects, brings to realization, the order of the New Creation. And in each instance, the order is characterized by the mutuality, the uniting in difference and interiority, and the enduring bond that is signified by marriage. It may be that there is an integration of individual consciousness in the liturgy, but only as the individual is a participant in the covenantal human substance. The unity of consciousness, Keefe writes, "therefore is not a private experience".

> Rather it is substantial, communal, and therefore public: it is the covenantal and nuptial integration of the free human community as free. This communal *ordo* can only be sacramentally actual in a fallen history, but its sacramental signing *ex opere operato* is public, historical, and free. Because it is liturgical, it cannot be imposed but only freely appropriated. As appropriated, it proceeds of its own efficacy to transform human society: it is thus that history is salvific.
>
> Consequently the sacramental efficacy of the Church's worship reaches far beyond the formal liturgical community, for its public character pervades the public, the "secular", life of the Christians who live by it; it cannot be compartmentalized or quarantined.[68]

Endowed in the liturgy with a freedom that is historical, communal, and public, we are sent forth at the conclusion of Mass with a share in the *missio* of Christ. For the one to whom we have been united in *amor* came not to be served but to serve and to give his life as a ransom for the many (Mt 20:28).

> We are freely given that which we have freely sought, and in that Communion with the risen second Adam and second Eve we enter into the love of Christ, whose mission is henceforth ours ..., for that solidarity with him which we have been given is free and must be freely appropriated in the free assumption of historical responsibility for the salvation of those for whom Christ died, if it is to integrate us into the fullness of the New Creation. The work of *amor* is to build the City of God: this is the task of the second Eve whose sacrament is the Church, and it is incumbent upon all who worship in her, for *amor* is concrete as historical responsibility. Our history, for Catholicism and so for Augustinianism, has no meaning but that which it has in Christ.[69]

[68] Ibid., 586.
[69] Ibid., 587.

Once more, Keefe identifies the bond that is brought about by the free consent of a husband and wife in marriage, in virtue of which it is the sacramental sign of Christ in union with his Church, as therefore uniquely imaging the Trinitarian unity that consists in the Father's gift to the Son and, through the Son, to the Spirit, who responds in gift to Father and Son with infinite depth, for which reason Augustine said that he, of the three Persons, is most appropriately named *caritas*.[70] So it is that in the closing passages of *Covenantal Theology*, Keefe underscores the critical role of sacramental marriage as the institution that secures the value of history, of the person in history, and of human freedom and responsibility. "It should be remembered always that this image," Keefe writes of the Eucharistically grounded Trinitarian image of God in man,

and the *amor* which for Augustinianism is its substance, is nuptial. It is this nuptial quality of *amor* that specifies the Catholic mission, the imitation of Christ. A nuptial love is historical and human; it cannot vanish into any sort of eschatologism or abstraction from the historical order, but is rooted in our historicity, our materiality, our corporeality. It is specified by the sacrifice of the last Adam for the last Eve, and by the responsive sacrifice of the last Eve: that is, by the One Flesh of the New Covenant.

Too little attention is paid to the enormous consequences of this conversion to history.... Its effect is social, the free public order, the free society, whose freedom, whose justice, whose common good has no other criterion than the marriage whose ground is the New Covenant.... Marriage, even in a post-Christian culture, is irretrievably imbued with a Christian significance. A vision of marital fidelity, of what the love of a man for a woman and of a woman for a man entails in devotion, in sacrifice, in celebration, entered the world with Christ, and it will not be removed by however meticulous an account of its unreasonableness on grounds economic, genetic, social, or otherwise cautelary. Such marital commitment, however dimly perceived, is a given in our world and will not be extirpated, for it rests not on man but on the death of Christ. For so long as the world endures, marriage will remain an effective and unwearying protest against all that affronts human dignity....

Marriage is the great social and political sacrament; sustained by the Church's Eucharistic worship, it is the proximately effective sign

[70] *De Trinitate* 15.5.29.

in the world of the Kingdom of God. It is primarily by marriage that the love of Christ is concretely perceptible in the world; it is by the effective symbol of marital love that the world learns of the meaning of the historical freedom which pervades it, however contested it be, and which alone is Christian.

We need not expect that the contest will cease, but neither does our mission to make the world free and holy in Christ. For most of us, this is by marriage; for all of us, it is by entering into the One Flesh of the Eucharist, that worship which is the nuptial imaging of God, *amor*. John the Evangelist has told us that God is love; so also, as made in his image, is humanity.[71]

---

[71] Keefe, *Covenantal Theology*, 590.

7

LAW, THE STATE, AND
CATHOLIC WORSHIP

Donald Keefe was the quintessential theologian. Nevertheless, he received his bachelor's from Colgate University in political science, followed immediately by a law degree from Georgetown University, two years before deciding to enter the Jesuits. Little surprise, then, that he made a career-long study of political thought and of the relation between law and theology. What follows are two selections that illustrate this combined interest. They illustrate, too, the application to political questions of his theological method. Human freedom, understood as free will, as the capacity to direct one's own actions, is characteristic of the person as a creation in Christ. It is a function of the openness and self-transcendence that arise from our existential participation in the Son's self-offering to the Father, a gift made perfect by the human Son in his Passion and made present to each of us in the Eucharist, the sacrifice into which the more perfectly we enter, the more expansively we are free. In human society, the unique, in fact the foundational, exercise of this freedom comes in the unqualified commitment to the genuine difference of another in marriage.

The first selection is taken from a paper Keefe presented in 1996 to a meeting of The Institute for Theological Encounter with Science and Technology (ITEST), in St. Louis. He argued that underlying the regard for the judgment of the ordinary citizen that is at work in the Anglo-American common law tradition, with its attendant practice of trial by jury, were both the Jewish teaching on the inherent dignity—antecedent to civil law—that belongs to each person as made in the image of God and the distinctively Catholic understanding of sacramental marriage as a union that binds into an indeterminate future, a union, then, that is a singular expression of the deliberative and responsible freedom that constitutes the person's dignity. With Hannah Arendt in her landmark "Reflections on Little Rock", Keefe maintains that the one and only basis for a free society is elective marriage. Political order on any other basis will be a testament to force.

The second selection is from an article that was also first read as a paper, at a seminar on "Capitalism in Light of the Social Objectives of Western Religions", held in Buenos Aires, Argentina, in 1981. It reflects the tension of that time, fewer than ten years before the fall of the Berlin Wall and the dissolution of the Soviet Union. Catholic theology had been paying scant attention to the problems of a postwar world when the Second Vatican Council opened in 1962, and into the vacuum stepped Marxist social theory, despite its suffocating immanentism. Nineteen years later, Keefe was calling for the now belated construction of a properly Catholic political theology and theology of history. The demise of public structures of injustice, Keefe states, must wait upon the overthrow of private attitudes of injustice. And generation after generation, there is one, central cause of renewal. It is the Eucharist, and in particular the reception of Christ in the Eucharist, that makes possible the dogged effort of moral conversion—above all for the laity, upon whose shoulders the burden of this work must inevitably fall—and that fuels the unceasing drive to shape a human society.

A final note. In both selections, Keefe makes use of a term that came into theology from the social sciences, "praxis". Praxis was originally a classical Greek word that meant, among other things, "action". But when it was adopted by theologians in the 1960s, it carried the meaning it had acquired in the nineteenth century, i.e., the process of effecting social change. Keefe, however, uses praxis with a different sense. For Keefe, true praxis is the Eucharistic worship of the Lord of history. Liturgical participation in the Son's offering to the Father secures the sense of one's own worth and dignity and of personal accountability for the single, human community that is, in history, the gift that the Father is receiving from the Son.

Marriage and the Free Society

That all men possess personal dignity innately, that personal dignity is constitutive of humanity wherever and however found, that it is not a creature of the law but of God's grace—this free communal conviction is the foundation upon which all free societies are based: there is no other free order than the covenantal imaging of God, and the common law of what Mr. Churchill has called "the English-speaking peoples" is firmly grounded in the hard-won conviction that all human beings as human possess this intrinsic, immediate, and inviolable dignity. The concrete exercise of this dignity, its praxis, is the rule of law, upon which rests the common-law tradition. This rule of law is constitutive, the concrete foundation of the constitutional law which is itself no more than the juridical recognition of the more immediate implications of the inviolability of human dignity, whose free and responsible exercise is the rule of law, the free ground of the free society.

Thus the rule of law is the radical expression of the dignity, freedom, and personal responsibility out of which all law arises and which it is the duty of all law to foster and defend. This rule of law is not a theory, nor is it a merely political consensus: it is constitutive of the public good, of the common weal. Therefore it is "constitutional", to use the more usual term, as no mere theory, no merely practical agreement can be. A great debate has arisen over the past decade or two over what the rule of law might be in the concrete, if we admit as we must that our personal dignity and free responsibility [are] no abstraction, no timeless ideal, but an objective historical fact. This great debate finds us in somewhat the position of the centipede who is quite able to walk, but unable to explain how he manages it.

From Donald J. Keefe, S.J., "The Law and the Covenant: An Overview of Law and Freedom", *Patenting of Biological Entities*, Proceedings of the ITEST Workshop, October 1996, ed. Robert Brungs, S.J., and Marianne Postiglione, R.S.M. (St. Louis, Mo.: ITEST Faith/Science Press, 1997): 56–118.

Only recently has the direct question been asked; there is no agreement upon the answer, save perhaps that the rule of law is more than theory, more than politics, more than a memory of a departed past, and yet is in some manner a concrete public fact, embodied in a consensus, in a communal memory, understanding, and love, and capable of, even requiring, a rational exposition.

We cannot dismiss the question over the reality of the rule of law. The customary juridical and political decencies by which a free society remains free and politically responsible for its freedom must govern our use of the otherwise unqualified power which the technological society commands. As we have learned to agree that war is too important to be left to generals and that health is too important to be turned over to doctors, even that law is not merely what the judges say, so neither can we permit scientists to decide definitively upon the propriety of the uses of technological power, for in all such cases the alternative to the rule of law is more or less well-meant coercion and the sudden elimination of the free society of responsible human beings by their submission to a similarly well-meant herding together of people whose freedom is regarded by their benefactors as centripetal and destructive of community, and whose social union is taken to be merely the product of coercion. When transformed by such coercion into intrinsically indistinguishable social atoms, human beings can know no responsibility and, thus, no law. Obviously, in the free societies of the West, the rule of law bars this simplistic dominion by an elite. It is important that we understand how and why this is true, for this century has shown us to be alert to the elitism ever waiting in the wings.

Here may be posed the hypotheses which will be spelled out in more detail in the pages which follow:

Covenantal marriage is the elective nuptial union of a man and a woman who are equal in personal dignity before God. Their nuptially ordered, nuptially normed dignity, authority, and responsibility images the God of the Covenant. As the imaging of God, the exercise of nuptially ordered authority is substantial: the man, the woman, and their covenantal union in one flesh possess it equally, irreducibly, and irrevocably.

Covenantal marriage is causally prior to the legal and political institutions of the civilizations grounded in the Judaeo-Christian tradition.

Covenantal marriage is their foundation, by reason of its concretely effective conversion of the pagan, monistic notions of authority, responsibility, and freedom by the countervailing efficacious praxis of covenantal, nuptially ordered authority and responsibility.

In marriage so understood, as it is by most Jews and most Christians, the man and the woman in marriage form "one flesh", a most mysterious union in which the personal authority of each is equally exercised in the affirmation of the full dignity and authority of the other. Marriage so understood immediately undermines those elitist and authoritarian governmental systems which suppose that the *princeps*, the law-giver, represents his people by absorbing the fullness of their free and personal responsibility into his public persona, and this without remainder, so that any spontaneous exercise of personal responsibility by a "subject" is equivalently traitorous and rebellious, the deed of an outlaw. All legality based on that postulate of a monist and unconditioned public authority—an authority which is liturgically grounded in the pagan view of salvation as achieved only by liturgical flight from historical existence—is debarred by Judaeo-Christian marriage, for reasons which can only be pointed to here.

Summarily, marriage is patterned upon the revelation of the covenantal, non-adversarial relation of God to the world, and of the world to God, while paganism takes for granted an adversarial divinity, who is offended by any claim to dignity or authority by what is not divine. For Jews and Christians, the opposite is true: the worship which is the imaging of God is the exercise of personal responsibility for the people of God. It is the explicit undertaking of personal responsibility for the other, and in no public institution is this undertaking as explicit as it is in marriage, which thereby specifies what freedom, authority, responsibility, and dignity are and how they are to be achieved or appropriated: viz., in worship. Once again, summarily, this is covenantal worship, the liturgical appropriation of free moral responsibility in history, the keeping of the Commandments.

On this covenantal, nuptial postulate, and its accompanying praxis of free marital responsibility, all free society is based. The corollary is that no non-covenantal society is free, for the Covenant, as nuptially imaged, is the only free social unity or order in our fallen world: all other societal orders collapse into some modality of monist necessity and induce a social devolution which finally involves the destruction of humanity itself. For that devolution is a counter-praxis, the coerced, impersonally—or servilely—exercised alternative to the nuptial keeping of the nuptially ordered Covenant, the marital imaging of God in one flesh.

The alternative to this free union of free people is the unfree union of unfree people; once again, no one has ever proposed any other form-free social unity. In fact, if free marriage is not the normative, the prescriptive social institution, it is hard to explain why every rationalization of society from Plato to Mao has found free marriage indigestible, a surd in need of rectification. Among the "English-speaking peoples", this devolution from freedom to servility began with Henry VIII, and the common law has never been the same since then, for its nuptially ordered rule of law, once submitted to and no longer limiting a coercive central authority, could no longer be normative for civil responsibility: its exercise could now be accounted criminal.

Within the past fifty years, the Constitutional law of the United States and that of much of the Western world has ceased to develop its understanding of fundamental human rights and obligations in terms of a society whose basic social institution is marriage as traditionally understood in the Western world and as grounded in the Judaeo-Christian religious traditions. Particularly, the secularizing thrust of post-World War II jurisprudence has called for the restructuring of society upon the rationalization of notions of freedom, authority, and responsibility—notions whose original meaning in Constitutional law rested upon a historical development of a free religious consensus which understood man and man's institutions to be warranted only by their being "under God".

The result of the post-modern rationalization of this historical legal tradition has been the now commonplace supposition that society is composed of unqualified, atomic "persons" rather than of maritally founded families. Correlative to this reduction of the nuptially and covenantally ordered, irreducibly masculine or feminine persons, to an impersonal, intrinsically undifferentiated and alienated androgynous existence, the understanding of personal dignity and personal responsibility is correspondingly transformed: the now ideally unrelated, absolutely irresponsible person-as-atom is anti-social by definition. "Socialization" can then be achieved only by coercion, by restricting the ideally unrestricted and random "freedom", mechanically conceived, of the person-as-atom and forcing an impersonal association otherwise abhorred. This exercise of force majeure is the single and unique subject of rationalized law in the rationalized state, whose authority is power simply and whose exercise of it is marked by no ultimate responsibility to any higher or correlative authority, for the authority of the lawgiver is there understood to be unqualified and absolute, resting upon the possession of supreme power.

This view of the human condition as atomized is abstract or ideal; the vagaries of historical circumstance, which condition and limit all power and which therefore bar the historical realization of claims to absolute or monist authority and dominion, have always prevented the full implementation of coercive law and the full atomization of historical human dignity and society. Nonetheless, since Plato wrote *The Republic*, the "administered society" has been presented as the uniquely rational ideal and the utopian manipulation of a dehistoricized, noncovenantal humanity, as the purpose of law....

Freedom, as it has been understood in the English and the American legal traditions, ratifies, develops, and celebrates the constitutive, covenantal, and nuptial differences among human beings. This more-than-axiomatic dynamic of free mutual affirmation of the goodness of the personal, nuptial, masculine-feminine differentiation flourishes among a people whose freedom is precisely their nuptial, their covenantal ordering; it is explicit and effective in marriage insofar as this still possesses a privileged and in fact a constitutional standing in the laws of this nation and of other Western societies.

On the other hand, all these personal, nuptial, covenantal, and qualitative differences and distinctions among human beings (of which those between men and women are at once the most radical in human experience and the most refractory to rational analysis and reduction) are nonetheless held by recent jurisprudence to be reducible finally to merely quantitative differences in power and, therefore, to be open to rational analysis in terms of more or less, greater or smaller participation in unqualified power. Thus all personal differentiation is interpreted as resting upon power, and a personal claim to power cannot but be an insolence, a threat to a public order whose monist raison d'être restricts all power to the *princeps*, to the possessor of absolute and unqualified power, the authoritative source of law: summarily, utterly irresponsible and unconditioned coercion.

Consequently, such personal differentiations as claim legal standing, legal significance and authority, are thought by contemporary jurisprudence—as they were by utilitarian rationalists such as Mill—to require a rational justification, one reciting either an ideal, nonhistorical necessity of thought or a practical necessity of rationalized government. These deterministic criteria bar the grounding of law in free custom as irrational. Under their influence, law is understood to deal with persons—mere social entities—whose freedom is perceived as at best a mere randomness, whose product is suspect if not incriminated a priori. In this guise, law becomes a subdepartment of classical mechanics, as Hobbes saw in the middle of the seventeenth century, following upon the subordination by Henry VIII, in the previous century, of marriage and, with it, of the rule of the common law, to the now irresponsible, absolute coercive power of the *princeps*. The centuries following that usurpation saw rationalized law coupled with the Cartesian rationalization of rationality itself. Since then, the logic of the sovereign's *ultra vires* exercise of the "raw judicial power" which Henry found inherent in the sovereign state has steadily been imposing his monistic merger of governmental authority and coercive power upon the public law of England and the United States.

More and more, the heretofore freely responsible member of the free human community, the "person", the human being who is nuptially ordered as a matter of obvious and objective fact, is being juridically transformed, intelligible in law only as a social atom to whom no *inherent* dignity, authority, freedom, or responsibility may be attributed without immediate detriment to its rationalized intelligibility: i.e., to its atomic unicity, to its absolute conceptual isolation, to that complete lack of intrinsic relatedness to any other similarly atomized person, which now is named privacy. Personal freedom more and more becomes intelligible merely as the quantum of physical motion assigned by law to this human atom; increasingly, personal authority is becoming comprehensible in law only as mere power, and power itself is intelligible, discussible, only in terms of quantified movement in space and time. In brief, human existence is coming to be thought inherently meaningless until submitted to external criteria, inevitably provided by the ideology imposed upon it by an elite, whose authority so to act is its possession of force majeure.

Differences in freedom and authority thus viewed are comprehensible only as quantified, as reducible to more or less range of movement, submission to more or less inhibition upon individual randomness, to limitations upon the social atom's otherwise unconditioned power, upon the aboriginal condition in which every such atom is the antagonist of every other: *homo homini lupus*, in Hobbes' famous description of the "state of nature", supposedly antecedent to the social contract whereby men abdicate the feral freedom of the jungle in favor of the passive peace of the cage. Within this rationalistic and indeed mechanical frame of reference, it is immediately evident that the existence of customary, historically instituted, differences in the power of "naturally" or ideally undifferentiated atoms cannot be accounted for or made comprehensible under rationalist criteria, whether of ideal or practical necessity, and are therefore condemned as irrational and consequently as unjust by the utilitarianism of modernity. Their irrationality—which is to say, their irreducibility to necessity whether rational or practical—is held to be unjust and oppressive, an arbitrary and prejudicial exercise of power; marriage has long been so condemned. No vindication of responsible freedom can consist with this monadic rationale, wherein all is either rational and necessary or irrational and mere randomness. It is evident that every distribution of power falls under this condemnation. Only an undistributed, single, absolute power is rationally comprehensible and, therefore, just. Such an absolute power is of course irresponsible by definition, but as absolute is also beyond the reach of criticism....

The rationalization of humanity in the name of monadic logic cannot but look to the abolition of all variety in the human community as a strict requirement of justice. It then cannot countenance [or] be at peace with the ancient covenantal world view of law as the product, the expression, of a customary consensus freely arrived at—the customary law, the common law, with its connotation of the legal propriety of the free community as maritally ordered and constituted, a society whose inherent, concretely nuptial specification of personal, covenantal responsibility for the future is radically incapable of rational reduction to any comprehensive utopian ideology, as it is radically incapable of being reduced to the necessary reasons of the autonomous, monadic rationality of modernity-as-ideology.

Particularly, it is the institution of covenantal marriage that is ideologically indigestible, the bone in the throat of every immanentized soteriology, as every utopian from Plato to Engels has known.

We have said that J. S. Mill, upon whose 1859 essay *On Liberty* most of the contemporary discussion of freedom still pivots, insisted

upon just such an atomized humanity, very Hobbesian in its theoretical composition, entirely dismissive of intrinsic or innate personal
relations, and subject to the imposition *ab extra* of such relatedness
by force of law only where it can be shown empirically that such
legal inhibition upon the otherwise unconditioned, absolute, and
irresponsible freedom proper to the human atom is demanded in
order to avert real physical detriment to the equally atomic interests
of another, a detriment which is not to be inferred from the mere
fact of its being recognized as such by custom or convention, but
which must be demonstrated empirically. This utilitarian criteriology
is clearly antagonistic to the free, customary, covenantal, and consen-
sual moral decencies which have until lately informed American law.
The assumption of the validity of the utilitarian criteriology accounts,
e.g., for the contemporary quest for a clinical "proof" of the conventional consensus that pornography is a cause of crime, that the penal
vindication of the conventional decencies is a deterrent to crime, etc.,
as though what could not be shown to be empirically necessary could
not be affirmed to be true....

It cannot be too much stressed that for the utilitarians such as J. S.
Mill in the nineteenth century and B. F. Skinner in the twentieth,
it is not the covenantally ordered civil responsibility of the Judaeo-
Christian culture that is constitutive for the good society but rather,
as has been seen, the uncivil irresponsibility of man-as-atom, whose
autonomous existence is that of an absolute, possessing no inherent or
characteristic or owed relation to any other atom. This atomization
and consequent impersonalization of humanity is the *sine qua non*, the
radical a priori postulate, of the ideal utopia whose abstract perfection
is achieved precisely by the elimination from it of the concreteness of
personal historical freedom and of personal historical responsibility.

Obviously, this abstract, non-historical, ideal of freedom-as-
absolute contradicts the free historical fact of freedom-as-covenant.
Just as covenantal or nuptial freedom presupposes and requires the
personal, sexual, nuptial irreducibility and uniqueness of historical
men and women, as the condition of their factual, intrinsic, free, and
nuptial community, the monadic ideal of freedom as pure autonomy
must refuse both the intelligibility of sexual differentiation and the
personal uniqueness of individual men and women, for atoms are fun-
gible. Any one of them can take the place of any other; their lack of

personal uniqueness is the single and all-embracive utopian virtue. For the covenantal community, on the other hand, the historical paradigm of the free exercise of free responsibility is *elective* marital love; marital commitment, marital self-sacrifice *exist only as elective*, as an unqualified covenantal self-donation to an utterly unique person, a man or woman whose sexual differentiation from oneself bars all narcissism from marriage and, so, from the praxis that is marital fidelity. For the utilitarian community, however, the only possible meaning of love is the nonelective, nonreflective self-love of the atomic self, which is equivalently the hatred of all that is not the atomic self. Thus atomized and idealized, freedom as power and justice as equality simply exclude the elective dimension of marriage, even as pagan, and, of course, bar the covenantal marriage of the Judaeo-Christian tradition as a most radical injustice, as a surd to be expunged from the rational society. Marriage can be justified, as by Plato, only on extrinsic grounds of a nonhistorical criteriology which must deform it to accept it, for from that rationalist point of view, marriage as historically realized has and can have no intrinsic value superior to any other irrational and random distribution of the social atoms which as "persons" are a priori unrelated and whose relation must be justified on universal grounds, which simply bar the nuptial election that is covenantal marriage.

When judged by the autonomous uncovenanted rationality of utopian idealism as the mere product or resultant of randomly distributed extrinsic forces lacking all justification, covenantal marriage must be condemned as a finally manipulative master-slave relation of oppression, for the presence of monadic freedom and monadic authority in the one atom is always expressed in the repression of the power of choice, of election, in the other atoms. This notion of authority is common to every pagan culture and underlies the cosmological obediential morality characteristic of those cultures, whether their paganism be old or new....

The commonsense refusal of ideological reduction which characterizes the American legal tradition is rooted in the customary, or conventional, or liturgically mediated wisdom of the Western world. Since Constantine, this wisdom, obscurely nourished by the Roman Catholic liturgical praxis of marriage, has been transforming the totalitarian dream of empire embodied in the Roman law, even while that law was being accepted as the principle of the rational organization of society in the centuries following the Gregorian reform. Already from the close of the fifth century, the bipolarity of the symbolic authorities of Roman law on the one hand and of the Catholic historical worship on the other had forced the old pagan Roman notion of authority as monadic or cosmological to give way, slowly and reluctantly, before the recognition that in fact the world is ruled by a non-coercive ecclesial authority as well as by the quite distinct power of political sovereignty and that, in consequence, authority could not be the simple abstract monadic principle, the *logos* alike of cosmic structure and of social unity, that the ancient Stoic ethic of the Roman law had assumed. This recognition was worked out in the perennial conflict between Pope and Emperor, and was for long a practical rather than a theoretical understanding, as in the running dispute between Anselm and the English monarchy under William II and Henry I. The theoretical implications of the practical failure to recognize the covenantal character of ecclesial authority and responsibility are manifest in the political philosophies which are the heritage of the federal Constitution, all of which take for granted what had been rejected over the nearly thousand years between Ambrose and Marsilius of Padua, the monolithic character of all authority.

John Locke, for example, put the final authority in the State, much as Marsilius had done in the dispute between papal and civil government which marked the early fourteenth century. Such rational resolutions of the historical Church-State bipolarity are clearly monist, concluding to the same cosmological understanding of the unity of society as is embodied in Plato's *Republic* and in every rationalization of the human community since then. We have pointed already to the consistent demand of such rationalizations for the revision of marriage in the sense of abolishing its irrational (because anti-monist, free, and finally Trinitarian) implications; the denial of the legitimacy of that Trinitarian qualification of the unity of authority is the evident implication of any rationalization of the human community. The intimation that the unity of authority, and of human community, is in fact covenantal, that it is *intrinsically* qualified and relative as imaging the Triune God, is mediated in the Church's public worship. Only in the inherently free praxis of that worship does it become manifest that authority not only is not realized but also that it cannot be realized by the suppression of freedom in those under authority; in that worship, public authority is authentically exercised only in supporting the freedom of all others. In brief, the historical actuality of authority in human society is in the Church's worship discovered to be covenantal and, therefore, maritally ordered.

The concrete social and juridical impact of the liturgical practice of authority as covenantal is scarcely given lip service in contemporary legal and political theory, even by the advocates of the natural law. If the problems now confronting the legal and political unity of the Western civilization, and more particularly those confronting the implementation of the federal Constitution, are to be resolved in a fashion which preserves that unity in its freedom, the only device which is capable of sustaining at once the freedom and the integration of human society must be exploited: this device is the nuptially ordered Covenant, whose dynamically and historically effective sociopolitical historical expression or praxis or liturgical sign is the irrevocable marital commitment, the radical imaging of God which is the worship of the Lord of history, the Lord of the Covenant.

This free marital commitment is a most radical rejection of all the cosmologically grounded monisms whose monadic paradigm for rationality still locks most Western minds into the supposition that the truth of reality is its rationally necessary cosmic structure rather than its historical freedom and that, consequently, the rationality and stability of public life, whether of the macrocosmic society or the microcosmic individual, stands in a most fundamental opposition to the incalculable and therefore irrational future posed by the exercise of personal freedom and responsibility. As Psalm 95 reminds us, so also thought those timid followers of Moses who, frightened by the grim prospect of the desert into which he would lead them, feared that free and uncharted future and grew nostalgic for the cosmic security offered by their Egyptian captivity. To rely upon the promises of the Lord of the Covenant, the Lord of history, to commit oneself to the freedom and responsibility that He offers, and to the covenantal society He offers, is precisely to disencumber oneself of those cosmic safeguards which above all are alert to ban the human freedom [needed] to effect the new—for to the cosmological consciousness the novel is by definition dangerous; it must be annulled by the eternal return to the timeless, the ideal and nonhistorical symbols of a universe immune to novel change. Law, insofar as embodying and relying upon such pagan symbolism, cannot but exist to annul historical novelty by annulling the freedom which causes it. . . .

It is necessary to point out in season and out that the egalitarian, atomizing premise has no standing in the rule of law, that it is not the basis of our liberties, and that to postulate it as the common ground of public debate is to endorse beforehand and a priori, without reflection, an elitist program designed to impose cosmological servility upon a historically free people. The civil equality and justice of the free community is not ideal; it cannot be egalitarian in the monist sense of condemning as unjust, because irrational, the free marital commitment underlying all free social unity. Rather, the equal dignity of free men and women has a covenantal, finally nuptial expression; in marriage their sexually diverse personal responsibility is concretely uttered in marital love, in the free and irrevocable election that is marriage. In sum, historical humanity is comprised of persons who are diverse as masculine and feminine, which is to say, as freely nuptial. Any jurisprudence, any politics, which rests upon some other notion of human dignity, freedom, authority, and responsibility than that which is covenantally ordered cannot support responsible personal freedom.

However, it is not enough simply to refuse the servility of the utopian society constructed by an anti-historical or cosmological rationality. Correlative with that refusal must be the confident praxis of covenantal marriage as publicly vindicated, as concretely, convincingly actualized and effectively realized in the free consensus of the maritally ordered polity that is the heritage of the Judaeo-Christian civilization. For only in a resolutely marital society is the freedom inherent in the Western legal tradition actually and routinely vindicated in terms of law and government. It is only when the radical ground of human existence is factually lived in freedom that it is inviolable, transcendent to all force majeure, in a free consensus that is historically and actually prior to all government [and] that the coercive power of the central government is limited in its jurisdiction, denied absolute standing, as the very condition of its institution by a nuptially ordered free people.

We may be very sure that when covenantal marriage is no longer the freely normative political praxis within a given society, the rationalization of that society, its reduction to logically indistinguishable atoms possessing only an extrinsic and coerced order, will be already in place: nature abhors a vacuum.

An essential dimension of the convincing demonstration of the centrality of marriage which is now necessary therefore consists in communicating the concrete historical significance of the nuptial or marital symbol. This communication cannot be theoretical, but must be the concrete and political: it can only be the free and public praxis that is marriage itself. The nuclear density of this symbolism, of the fundamental free nuptial unity which is the sacramental marital commitment, at once affirms concretely into history, and publicly demands and causes, an open future and an open society. The marital symbol is a dynamic, a historically concrete refusal of all limitation upon the free association of men and women within all the dimensions of their society and upon their free access to all those dimensions: cultural, economic, political, and above all, religious. Further, the marital symbol is liturgical, in that it affirms, causes, and in practice presupposes the equal dignity of all human beings, by reason of their objectively nuptial reality—which does not at all depend upon its recognition or its vindication, for it is given in [the] creation of humanity in and to the image of God. This free nuptial order is a reality transcending all possible calculation, all human devices. Its truth and reality lie beyond all the rationalist and utilitarian criteria which might presume to measure it. Where any of the nuptially ordered elements of human freedom are denied or submitted to supposedly higher values, so also is the freedom to marry and be married; with the submission of the covenantal symbol upon which our freedom rests to the servitude of self-enclosed and self-imprisoned microcosmic man and the consequent suppression of its dynamic historical utterance, the cosmological servile state emerges.

"Privileged" is therefore an inaccurate description of the relation of marriage to the free civil society, for "privilege" connotes the prior existence of a source of law transcending marriage, transcending the freedom of its praxis, and thus transcending the freedom to marry. Rather, marriage is the concrete ground of that free civil society and cannot be put in question by it without rejecting the constitutive, the constitutional base of all free society. However, that constitutional foundation of political freedom is now being put in question. The rationalist reductionism of man to political atom and its rejection of the constitutive covenantal notion of society [underlie] that *dubium* and [provide] the content of its rationale. . . .

The subject of the law of a free people is a free community, whose freedom is not an idea but a free praxis and so an event, the event which is self-commitment to the unconditioned dignity and worth of another human being who is personally and covenantally—which is to say, nuptially—irreducible to oneself. Only in this event does freedom, whether as masculine or as feminine, reach its adequate historical expression: the unconditional self-bestowal upon an irreducible and complementary other and a simultaneous joyful affirmation of the self-bestowal [in return] of that other as the supreme gift, the completion of one's own full dignity as man, as woman. There, in that self-sacrifice and celebration, all freedom finds its adequate expression, all free society its covenantal ground, and the equality of all people in personal dignity, freedom, and responsibility, which undergirds any free legal system, is concrete in the nuptial ordering of humanity.

Political Freedom and Liturgical Life

When, at the time of the [Second Vatican] Council, Roman Catholic theologians were suddenly awakened to the reality of institutionalized oppression in the Western world, there existed no well-integrated critical Catholic theology of society and social institutions. Such energy as had been expended in this realm had been exhausted in studies of the natural law (Mounier, Maritain), in studies of the interrelation of church and state (Murray, Sturzo), in the examination of the morality of war (Murray, Ford) and the interrelation of morality and law (St. John-Stevas) and the like, problems of a peculiarly abstract academic interest, the practical solutions to which had habitually been arrived at without much benefit from moral theology. The few Catholic scholars writing in specifically social areas (John A. Ryan, O'Dea, Furfey) wrote less as critical theologians than as sociologists and political scientists; the impact of their work upon Catholic thought never was sufficient to prompt the articulation of a theology of politics. In the absence of an identifiably Catholic political theology, the postconciliar theologians found themselves unable to resist the claims of the new theology of secularity. This had a base in the work of the martyred Lutheran theologian Dietrich Bonhoeffer, whose critique of immature Christian pieties had been underwritten by his own heroic death. The Second Vatican Council, having demanded of Catholics a new openness to the world and having affirmed the legitimacy of a kind of secular autonomy, seemed also to suggest the ultimately Christian character of many secular goals and programs. The prospect of a Christian maturity freed of ecclesial oversight suggested also the illegitimacy of much of what had passed for Catholic practice heretofore: this practice was tinged, suddenly, with the character of a childish obedience. The identification of "religion" and paternalism, already proposed by Bonhoeffer, found a ready acceptance in

From Donald J. Keefe, S.J., "Liberation and the Catholic Church: The Illusion and the Reality", *Center Journal* (Winter 1981): 45–64.

Catholic circles whose intellectual energies had in fact long been suppressed in the name of Catholic orthodoxy.

This was also the decade of the radical theologians: Harvey Cox's secular enthusiasm seemed to many Catholics no more than a prolongation of that optimism which the Council, following Pope John XXIII, had popularized as *aggiornamento* [modernization]. Driven by this optimism, the radical theologians developed a theology of secular hope profoundly influenced by neo-Marxist thinkers such as Bloch and Garaudy. This new theology rested upon a Marxist social critique whose political implications soon became explicit. This development, which passed from a theology of secularity to a theology of hope to a political theology of liberation, took place under auspices owing little or nothing to the Catholic doctrinal and moral tradition. If some of the leading voices in the new theology were Catholic, such as Metz and Dewart, they were so in the new mode: their inspiration was secular and ecumenical, and their attitude toward the Catholic tradition was negative. It had become the hallmark of the contemporary Catholic theologian that he avoid at all cost the despised role of "court theologian", and any manifest concern for official Church teaching was suspect of a servile betrayal of *aggiornamento*. In such circumstances, liberation began to be understood in a context in which Catholic orthodoxy was charged with an ecumenical obligation which amounted to accepting the Marxist social critique—and all the implications of that critique, fundamental to which is a rejection of the free market and of the private ownership and control of capital investment. Equally fundamental is the criticism of religion. In this dialogue, it now became the obligation of the Catholic partner that he acquit himself and his Church of the charge of providing an ideological defense of those "structures of injustice" which are the object of the Marxist social critique. Thus, at the outset, it is Christianity which is suspect, and it is suspect precisely because of a concrete historical institutional presence which impedes and is an obstacle to the liberation of the oppressed from the original sin of private property. Thus, for the Catholic Marxist, any aspect of Catholic life which can be interpreted as an obedience must be expunged. The entirety of the doctrinal and moral tradition is to be reviewed in the light thus cast upon it by the new ecumenism, and, to the extent that it cannot be integrated into the Marxist future hope, it must be discarded. This ordinarily amounts to its restatement in some theological format which deprives the Catholic tradition of its own historical concreteness, for it is the Church's historicity that is the problem, precisely because it competes with that philosophy of history which is integral with Marxism.

Had the liberation theologians' criticism of the Church focused upon factual abuses—for example, upon the centuries-long complicity of the Catholic hierarchy with European colonial governing classes and their successors, or upon the long and shameful record of clerical indifference to the suffering of the poor—no objection could be made to such passionate and angry protest. The easy complaisance with which the conventional middle-class Christian has accepted and accepts the conventional indignities done to the poor and to the helpless is a loathsome thing, excoriated in the Old Testament and personally condemned by Christ in the New Testament; the implication that Christianity lends support to this oppression can only nauseate, and the more so the more one is aware of the massed misery which avowedly Christian and Catholic countries can countenance, have countenanced, and still countenance. In saying so, I do not speak *de haut en bas*; it is my own country's slaughter of the poorest of its poor, the weakest of its weak, a slaughter institutionalized by our abortion laws, that I have here primarily in mind.

Unfortunately the liberation theologians were not intent upon the bishops' return to the manifest duties and responsibilities of their office; this was the last thing desired, for that office with its teaching and governing functions had been sacrificed to ecumenism and could hardly now be called to account. Instead, the remedy proposed amounted to the rediscovery of an ancient doctrinal aberration, one which over and over again has proven itself to be no more than the reinvocation of an antihistorical despair, a despair of the goodness of the world God made good and a flight from the terrors of a history whose only hope is that it will end.

This new consciousness, identified by the Christian Marxist as that of the oppressed, experiences history as class conflict, yearns for the end of that struggle, and so longs for the end of history as such. The experience of class struggle is the experience of the proletariat, at least ideally, and, insofar as the liberation theology of the Marxist is concerned, it constitutes the normative truth or, better, the normative criterion of all reality. This criterion is not an abstract truth, but an activity, the praxis which liberation jargon refers to as hermeneutically privileged and proposes as the single touchstone by which any expression of Christianity is to be judged. Quite clearly, this judgment amounts to a reduction of Christianity to the contours of that Marxist philosophy which [seeks, not] to understand the world, but to change it: only that Christianity is valid which is participation in the class struggle. Liberation theology lives upon the identification of valid historical existence with praxis and upon the further identification of praxis with involvement in class struggle, i.e., against the alienation of the oppressed. To share in the struggle of the proletariat against the oppressor class is to be involved in that praxis which is for the Marxist the reality of historical truth; it is to live toward that goal of liberation from oppression and so from class warfare which is the goal and the end of historical existence. This goal includes the end of all alienation of humanity from its proper reality; it marks the disappearance of all inequity, of all injustice, of all differentiation in human existence. Until that goal is reached, the Christian Marxist must recognize that both God and man are submitted to the alienation and anguish in which the substance of history consists. Short of that goal, it is maintained, no Christian may regard any Church institution, any office or doctrine or moral law as possessing any validity of its own. Such a claim would immediately resist the class struggle and would amount to oppression, to an ideological resistance to history. To live in history, for the Christian Marxist, is to live toward the ultimate union of God and man; short of that eschaton, the parousia, no historical reality is able to mediate God to man—for history is precisely that which separates God from man. This realization, of course, amounts to the abdication of the sacramental principle: history, for the Marxist, is the realm of total insignificance. Consequently, the sacramental worship of the Church is radically incompatible with any kind of Christianity which wishes to be Marxist. For such, there is no actual sacramental presence of salvation in history: history is intrinsically vitiated, opaque to the truth and to the justice of God. The only Christian virtue, supplanting faith, hope, and charity, is that praxis which seeks the destruction of all historical structures which claim any intrinsic validity. The Gospels have no other meaning than this, and their truth is available on no other basis. Only this praxis is truly Christian, because only it is truly liberating. Thus the Christian Marxist.

The imposition of the prior truth of any non-Christian historical consciousness upon Christianity is always the perversion of the faith. This, in fact, is the one heresy—the refusal of conversion to the Christian historical consciousness. The conversion which Catholic Christianity requires is precisely that which worships God as the Lord of history. The entirety of Christian doctrine and practice is no more than the expression of this new historical consciousness, a consciousness which has demanded of every generation of Christians from the first century onward a rejection of all the varied intimations of historical futility which have been and remain the alternative to the worship of the Lord of history. Every attempt to reduce the terror of a history experienced as ambivalent and absurd, every salvation scheme responsive to that pagan experience of history, must be foresworn. The Christian experiences, not the terror, but the order of history under the dominion of the Triune God, and the salvation which is promised him, which he seeks and makes his own in the sacramental worship of the Church, is [a redemption, not] from history, but from sin. History is God's creation in Christ; it is very good, and not all the vice by which humanity has deformed it has been able to obliterate its splendor, its mediation of God. Between God and his creation there is no alienation. History has no autonomous dynamic, no intrinsic struggle between good and evil upon which even God would be impaled. God transcends history as its creator, its redeemer, its saving Lord. To speak of his alienation from history is to introduce a primordial dualism which is the very stuff and substance of a despairing paganism....

Yet the cause of the poor remains as it has been, the cause of the Church. This is not politics, but Catholicism. A Catholic theology of politics, which recognizes the reality of economic oppression and responds to it, not with an even more complete disenfranchisement of the poor, but by advancing the cause of a real social and economic liberation, is not a mere academic option, one among many; it is a real necessity for the contemporary Church. The pity is that so many well-meaning efforts to formulate such a theology rely now as in the past upon some secular device whose relation to the Christian reality is at best haphazard, and more often is antagonistic. Such was the fault of the Aristotelian sociology of the "perfect society" so much relied upon by scholastic thinkers: such was the panoply of juridical constructs so unthinkingly assumed to be Christian because Roman and thus written into much of what passed for "natural law". Such also is the social theory out of which much of the talk of freedom and justice today is drawn. Any attempt, now as heretofore, to apply such concepts theologically is doomed, for they lack all theological foundation and, therefore, theological legitimacy. A Christian and Catholic political theology can have no other foundation than the social reality, the praxis, which is the worship of the Lord of history. Only this is responsive to the reality of our human existence—for our existence is in Christ, as Paul insists. We must take this fact with an absolute and literal seriousness. The only meaning which freedom and justice and dignity have is that which they have in Christ, and this they have, not in clear and distinct ideas, but in sign and in sacrament. The fullness, the *pleroma*, as St. Paul calls it, of our humanity waits upon the parousia, the second coming of Christ. Short of that completion and creation of ourselves and our world in integrity, the justice and the peace and the freedom of the children of God are present in this world only sacramentally, in the worship of the Church. But that *pleroma*, that fulfillment for which we long, is actual and real, with the reality of the risen Christ, the reality of the Eucharist, by which our historical existence in Christ is sustained in Christ. This is a sustenance in truth, in freedom, in dignity, in justice; it is the single source of our legitimacy; it is the gift of a future which fulfills and does not nullify the present and the past.

This gift has caused and causes the radical human community which is the Church. It makes to be present in the world the freedom without which the Church cannot worship, cannot exist. Out of that worship, in which the gift is appropriated by the people of God, a new understanding of the dignity and meaning of our humanity has entered the world, against an enormous resistance—the resistance which is our fallenness, our fear and dread of our own reality, our own history, our own freedom and responsibility. Over the nineteen hundred and fifty years of this Eucharistic worship, the pagan despair of human worth has been pushed back, not by theory, not by law, not by charismatic leadership, but by the continual and cumulative appropriation by the people in the pews of the reality which is given them in this worship. It is this dawning consciousness of the reality of dignity and freedom which has been and continues to be the one principle of novelty and ferment in the world: it is this which Church doctrine and law and mission articulate and defend and propagate, but do not create. This slow, often hesitant, often betrayed but finally irreversible and indefeasible history of our common salvation is at the same time the entry of every human being informed by that worship into that realm of responsibility for a uniquely personal concreation of the promised Kingdom of Christ; it is an acceptance of personal responsibility for the future which bars as sinful, as a rejection of the good creation, every resubmergence of that individual into the anonymity of a faceless mass and a featureless, meaningless present. The Church's worship demands and forces a community of freedom, each of whose members has an incalculable and irreplaceable dignity, value, and destiny.

This Catholic worship, which begins with baptism and which is sustained by the Eucharistic sacrifice, is that by which our fallen time is nonetheless good, and therefore is history, significant and meaning-bearing time, whose meaning is the New Creation, whose first-fruit is the Resurrection of our Lord. This history is complex in structure: it is the history of the people of God and includes the history of the Church and the history of the world. For those Catholics whose lives are structured by the sacrament of orders and the vows of religion and whose office is one of a primary responsibility for the formal or liturgical worship of the Church, historical freedom and responsibility [are] ecclesial primarily, and only secondarily [have they] any public dimension.

For the vast majority of the laity, whose office is to bring Christ to the world, sacramental existence is primarily marital, and lay responsibility of Catholics is measured and filled by what the sacrament of marriage is. In this sacrament, the formal structure of public life in all its dimensions is given, for the reality of communal life is grounded precisely here, in this marital worship. The implications of this sacrament for public life, and so for the political, economic, legal, and cultural structures of society, are of fundamental importance; to neglect or ignore them is to set up an antagonism between the dynamics of Catholic worship and those of public life, with isolation of each from each the only alternative to open conflict. Such isolation breeds the totalitarian state, for it requires that a substitute intellectual base be found upon which to ground the public life, and that base is always a rationale, an ideological deformation of the mystery of the human and the free. One does not avoid this by some doctrinaire imposition of Catholicism upon the world; one avoids it only by refusing the isolation of the faith, by taking the truth of Christ, the worship of the Church, into all the dimensions of public life. It is the failure to do this, on the right as well as on the left, that has established real injustice and oppression in the Christian world, and the only liberation from such social structures that is real is that which is dynamically present in the worship of the Church. The reality of liberation is the reality of the New Creation. There is no other, and all its counterfeits are finally idolatrous.

Marriage, taken seriously, forces into historical reality the universality of political freedom and of private property; it does so because the marital commitment to another qualitatively different human being defeats all rational analysis. It produces a host of mediating social structures which effectively impede any arbitrary use of governmental power and which stand as absolute obstacles to the bureaucratic rationalization of society, which is today, in the technologically advanced countries, on either side of the Iron Curtain, the single important threat to personal freedom in public life. The permanent and exclusive and total commitment of a man and a woman to each other and to their children is utterly repugnant, absolutely resistant to the despotisms old and new which seek their goal by means of the reduction of human beings to faceless rationalized integers, to units whose only dignity is that of the function they perform. Upon this all the utopian dreams agree, from Plato's *Republic* to Marcuse and Skinner in the visions of our own day; from the Spartan oppressors of the Helots to the slave-holders and feudal landlords of the new world. Aldous Huxley's satirical *Brave New World* and George Orwell's prophetic *1984* alike recognize the incongruity of such a marriage commitment with the schemes of those who would save a free humanity from the risks of freedom. Orwell's "Big Brother" provides the paradigm of the modern social engineer, the exponent of the secularized society whose radical requirement is that marital fidelity shall be betrayed, that the nuclear family shall give way to a secular social arrangement. The secular stress upon the legitimacy of abortion, upon the sundering of the marital bond on grounds of privacy, the intrusion of the abortionist in the parental function, the secularization of sex education, even the widespread demand for "day-care centers"—all these speak of the social planner's need to displace sacramental marriage with a casual functional relation to which even the sexual differentiation between men and women is being found obnoxious, finally unjust. The secular reduction of men and women to personal insignificance, their seduction by the prophets of liberation from their most fundamental historical responsibility, from the possibility of the radical personal commitment which is marriage, has gone very far. It is not too much to say that it has invaded the very marriage tribunals of the Catholic Church, where the dehistoricization of such commitment, its reduction to a mere ideal not realizable in the concrete, is now widely accepted.

One should not think, however, that it is only the avowed secularist who poses a threat to sacramental marriage. An equivalent threat is posed by every refusal to pay the wages which permit a man to fulfill such a commitment, which enable him to enter into that future of fidelity to which he is pledged, which do not foreclose his social freedom by forcing upon him a sub-Christian life of unremitting toil. If it is true that a free society cannot submit to the bureaucratic programming of its destiny, if it is true that Christian and Catholic worship must finally reject the historical pessimism which now finds expression in the advocates of a Zero-Sum Society as the basis for such economic planning, it is also true that with less fanfare many a capitalist entrepreneur is quite as fearful of a free society, of a free polity, of a free economy, and of the rule of law as his bitterest bureaucratic opponent. He, too, seeks insurance against a future which he cannot control and finds himself in consequence engaged in the same reduction of society to a faceless mass of economic entities whose personal insignificance is the price of his own security. We must all remember that the obstacle to liberation is finally human sinfulness, not some group of enemies. It is not a demonology that we need, but the recognition of our own sinfulness. It is not accidental that the sacrament of penance is integral to Catholic worship; if we do not worship as sinners, we cannot worship at all. Moreover, if we do not take that worship into our public life, it is not Catholic worship, it is not sacramental, and we ourselves are removed by that infidelity from the history which is our salvation.

Twenty-five years ago the great Swiss theologian Hans Urs von Balthasar remarked that, while it was quite possible for a medieval man to pray fervently and in good conscience while a few yards beneath the chapel his captive enemy rotted away his life in an oubliette, such innocent savagery is no longer a Catholic and Christian possibility. The love of Christ, manifest in the Church's worship, has urged us past the point where we could contemplate without guilt the denial of dignity to those for whom Christ died. Any economic and political freedom we exercise must be not that of a lonely entrepreneur or a feudal landholder isolated from humanity by his wealth, but of men and women charged before God with promoting the dignity and beauty of the world he made good. This dignity and beauty finds its ultimate symbol in the One Flesh of the Eucharist, the marital sacrifice in which Christ gives himself totally to and for his bridal Church. This marital reality is the utterly fundamental ground of all we are, of the New Creation itself. Upon it rests all history, all freedom, all justice. We make these actual in our lives only through the worship of the Lord of history, wherein we receive our own history as gift. But we receive it as a people, and we cannot receive it otherwise. When any of us are prevented from a full entry into this worship, the rest of us cannot be at peace until the impediment is removed. We are summoned always to our own liberation, away from those idolatries of power, of money, of lust which are the permanent temptations of our fallenness. By the same summons, we are called to the sanctification, the healing of the world. This is the summons to worship God, and there is no dimension of our lives which that worship must not pervade. It leaves us free: there is no formula for action by which we may be delivered from the daily responsibility of love. However much we do, we remain unworthy servants; there is always before us another summons, a still greater love. Until Christ shall come again, there shall be before us the face of the poor, of the sick, the imprisoned, the oppressed—the face of Christ, the face of our brothers. If we turn away, wearied, disgusted, angered, let us remember from whom we have turned; let us confess our sin in having done so, and let us take up again that burden which is our petty share in the redemption of the world, the one dignity we possess, the only liberation that is real.

8

THE CHURCH IN HISTORY

Keefe often observed that the very moment in the twentieth century when theologians first began to appreciate the historicity of the Church, her place in the flow of human events, they were increasingly falling victim to the distortions of historicism, the claim that to belong to history is to be trapped by history, each period essentially closed off to every other, as if there really were no history at all but only the succession of discrete units of time. One may speak of the first-century Church, then, or the tenth-century Church or the seventeenth-century Church and describe the ritual and observance, ministries and offices, just as the music and architecture, dress and style as so many cultural products, reflective of the very same currents that shaped every other social and cultural product of those eras. There is nothing of the Church that is not time-conditioned, nothing that transcends, because there is nothing of the Church that is transcendent.

The same extrinsicism underlying this view of time, when applied to the question of authority in the Church, has the effect, as also in the state, of reducing authority to power. In the following selection, Keefe makes his point by noting that the language of *ius divinum* and *ius humanum*, first borrowed from Roman law, was still being used after Vatican II in debates over the nature of the Church. *Ius*, meaning "right" or "law", carries the connotation of something that binds by virtue of assertion. So understood, whether one argued that structures of authority in the Church were simply matters of the tendency inherent in any human organization toward centralization (*ius humanum*), or, having conceded that although that might be true in the case of, for example, an institution like the College of Cardinals, nevertheless it was Christ himself who, at least by implication, established the episcopacy when he first sent forth the apostles (*ius divinum*), the basis for the bestowal of authority is pure decree. Absent is any sense of an intrinsic connection between what Christ had done and what he was commanding his apostles to do, or their successors, or any member of his Church. It is a view bereft of the teaching that the Son had been sent, had united to himself human life, in order that he might bring life abundant (Jn 10:10), that by their love they who believe might abide in the Father by abiding in the Son, who remains in the Father (Jn 14:10–11, 20).

This was abiding not simply on the level of intentionality, but a literal sharing in the life of the Son and, therefore, of the Father. Even if the gesture that would effect a participation in the action of Christ was no more than a borrowing by Christians of a Jewish practice, the laying on of hands, still it was understood that in this convention of their own choosing it was Christ himself who drew the believer into his role as the Son transmitting life, in the Spirit (Rom 15:15–19; Acts 6:6; 13:2–4; 1 Tim 4:14; Jn 20:21–23). For it is the living who transmit life, and only Christ could join to his life one who would be enabled to make Christ's life present to others. This life, from beginning to end, was a sacrificial life in which everything that was given to the Father meant a loss to himself, thereby inverting the movement of sin; an inversion that, adopted by the penitent, makes possible the only adequate demonstration of remorse a sinner's dignity demands. The Eucharist, then, is Christ's sacrificial life made present in an offering that he himself instituted, carried out by one whose authority derives from Christ's, joined in by those whose authority to provide the elements and lives that are to be transformed comes of their entry into the life of Christ in baptism.

The Catholic doctrine that in each and every celebration of a sacrament the grace of Christ's life is infallibly at work, *ex opere operato*, in virtue of the celebrant's action, performed according to the intention of Christ's Church, was denounced by Luther in his *Explanations of the Ninety-Five Theses* (1518) as an illustration of the pride-driven perversity that lay at the heart of the Church's institutional corruption. Broken by sin, the human person can have no share in the work of salvation, however that is understood. What followed as a matter of course was his conclusion that roles in the Church, like their counterparts in the state, are simply generated and assigned by the community for the sake of good order, the position he took two years later in *An Appeal to the German Nobility* of 1520.

Yet the draining of sacramental meaning from Church authority long preceded Martin Luther. In the first of the two selections that follow, Keefe draws upon the research of Henri de Lubac to trace the cause, and note the consequences, of the detachment of authority in the Church from its Eucharistic ground. More recently, the sacraments and the authority they confer have been taken as the proper subject of the social sciences and so subsumed under such categories as "functionality" and "functionalism". The result, Keefe argues in the second selection, taken from a draft of an article that appeared in the journal *Faith*, has been to expand on the pessimism of Luther and to strip the believer of any capacity to speak a word that binds, to commit himself unreservedly, or of himself absolutely to be changed, for the believer, too, is a creature of history, and there is nothing in history that endures.

Sacramental Realism and Office in the Church

During the fifteen years since the close of the Second Vatican Council, novel emphases initiated or accelerated by the Conciliar program of collegiality, ecumenism, and lay responsibility have placed such strains upon the conventional understanding of Church authority as to transform the task of justifying that authority into a practical summary of all the theological difficulties with which the contemporary Church is faced. For better or worse, it is here that the burden of explanation has accumulated. The authority structure of Roman Catholicism now seems to many not only inadequate to the stresses imposed upon it. It has become for them an obstacle to faith, rather than its support. The public expressions of sympathy for the democratization of Church governance, for the elimination of doctrinal impediments to Church union, and for the removal of all differentiation of liturgical office within the people of God are joined to an impatience with the authority which stands in the way of these goals, and whose reasons for so doing are less and less attended, less and less understood.

The upshot has been that the extrinsicist conception of Church authority has had a notable revival, and this in surprising places. Liberal and conservative alike seem to agree upon the essentially arbitrary character of any exercise of Church authority. If schooled in the philosophy of history, the contemporary theologian or canonist is unlikely to dwell long upon the possibility or likelihood of any intrinsic necessity for such exercise. It will be preferable to speak rather of *jus* [right], whether human or divine, but in either case in dissociation from any immanent reality in the Church and therefore in the last analysis a matter of command, arbitrary and susceptible of demythologization.

The language of *jus divinum, jus humanum* is part of the vocabulary of Vatican II, as well as of a good deal of current theological writing;

From Donald J. Keefe, S.J., "Authority in the Church: An Essay in the Theology of History", *Communio* 7 (Winter 1980): 343–63.

it is often used in the context of a question concerning the origin of the Church, a question which looked to that origin as a fundamentally juridical act. Few theologians today would maintain that the Church originated in an express juridical act of the Christ, whether or not they consider it to have been established by him rather than by his followers. The naiveté of a literal juridicism could not survive the results of biblical and historical criticism, but to say this is by no means to abandon the point which that naiveté intended to defend: the founding of the Church by Christ and by him alone. Nonetheless, the *jus divinum*, *jus humanum* language tends to the logical isolation of the divine and the human, an isolation worked by the employ of the categories of a non-mysterious and logically manageable discipline, the law, which, until converted to theological purposes, can have no interest in or reference to the sacramental reality which is Christ in his Church. It is all too easy to demythologize a claim to *jus divinum*, for the very concept of a divine activity in history is alien to the contemporary historical method. *Jus divinum*, under this challenge, falters, evanesces, to become mere *jus humanum*. The process is facilitated by the success of the lower versions of Christology which, under a similar impetus, have become mere anthropologies. One is then left, for practical purposes, with a merely human institution, like any other. If more is claimed for it, the claim must be proven to the modern historical consciousness. This demand for proof before the bar of reason is simply a renewal of the Enlightenment challenge to the historical Church, to which the Church unfortunately responded by taking up the impossible task of "proving" herself worthy of the mediation of Christ to humanity. This "old apologetic" having some time since been abandoned, and for the soundest of theological reasons, there can be little point in taking seriously a challenge which would require that it once more be assumed. The viewpoint from which such demands are made has nothing to say to the Church. The language of *jus divinum, jus humanum* is no necessary part of the claim of the Church to [be] a divine institution, and in fact impedes that claim all too often, for it can too easily invoke the late medieval nominalism from which the Enlightenment sprang, the mentality which thought all created reality, the Church included, to be without any intrinsic meaning or value, to be intrinsically dissociated and atomized, and so to draw its significance solely from the extrinsic relation imposed upon its disintegrated parts by the inscrutable will of God: a *potentia ordinata* [determinate, orderly power] no doubt, but of an order radically extrinsic to the world and to the Church, and so depriving them of any immanent necessity or truth, as also of all historical significance or efficacy.

This mistake is far older than Ockham and his heirs. De Lubac has traced it to the dissociation of Church and Eucharist worked by the medieval reaction to Berengarius's "symbolist" interpretation of the Eucharistic presence of the sacrificed and risen body of Christ. This orthodox and defensive reaction so stressed the realism of the Eucharistic body as to neglect or ignore that of the Ecclesial body of Christ, thereby severing a dialectic which had been for a thousand years the bipolar and unitary subject of the Church's worship and meditation: the Augustinian *Christus integer*, the Pauline "one flesh" of the Eucharistic sacrifice.

The theological consequence of this reaction was that the Church and the Eucharist began to be understood as separate realities, no longer mutually implicatory, mutually causative. While St. Thomas continued to see in the Church the *res sacramenti*, his explanation of transubstantiation ignores the Ecclesial body of Christ: it is the physical, risen body which is *res et sacramentum*, with the consequence that the ecclesial body of Christ, the Church, is not seen as *sacramentum*, but only as a final effect of the sacramental efficacy of the Eucharistic body, hence, as *res tantum sacramenti*, without any sacramental significance of its own. This effectively isolates two elements of a single reality, and the subsequent Thomist theology of Eucharistic transubstantiation often preferred to drop any consideration of the Church, even as *res tantum*. The theology of the Church which conformed to this isolationism began to speak of the Church in language borrowed from Aristotle's *Politics*, which was as little capable as the language of Roman law to speak theologically. The Church thus became a "perfect society" whose perfection was the possession of an authority adequate to its needs. A familiarity with the works of Jerome and Ambrosiaster had accustomed the middle ages to think of the episcopacy in terms of "power": power over the Church, it is true, but nonetheless power rather than grace, and the Gelasian[1] parallel between *sacerdotium* and *imperium*, although valid and

---

[1] Refers to the distinction made by Pope Gelasius (d. 496) between priestly authority and imperial power, in his letter *Famuli vestrae pietatis* to Emperor Anastasius I.

valuable enough in distinguishing secular and Church authority, could not but, if taken literally, contribute to the impression that what distinguished hierarchy from laity was much what distinguished nobility from commoners—power, rank, dominion. Gregory VII, returning to this Gelasian analysis after the Carolingian and Ottonian ventures in Caesaropapism, and rescuing the authority of the Church from the Empire into the hands of whose minions it had largely lapsed, again emphasized the distinction between temporal and spiritual authority, but without providing the high middle ages with any deeper insight into the Church's authority than had Jerome and Gelasius. The power of the keys, received from the apostles, was fundamentally the power to rule, from which depended the sacramental and teaching office of the *sacerdotium*. This statement of causal priorities leaves the Church's power to rule without any intrinsic support, without any explanation. It becomes understood as arbitrary, rooted finally in the will of the risen Christ, without doubt, but without inner intelligibility. From this, it is an easy step to that spirituality from whose viewpoint all religious response is obediential, finally passive, and all hierarchical authority finally despotic, whether its expression be provisional (*jus humanum*) or definitive (*jus divinum*).

The neglect of the Eucharistic foundation of Church authority in the medieval period, which de Lubac accounted for in terms of a kind of inadvertence, finds little remedy in contemporary theology. It is further unfortunate that the bishops themselves have become so accustomed to the juridical account of their office, for it has turned in their hands. Quite as centuries of juridical, natural law moralizing have at last undone moral theology by the continued insistence that it be not theology but philosophy and law—an insistence which had isolated morality from its intrinsic intelligibility as sacramental-historical existence *in Christo*—so the traditional canonical-juridical approach to the theological reality of Church authority has finally also come to term.

The result has been that the demand that freedom be taken seriously and respected has been found to be revolutionary in its implications. The reasons are simple enough: when the truth of Church authority is no longer grasped, the correlative truth of freedom in the Church is no longer understood, for it is in their correlation that their truth subsists. Taken out of this correlation, they each become clear and distinct ideas, detached from historical reality and open to ideological exploitation.

Where authority is thus absolutized, it becomes despotic and destructive of freedom; where freedom is made absolute, it becomes centrifugal, destructive of all community, demonic. Where authority is rejected because it is despotic, the revolution is torn between a continuing anarchy and the re-establishment of a despotic society.

The single solution to this dilemma is the return to the realities of historical existence, to the sacramental worship of the Lord of history, to the worship which has been subordinated to what it alone supports, the coincidence of freedom and responsibility which is truly historical existence, existence *in Christo, in ecclesia*. And, as John Paul II has made clear, such a return is inseparable from a renewal of Eucharistic worship, for it is not authority, or freedom, which is primary in the Church, but worship. It is in the Eucharist, the central act of the Church's worship, that the basis and meaning of Church authority, of Church freedom, is to be found.

It is the Eucharist which causes the Church, which gives the Church its intrinsic unity and meaning, as it gives intrinsic unity and meaning to the personal and communal lives of each of the people of God. It is here then that must be sought the ground of the Church's authority. As has been seen, to seek it elsewhere is to dissociate authority from the life of the Church, from the freedom of the Church, and to subordinate both to an ideology which must pervert both. Given that distortion, the hierarchical power becomes absolute. It can order intercommunion regardless of the absence of a faith consensus; it can institute divorce; it can ordain women; it can dispense with any and all doctrine; it can, in a word, exercise a despotic manipulative role over a supine worship, a worship without sacramental significance, but essentially servile.

Once the Church historian is committed to this version of ecclesiology, it becomes necessary to suppose that Church authority has in fact been exercised in this entirely despotic fashion and that in consequence the entirety of the Church's doctrinal tradition is a composite of fiats blindly imposed upon an otherwise unstructured worship. In sum, the doctrinal sacramentalism of Catholicism is an all too human invention, one in radical contradiction to the aboriginal protean faith of the primitive Christian community. It is then clear that only a dehistoricization will discover the primitive faith, a dehistoricization which is no more than the implementation of the absolutely transcendent truth of an historical-critical methodology, total commitment to which, total obedience to which, amounts to the new gnosis by which salvation is attained. And salvation, as Anaximander knew, is a matter of the elimination of all the qualifications by which finite things are distinguished from one another and from the utter unity which is justice.

The discovery of the absolute unworthiness of all the structures of finitude, the proclamation of their inability to mediate the infinity of God, these light our contemporary return to the ancient denial of the goodness of the human condition, our contemporary reappropriation of a pagan pessimism, and of the salvation which is extinction. This rediscovery belongs to the Reformation. It is fundamental to Luther's insistence upon the total corruption worked by the Fall, as it is to the Calvinist maxim, *Finitum non capax infiniti*. The evacuation of sacramental worship which with the Reformation is a matter of instinct began with Luther's denial of the sacrifice of the Mass, that Babylonian captivity in which Catholicism had languished for fifteen centuries. The rethinking of the Eucharist which followed this denial concluded that the presence of Christ in the Church is given by faith alone: this conviction, with whatever logical extrapolation may attend it, specifies the Christianity of the Reformers, as its secularization specifies the scholarship of the *Aufklärung* [Enlightenment] and the Romanticism which is its continuation. Whether from the vantage point of Luther or of the secularization of his *sola fide* which is contemporary historical criticism, the one blasphemy to be reprobated and utterly condemned is that Catholic optimism which asserts the eschatological significance, for better or worse, of all human acts in history. Luther condemned such deeds as "works", as the haughty insolence which is synergism. For the historian tutored by contemporary philosophies of history, all such deeds are of a merely relative value: academic history knows no eschatology. In either case, the Catholic doctrine of objective sacramental efficacy *ex opere operato* is a matter of scandal, whether the scandal be religious or academic.

The remedy for this scandal, by which the religious and intellectual immaturity it betokens is to be exorcised, is the program of secularization which a Pietist exegesis launched against dogmatic Lutheranism in the 17th century, which Bultmann and his followers have continued in our own time. For its adepts, schooled by the Reformation, Catholic sacramentalism is identified as the immaturity of sacralism, the outworn piety which lends cosmic value to customary institutions. Their desacralization by critical reason concludes to their secularity— for the notion of a truly sacramental institution in the Catholic sense has been dismissed by a radically confessional *a priori*. As demystified, desacralized, the Ecclesial tradition is seen at last to have no value which the mature Christian need respect. His dissociation from its merely sacral authority need occasion no misgiving. Rather, it is a matter for congratulation: the dissociation amounts to an emancipation from the oppression by sacral authority by which the rightful freedom of unstructured worship had been denied him.

The mentality which is at peace with such conclusions is too familiar to need a refutation. For nearly two millennia it has provided the perennial alternative to the Christian faith, an alternative which throughout all its permutations, from the docetism of the first century to the revisionism of the present, has held fast to one unwearying absolute: the impossibility of an historical mediation of God to man, whether that mediation be the "whole Christ" of the Eucharistic sacrifice or some expression of the existence of the people of God in history which that worship sustains.

The Church then has its own *a priori*, concrete and not abstract, event rather than idea: the worship whose focus is the Eucharist. This worship has been accounted the cause of the Church from the time of St. Paul to that of Vatican II. If we wish to understand whatever aspect of the Church, it is with this worship in its historical concreteness that we must begin, for any attempt to find a rationale behind it will inevitably prefer that abstract clarity to the nuclear density of the Eucharistic mystery and cannot but undertake again the too-familiar program of dehistoricizing the actuality by comprehending it within the critical method or idea—which then is made to be the primal truth of man in the world.

That such divagation is now common, even *de rigeur*, in contemporary theology is the result of the exaltation of an abstract idea of academic freedom which has inevitably established an adversary relation between those who accept its logic and the magisterial authority whose doctrine is subordinate to a religious rather than a secular norm of truth. The theological community thus emancipated from the heteronomy of an historical revelation is now earnestly engaged in the excogitation of a non-historical Church in which their non-historical autonomy will be at home. That this requires, precisely, the dismantling of the Eucharistic worship and of the Catholic tradition most recently reaffirmed in *Lumen Gentium* need occasion no surprise. Integrity in theology, as in all things Catholic, has no autonomous canons, no warrant or criterion which is not the Church's worship, *norma normans et non normata* [the rule measuring and not itself measured] of all authentic existence in the Church. It is by participation in this norm, and not otherwise, that theological scholarship is free, is historical and responsible—and not otherwise.

The recognition that the Church has its ground in the Eucharist carries in its train the recognition that the reality of the Church is intelligible only by reference to that mystery. And it then must follow that the two most neuralgic issues in contemporary ecclesiology, Church authority and Church history, are finally matters whose resolution has Eucharistic overtones. Both hinge, in fact, upon the numerical identity of the Eucharist with the sacrifice of the High Priest on the cross. Where this identity is affirmed, in the Catholic tradition, the Eucharist is offered as the sacrifice of Christ. Such offering is evidently impossible apart from an enablement by Christ himself. This is the root meaning of apostolicity in the Catholic tradition, and it is obviously a meaning inseparable from Catholic worship. The ecclesial community is radically incapable of providing such an authorization. To maintain the contrary is to meld the Church, for whom the sacrifice is offered, with the Christ, who offers it, as the Reform theology insists upon doing. This latter position is summed up in the assertion that apostolicity is proper to the Church, not simply to the bishops. A willingness to accept this view is *eo ipso* a willingness to dilute, ultimately to eliminate, that by which the Eucharist is numerically identical with the sacrifice of Christ, i.e., the institution of the Eucharist by Christ and simultaneously, as its consequence, the institution of the Church. That this institution cannot be understood as merely juridical is evident. The impossible is not the subject of law or command, and it is impossible to offer the sacrifice of Christ unless the intrinsic ability to offer it is given, instituted, as a permanent historical reality, continually present to the Church, by whose exercise the Church comes to be. Only then can Peter and the others to whom the command was given feed Christ's sheep, and this obedience can perdure through history only if their episcopal charism is the subject of a personal succession.

This succession, this power to offer sacrifice, is easy to parody. It has been mocked as "hocus pocus" for four centuries. But when it is seriously discussed, there are only two conceptual possibilities: the Church is apostolic by reason of episcopal succession to this apostolic *munus* [office], or it is apostolic on some other basis. The latter option has been too often explored to leave its issue in doubt. A non-episcopal apostolic succession entails the denial of the Eucharistic sacrifice of the Cross as distinct from the Church's *sacrificium laudis* [sacrifice of praise]. When this step is taken, the denial of sacramental historicity is inescapable. The concrete-historical or sign element of worship is increasingly isolated from the worship itself, and the latter soon finds itself as impatient of doctrine as of ritual: neither is adequate to a faith which understands itself, increasingly, to be incapable of an historical mediation, of an historical expression. The unity of the Church is more and more independent of any concrete manifestation, and those who insist upon such are labelled as fundamentalists, unappreciative of the need for an "historical" consciousness of the provisional character of all that is touched by time.

The Catholic doctrine of the sacrificial character of the Mass is then a most fundamental affirmation, for it underwrites and requires the institution of the Eucharistic worship by Jesus as the High Priest, who could alone enable the sacramental re-presentation of his Sacrifice. This institution is equivalently the institution of the Church as the unfailing consequence, *ex opere operato*, of the Eucharistic worship. And the Church, so caused, cannot exist apart from the succession by the bishops to the apostolic office, which is radically Eucharistic. The episcopal responsibility and authority, whether to govern, to sanctify, or to teach, have no other source than this, and no other finality. Authority in the Church is totally ordered to the worship of the Church and totally measured by what that worship is: the sacrament of the Son's obedience to the Father, of the sacrifice by which the Father is glorified and the Son receives again that glory which was his before the world began, that glory wherein the *Creator Spiritus* who raised him from the dead raises also from the dead his Body, the bridal Church for whom he died and for whom he now lives to die no more, *semper interpellans* [always importuning for us; cf. Heb 7:25, Vulgate]. This sacrifice is the *Christus integer*, the holy society by which we are in union with God, the New Covenant whose intrinsic structure, like that of the Old Covenant, is marital. In it, by it, time is redeemed, to become the history of our salvation. Here the structure of episcopal authority and the spontaneity of the freedom of the children of God meet: only in this mystery are both compatible, for by it both are sustained. It is in this worship of the Lord of history that the reality of history, salvation, is encountered and appropriated in the freedom which is given there, as the gift of the New Creation. For this worship is at once the gift and the self-appropriation of the world which God made very good. Man and his world have no truth other than the mystery of the Eucharist and no meaning or significance which does not find there its source and its culmination.

There is no need or place to spell out here the further correlations between hierarchical authority and the entirely sacramental historicity of the worshipping Church. It is enough to have pointed out that these are inseparable and that the derogation of the Church's worship cannot but be also the rejection of her historicity and her authority.

If the shift from theology to politics be so pervasive, it need not be wondered at that it is dominant in the American theological community, whose members are nearly at one in their demand for an authoritative role in the teaching Church, a role quite incompatible with the primacy of the episcopal college and the papacy. This academic community is marked by a fundamental concern for power rather than for truth—and in fact, it has no alternative, given the denial, on grounds of historical consciousness, of any significant doctrinal tradition in the Church. For, once all the moments in the temporality of the Church's existence are dissociated, each intrinsically unrelated to each, there is no longer any issue of permanent, because intrinsic, truth with which Christianity may be concerned. The Church has then ceased to be historical, time is no longer salvation history, and salvation must be sought elsewhere, in the will to power.

If this academic *ressentiment* has a single object, upon which all its anxieties are brought to their sharpest focus, it is the Tridentine dogma in which the infallible historical efficacy of the Church's worship is solemnly proclaimed: the doctrine of sacramental efficacy *ex opere operato*. This is the fundamental scandal, the rock upon which is broken every attempt to relieve the Catholic of the burdens of sacramental historicity. It stands in the way of every project which would reduce the Church's worship to faith, and faith to a *sola fide* ineffability. It

specifies the Church as irremediably historical, and history as irrevocably salvific. Its first exemplification is the "one flesh" of the Eucharistic worship, the Sacrifice in which all salvation, all worship, and all
history has its ground, and in the inseparable authority to offer that
sacrifice vicariously, to feed Christ's sheep until He shall come again.
This is a single Rock, Christ with his Vicar, and in its particularity, its
historicity, a single scandal, felt most poignantly where ecumenicity is
confused with the universality of an idea rather than understood as the
universality of worship.

The grounding of the authority of the Church in the here and now
of its worship is the begging of an enormous question, one whose
answer has been so unblinkingly presumed to be otherwise that *that*
begging passes for commonsense and so goes unnoticed, until the inevitability of its being begged, in whatever direction, is pointed out. The
question is the utterly radical one of the meaning of the experience of
time. The so-called world religions outside the Judaeo-Christian ambit
have consistently interpreted time as destructive rather than creative
and salvific, while the Judaeo-Christian and Western experience has
been of a "good creation" in which the Lord of history manifests his
lordship through the radically new events by which he directs his covenanted people to a continually open and incalculable *kairos* [due time]
of salvation. Since around the beginning of the seventeenth century,
however, the older and pagan experience of time has re-entered the
universe of discourse which is contemporary culture, to the point that
this experience is symbolically actual to a dominant degree in the popular media of communication and entertainment, where "controversy"
is the daily fare, and the exorcism of the Christian consciousness the
daily denouement. We cannot here be concerned with the manifold
pseudo-salvations, the utopian prospects, which would wean the other
professions from their ancient fiduciary responsibilities for the City of
God. It is with the anti-historical surrogates for the Church's sacramental worship now fascinating the theological community that we must
deal. These have their proximate ground in the dichotomy between
faith and history which emerged in Western consciousness with the
Lutheran Reformation and which became progressively more stark in
that consciousness as it passed from orthodoxy to the contemporary
liberal "historical consciousness" by way of Pietism, the Enlightenment, and Romanticism, with their progressive proclamation of the

religious, the rational, and finally the subjective emancipation of the individual from the thrall of the historical and sacramental worship of the Lord of history in his Church. The proclamation is eminently pagan: it proffers the same freedom from the incalculable demands of historical responsibility as was sought by those who rebelled against Moses in the desert, the same refuge from a future which cannot be controlled. Those who murmured against the improvidence of Moses are of one mind with those who today object to the Church's demand for a "blank check" commitment to its teaching, future as well as present. Some lesser, safer donation which would leave a prudent level of reserve and relativity in the account certainly consorts better with the conventional wisdom, but the paradigm of Christian commitment is still the widow of Mark 12:41–44, who gave all she had: this is the currency of faith, and there is no other.

The temptations to infidelity which Christians encounter and have encountered are all presented by the suffering inseparable from existence in our Fallen history and its stark tension with the Trinitarian Redemption of that history, its stark tension with the Church's authority to mediate that Redemption in its sacramental worship. This tension translates into equally starkly distinguished options: the commitment to the Kingdom of God which is the culmination of the saving history of the Good Creation, or the commitment to salvation through a non-mysterious history, a salvation which is the rationalization of history through its submission to the scientific image of man. Between these there is no bargaining space. The Catholic commitment to the Kingdom of God in and through existence in history, i.e., in time qualified by the immanence within it of the eschatological King in his Kingdom, the *Christus integer* of the Eucharistic presence, is therefore a commitment to Eucharistic time. It is this worship by which time is significant of the eschatological fulfillment which is the Kingdom of God: it is this worship by which time is history. The Church's unity in an otherwise relativized and disintegrating temporality is Eucharistic: it is by this worship that the Church is one, that it is holy, that it is universal, that it is apostolic. In this worship the Spirit is continually given, as the finality of the Mission of the Son by the Father, and apart from this worship, *per impossible* [sic], the Spirit is not given. All grace is *gratia Christi*; the Church knows no *extra Calvinisticum*.

From this standpoint, which simply takes seriously the *prius Eucha-risticum* of Vatican II, the Church's confidence in her own historicity is alone to be justified. All other criteria by which that historicity might be judged are alien to it, finally non-historical. We are concerned, at bottom, with the valid and true interpretation of reality itself, of the "Good Creation", the temporal and spatial context of redeemed humanity. The Church's interpretation is sacramental. The world is holy by its effective signification of the Kingdom of God, a sign-value which is effective by reason of its Eucharistic center where the Creator is present to his People. To share in this worship is to share this inter-pretation: they are the same, the celebration of the sacrifice, *omne opus quo agitur ut sancta societate inhaereamus Deo.*[2]

Finally, this worship, this sacrifice, has a marital structure, the struc-ture of the New Covenant, as of the Old. The preoccupation of nearly two millennia with legal and sociological explanations of Church authority and of marriage have obscured the "one flesh" typology with which Paul associates the Eucharistic sacrifice to the marital society and to the good creation in Ephesians 5:21–33. The richness of this typol-ogy is obvious. We can do no more here than suggest its availability and pertinence to the rediscovery of the meaning of authority in the Church. If we begin with the understanding of the apostolic office to which the bishop succeeds as that by which the bishop is authorized, ontologically made capable through a laying on of hands, through his succession to the apostolic mission, to offer the One Sacrifice of Christ, it is evident that whoever offers this sacrifice by this authority does so vicariously, *in persona Christi*. He stands, then, in Christ's rela-tion to the Church, and does so precisely by his Eucharistic authority. His relation to the Church is then marital, and his authority is then understandable only in marital terms. What these are is detailed in the New Covenant fulfillment of the Old Covenant hope for the eschato-logical union of Israel with her God: it is this which Paul summarizes in the Letter to the Ephesians. From this source, some few conclusions are immediately available, the first of which is that the sacrifice, the *Christus integer*, by which the Lord of history is united to his People, is an irrevocable achievement, irreversible in history, not to be undone.

---

[2] Augustine, *City of God* 10.6: A true sacrifice is "every work which is done in order that we might cling to God by a holy companionship".

It is a Trinitarian achievement: the Father's sending of the Son by which the *Creator Spiritus* is poured out in the Good Creation which is good because in the image of God, and in the image of God by reason of its marital structure. Here Karl Barth's insight into the meaning of *Imago Dei* is far preferable to that of St. Thomas. This insight does not place matrimony in God, but simply recognizes the ground of its liturgical significance: the created celebration of the uncreated *Herrlichkeit* [glory], as Eucharist, as marriage, as Covenant. What is celebrated is Trinitarian, not marital. From this it is immediately evident that the model for the bishops' authority over the Church, as for the Church's subordination to that authority, is a Trinitarian model, the Mission of the Son by the Father, the obedience of the Son to the Father: the authority of God revealing himself, which is not other than the object of our worship, the cause of our redemption, *Christus integer*. By his obedient sacrifice, the Son was not diminished, but glorified, for the glory of the Father is not apart from the glorification of the Son. And his glorification, this plenitude of the uncreated Splendor, can only be the created splendor, the New Creation, the Kingdom whose historical symbol, manifestation, and sacrament is the Church, the Bride, the created beauty and wisdom by which we belong to God, who dwells in Light inaccessible. This beauty and plenitude is then for celebration. By it we share in the creative and redemptive work of God, for our freedom as his children, received as gift, is salvific of our selves and the world. By this freedom we are historical in the history of the Good Creation, the history of salvation. There is no other history than this. If *this* history does not pervade our consciousness, not as a method but as worship, we shall not be free to encounter Christ in his Church, but only others like ourselves, without authority, locked into our own futility in an endless and mindless contestation.

Promise and Priesthood

With the extension of the competence of sociological analyses of sacramental realities, particularly marriage and the priesthood, the sociological category of "dysfunctional", a doubtless useful label for troubled families in which the relations between the members are perceived as abusive and destructive, has been enlarged to include the sacraments of the Catholic Church. We began to hear, some forty years ago, of "dysfunctional" marriages: i.e., of marriages seen to have "died" by reason of comparably abusive relations between husband and wife. The use of this term arbitrarily subordinated the sacramental efficacy of the sacramental symbolism of marriage to historical conditioning, to the circumstantial casualties and erosions that are the commonplace of daily experience, with the result that the irrevocability of the sacrament of marriage had been dismissed ex parte, without discussion. No marriage, within this facile convention, could henceforth be considered transcendent to circumstance, for it is evident that sociologically normed realities cannot transcend their social contexts, as a matter of definition.

Consequently, to employ this idiom is to dismiss the intrinsic efficacy *ex opere operato* of the sacramental signing by which the Catholic liturgy is Catholic.... In the end, the assertion of a "functional" sacrament is the denial of the Catholic doctrine affirming the realism, the concretely historical efficacy, of that sacrament and the inescapably eternal as well as historical significance of the actions which attend it. By the glib attribution of "functional" to the sacraments, [the] realm of the holy is overcome and, with it, the significance, the dignity, of human existence in history....

The foregoing of all claim to personal dignity, personal freedom, personal responsibility, and personal authority has long been seen to be the price of entry into the civic responsibility proper to the secular

From an unpublished essay of Keefe's, a version of which appeared under the title "Reflections upon the 'Functional' Priesthood" in *Faith*, 32/2 (March–April 2000): 13–18.

society's apotheosis of humanity. In that society of dissociate and morally irresponsible, personally insignificant individuals lacking all dignity because lacking all relation to each other, the society which, fifteen centuries ago, Augustine dubbed "the City of Man", the submergence of the responsible self in the we-saying reflex of the mass, collectivist quest for a secular, technologically secured salvation, relieves one of all responsibility. Thereby, with the dehistoricization of consciousness, God is dead, and everything is permitted.

In this "New Age" renewal of the ancient pagan pessimism, salvation is appropriated by personal extinction. Immersion in the mass consciousness of modernity has no other goal, for in that City, the exercise of personal responsibility has become incomprehensible, the exercise of personal authority, criminal, and the affirmation of personal dignity, absurd.

Because sacramental marriage is the coalescence, into a single, highly efficacious and attractive public expression, of those historically optimistic aberrations by which men and women actually accept unconditioned personal responsibility for each other in the mutuality, the "one flesh" of elective, nuptial love, modernism attacks sacramental marriage from an animus as mindless as it is unrelenting. The instinctively *ad hominem* response of modernity to the inherent truth and dignity of men and women who give it public utterance in their nuptial fidelity bars from the outset all discussion of its merits: they have become the subject, at best, of a humor no longer jovial but demonic.

Modernity finds the same absurdity in the young man who, in the rite of ordination to the Catholic priesthood, assents to the call from the ordaining bishop. By that response, he announces his free acceptance of priestly orders, his free undertaking to offer the One Sacrifice and to forgive sins in the person of Christ, to serve the Church and her alone, in celibacy, for the rest of his life—a life whose difficulty is underwritten by the decline of candidates for it to a near vanishing point.

For the Catholic priesthood has no natural attractions which could militate against those offered by comparable careers in the learned professions. Nonetheless, despite the powerful attractions of marriage and family, of career, property, and independence, young and not so young Catholic men continue to present themselves for ordination to the priesthood, knowing that by that ordination they will be forever changed, set apart, committed for the rest of their lives to a course of conduct sustainable only by seeking and finding an ever-closer bond in the worship of the Church with the Lord they will be vowed to serve by accepting responsibility for that worship.

Sacramental realism assumes that in baptism we are given a dignity, a personal word to utter which, as a personal participation in the Church's historicity, in her worship in truth, transcends the ephemeral chatter otherwise marking our fallenness. In that worship we each appropriate the Truth that is Christ, given to each of us as our food and drink, for in him we are members of a priestly people, entitled to the support of the altar. In this Communion with the risen Jesus the Lord, we are ourselves affirmed by the Second Adam who is our Head, who has named each of us in the naming of his bridal Church, and who, by that naming, has summoned us, given each of us our vocation, our uniquely personal truth to utter into the world. In that free utterance of covenantal fidelity, we appropriate the gift of our own free truth, our personal imaging of God in the freedom that is the worship of the Church.

To worship there is to appropriate as one's own that sacred symbolism, that utterance into public life of the truth of the good creation, made effective *ex opere operato* by Christ's institution, which stands radically athwart the propaganda and the project of modernity, within whose irresponsible society no man or woman has a personal word to utter and, so, has no truth or dignity which could be profaned. Each depersonalized individual has nothing to betray, nothing to honor, nothing to regret, nothing to praise or to blame, nothing over which to rejoice, nothing of which to complain. To enter this impersonal realm of absolute irresponsibility is to live without hope, without love, without a future or a past. This is life in the world of man, built by the faithless for their own oppression. Only death can solace its misery, and death is lavishly to hand, the remedy for all social ills, the efficacious quasi-sacramental sign of that salvation which is oblivion, "the abolition of man", the soteriology of sin.

The imperceptible inculcation over the past thirty years and more of the connotations of sacramental "functionalism" have deeply eroded much of the confidence of Catholics in their liturgy. For example, although "functional" is not often said of the Eucharist, theories which would submit the Real Presence to political or sociological criteria abound. For example, liturgists who should know better commonly

insist upon the distribution, at any given Mass, only of hosts consecrated during that particular Mass, as though those consecrated at any
earlier Mass were by the passage of time rendered no longer capable
of mediating the Sacrificial Presence of the risen Christ. Consecrated
hosts which once were held in ciboria of precious metals upon which
artists lavished their skills are now to be kept in baskets; the gold and
silver of which chalices were made has been replaced by pottery of at
times remarkable ugliness. For the contemporary liturgist, the Mass
which the Church proclaims to be the Offering by the High Priest of
the One Sacrifice has become merely a meal, and a folksy one at that.

This pseudo-liturgical piety manifests the antisacramental consciousness of the Lutheran Reformation, which regards the Eucharist
as "dysfunctional" apart from the Mass in which the hosts were consecrated: the consequent nullification of all other forms of Eucharistic
devotion follows as of course, a consequence unworthy of remark.
The Reformation's aversion [to] such devotions [have] become fash-
ionable in Catholic circles since the [Second Vatican] Council for reasons having nothing whatever to do with the Council; but today we
find Benediction, Perpetual Adoration, [and] the Forty Hours [aban-
doned out of fear of] a supposed competition between the tabernacle
and the altar, thought to have been recognized by Vatican II, although
the conciliar documents know nothing of it.

The result is the removal of the tabernacles in our parish churches
from their traditionally immediate proximity to the altar, with its corollary, the practical disappearance of Eucharistic piety. Obviously,
this is not the product of any Magisterial decision or policy whatever. Rather, it is insisted upon by self-proclaimed liturgical experts
whose focal aversion—again Lutheran—[to] the Catholic doctrine of
the Sacrifice of the Mass has become increasingly evident over the past
decade. That aversion focuses upon the priesthood: upon its masculinity, its celibacy, its office to offer the One Sacrifice in the person of
the Christ.

One hears rather less of functional marriage of late, perhaps because
annulments have become so common as to be perceived by many
as "Catholic divorce". When marriage thus understood becomes a
commonplace, all those virtues which the sacramental sign of matrimony underwrites, and whose lack unravels all free social unity—
chastity in and out of marriage, fidelity in marriage, and that subtle

but indispensable, sacramentally signed differentiation within the equal dignity, authority, and responsibility of the man, the woman, and their covenant, together with the irreversible personal interrelations which that differentiation connotes and supports, within the one flesh of marriage—all these also soon go by the board....

The currently popular advocacy of the "functional priesthood" is therefore in the service of an agenda: its program is familiar. It came into fashion some thirty years ago, coincident with the reversal of the altar and its dissociation from the tabernacle, with concern for use of hosts consecrated at the Mass attended, with the henceforth ordinary use of "extraordinary" Eucharistic ministers, with fastidious avoidance of concelebration as offensive to women, with an animus against the reservation of the priesthood to men and against priestly celibacy. It was at this time that a new paradigm of the priesthood became the object of a popular quest: "professionalism" was in, usually in some sociological guise, and [the] tradition of a distinctively priestly spirituality was out. The new liturgical translations from 1970 onward began to reflect this new paradigm. Any language intimating a liturgical differentiation between the "presider" and the people in the pews was suppressed, for now it was understood, without any felt need to explain, that in the liturgy of the Mass they were all doing the same thing. Implicit in the new paradigm was the discountenancing of the priest's customary daily celebration of the Mass. This had become meaningless apart from a congregation, for it was now the faith of the congregation which would effect the new "transubstantiation", no longer of the bread and wine of the Offertory into the sacrificial Body and Blood of Christ, but rather that of the "assembly" into the Body of Christ that is the church. Soon religious communities, in which every priest had celebrated daily, became congregations, in which one would celebrate for all. Priestly garb became superfluous; the clergy soon became indistinguishable from the laity, apart perhaps from a certain modishness in dress.

Henceforth, an empirical criteriology for the new priestly professionalism was in view. First, the priest's novel presidential function needed elaboration. It would not be enough to be seen as a mere occupant of the chair at the liturgical assembly, who would cease to "preside" and vanish into the disassembled assembly at the end of the liturgy. We began to hear of the priest as "leader", a notion requiring an interpretation by "inculturation" for it to be understood—for there were other candidates for leadership—and a consequent education in "leadership", in "listening skills", etc.; and those found not up to the new standards, particularly of the novel histrionic liturgical performance thought to be implicit in the strategic reversal of the altar, were invited to reconsider their vocation. Whether the invitation was heeded is hard to say. Certainly the vocation crisis was not thereby resolved, but it was effectively confused.

The application of the term "functional" to the priesthood immediately announces an interpretation of the sacrament of orders which rejects the sacramental character imparted by ordination, as its application to marriage announces an interpretation of marriage that rejects the irrevocable bond between husband and wife infallibly caused by their free, sacramentally signed personal commitment to each other.

In either case, the mentality at work is Protestant: a "protest" against the astonishing, even absurd Catholic doctrine which maintains that adult baptized Catholics are capable, by their participation in the Church's worship, of historically unconditioned self-assertion; capable, then, of giving their word irrevocably in despite of all that may occur in the future.

The sublime arrogance of a young man and a young woman ... thus pledging themselves to each other for all their lives, come what may, "forsaking all others, for richer, for poorer, in sickness and in health, for better and for worse, until death do us part" must horrify any actuarian: the odds against such absolute fidelity are overwhelming. From the pragmatic and pessimistic stance of the circumambient modernity, the pledge of unqualified fidelity to the Church, the Bride of Christ, which sacramental ordination entails, is an even worse case. For a man thus to forego what modern secularity regards as his birthright, impersonal access to women liberated for his use by the Pill, by legalized abortion, by feminist ideology, is a radical abdication of manhood itself. This becomes the more obvious when it is considered that by ordination the priest places himself under the personal authority of his ordinary, who thenceforth will determine where and how he will serve his diocese. For a man thus deliberately to place himself under authority is seen to have foregone thereby that individualistic autonomy and irresponsibility which modernity so prizes, which it associates with the acquisition of the wealth—i.e., with power, that counterfeit of responsible freedom—by which the modern, atomized man may isolate himself yet more fully from his fellows, and so approach more nearly that transcendent standing which befits the Atom as Absolute. Clearly, priestly Orders are countercultural these days, even more radically so than is marriage, which is so easily camouflaged as romance. But the romanticization of the priesthood as functional proceeds apace.

In fact, it is only the Church's sacramental worship that recognizes such radically unconditioned, unsentimental personal commitments for what they are, integral and integrating elements of the Church's worship in truth, which is to say, of the Catholic [worshipper's] sacramentally objective imaging of the Triune God. Only in that worship is there validated the traditionally commonplace supposition that adults do in fact have an absolutely true word to give and that, once given, it can be broken only by a failure of personal integrity—which is to say, by the grave sin of covenantal infidelity. In short, it is only in that worship that full personal responsibility, full personal significance in history, can be appropriated, for only there is the imaging of God understood in its full nuptial meaning.

The assumption of the inviolable personal dignity of all human beings, and of the correlative personal responsibility and authority of adults, is inseparable from the Judaeo-Christian culture of the Western world, but it is an assumption entirely open to the actuarial, pragmatic criticism which sees in the claim of the sacramental symbols of Catholic worship to an *ex opere operato* efficacy an utter absurdity—e.g., the absurdity which a physicist would find in the defiance of entropy by the purported inventor of perpetual motion. Every pagan, whether the *dévot* of a bygone cult or a convert to the contemporary secularity, knows that time devours its children, that it erodes the one, the good, the true, the beautiful, and that salvation is given only by flight from time, not by immersion within its futility. But ordination to the priesthood is a radical personal immersion in the history of salvation precisely as salvific. The man so ordained accepts and affirms the final significance of history, the Kingdom of God, as the very objectivity of the historical order. For the Catholic priest, the life, death, and Resurrection of the Second Adam is the unsurpassable fulfillment of von Ranke's criterion of historicity: the Resurrection, with all it implies, is "that which actually happened", the Event which unites the past, the present, and the future into a single indefeasible sign of the Christ's victory over the otherwise fatal fragmentation of time and space.

Only Catholic Christianity supports the historical optimism which sees in history itself the medium of salvation. For the Catholic, salvation history is history as objectively understood, in the appropriation of a free historical consciousness which is available only as a gift of truth, freely to be appropriated, freely to be affirmed. This appropriation-affirmation is liturgical. The time into which one enters, in which one lives by that appropriation, is the time which the Christ's sacrifice redeemed and which, as Eucharistic, his sacrifice orders by giving it that free unity, the sign of its fruition in the fulfilled Kingdom of God, by which it becomes history, possessed of an objectively significant content.

By this personal participation in the Catholic liturgy, the gift of personal dignity is freely appropriated and freely uttered into history—a history which is fallen, but which is irrevocably changed by that utterance, which is participation in the mission of the Word, who does not return to the Father without doing that for which he was sent, the redemption of fallen history. The priest, under the bishop, is ordained to authority over and responsibility for this liturgy. His authority and responsibility are not his own: he can exercise them only in the Person of Christ, the Second Adam, the Bridegroom of the Second Eve who is the Church. In Christ's name the priest offers the One Sacrifice which causes the Church to be, which institutes that One Flesh of the Second Adam and the Second Eve that is the New Covenant. This is his primary authority, his primary responsibility. From this Eucharistic authority flows what ancillary authority he may have: to preach, to baptize, to forgive sin, to confirm, to anoint. His office is then Christ's, to recapitulate all things in the *Caput*, the Head, in whose Name he acts. This recapitulation is the bestowal of the free unity of the One Flesh of the New Covenant upon a fallen world, the flesh whose cause is sin and whose sign is death.

The priest can do this only because he has by his ordination become what he was not: i.e., he has become capable of offering the One Sacrifice in the name and with the authority of Jesus, the High Priest and the Victim of the Sacrifice, and capable of forgiving sins in that same Person and with that same authority. This priestly capability is constitutive, never to be lost. That it survives even his own sinfulness, his willful abandonment of its responsibilities, was settled by the condemnations of the Donatist heresy in the fifth century. Therefore the priestly character is not a metaphysical accident: it exists on the level of substance, as does all grace.

The priesthood is then not a function, any more than the baptismal *character* of the baptized is a function. As one cannot take a furlough from the consequences of one's baptismal *character*, so also one cannot have a vacation from the responsibilities of one's ordination, i.e., of one's priestly *character*. Even formal laicization does not remove the priestly *character*, the priestly authority and responsibility to act *in persona Christi*. The laicized priest is of course forbidden under pain of grave sin to exercise that authority, barring cases of extreme necessity, but he cannot be deprived of it—by anyone, even the [pope]—nor can he abdicate it on his own responsibility, whether the abdication be temporary or permanent. The priesthood is constitutive of his very person, of his exercise of free responsibility and authority; and the priest's fidelity to the priesthood—which is nuptial fidelity to the Church *in persona Christi*—is the intrinsic criterion of his personal conduct and his life. This consequence is not a matter of Church law. It is the reality of his priestly Order. Freely and responsibly undertaken, this fidelity is inseparable from the priest's capacity to act in the Person of Christ. To have accepted that Personal authority is henceforth to live under it. He lives, in Paul's words, not for himself but for Christ, whose fidelity to the Church in the One Flesh of the New Covenant is irrevocable. The priesthood is not an accident, a function. It is the priest's very substance, his existence as a man whose fidelity is his *raison d'être*.

9

MARY THE MOTHER OF GOD

Any Catholic systematic theology will take special note of the Marian teachings. Keefe, however, maintains that these teachings, taken in their full implication, accord Mary the place of a first principle in the created order. For the Genesis author in 1:27 places humanity, male and female, first, at the summit of creation, alone said to be in the image of God. Then, in virtue of their exclusive capacity both to hear God's word and to be commanded to keep it (1:28–30; echoed in 2:16–17), they are placed at the center of creation. Finally, in the second chapter, the first couple are said to provide the framework of creation; the man in 2:7 inaugurating, and the woman in 2:22 concluding, God's formation of life, with the framework made complete in their free, "one flesh" union (2:24). But Paul, in Ephesians 5:31–32, states that the talk of a man leaving his mother and father to cling to his wife in one flesh is a "mystery" that he takes as referring to Christ and the Church. And Christ does indeed cling to his Church, as the Church lives by clinging to him. But underlying this uniting is his union with humanity, which he joined to himself in being conceived from Mary. Christ is one with all human flesh because of her free assent to her Lord's word, recorded in Luke 1:38: "Let it be to me (Latin, *Fiat mihi*) according to your word." Keefe, following Paul's teaching that creation was in fact made through Christ (1 Cor 8:6) and in Christ (Col 1:16), reasons that the goodness Genesis attributes to creation in the beginning rested on its being centered on this man and this woman, Christ and Mary, and their bond, which is the bond of the New Covenant.

The full goodness of creation residing in the goodness of life, the bond of the New Covenant is, for Keefe, best signified by the bond of masculinity and femininity in marriage. Christ's masculinity expresses the matchless gift of himself, the divine Son, to one who, as creature, is completely other than himself. Mary, in her femininity, expresses the interiority whereby personal life is brought about in and through a person. Yet she does so with the integrity that belongs to femininity in its primordiality, as unfallen. Hence, as Louis Bouyer remarked in *Woman in the Church*, she possesses her femininity in all its dimensions, all its facets, as integral, united, as diverse but not divided. Thus, the range of titles she has received in the tradition.

Chief among these is *Theotokos*, "God-bearer", in the sense of having borne, having given birth, to God. The title was formally taught at the Council of Ephesus (431) but had been in use for Mary from the third century. Nevertheless, Mary, who had conceived as a virgin in an event that marked a new beginning, retained her virginity even as she gained maternity. As early as the fourth century, she is referred to as "Ever-Virgin" (*Aeiparthenos*), and the Second Council of Constantinople (553) called her "the holy, glorious *Theotokos* and *Aeiparthenos*". Over time in the West, it came to be said that Mary remained a virgin *ante partum, in partu, post partum*: before, during, and after giving birth. The point was to claim that Mary in her perfect femininity at once signifies, as virginal, the breadth of life that it is possible for one to bring forth and instantiates, in her motherhood, the actual bringing forth of life, of a specific life, the Author of life.

The undivided, unreserved freedom with which Mary gives herself in turn to Christ, and thereby becomes *Theotokos*, is human freedom as it was before sin, hers as a gift bestowed from the moment of her conception, she who is "full of grace" (*plena gratia*), the fruit of her uniquely intimate union with the Son. Thus, the doctrine of the Immaculate Conception, defined by Pius IX in the papal bull *Ineffabilis Deus* (1854), is intrinsically tied to the teaching of the *Theotokos*. Similarly, Pius XII's definition in *Munificentissimus Deus* (1955) of Mary's bodily Assumption, declaring that she entered immediately into the order of transformed life effected by her Son's Resurrection, follows from her role as the woman who, in her response to Christ and to the Father who sent him, collaborated in establishing this order, which is human life joined to the divine. As the tradition came to refer to Jesus as the New Adam, led by Paul's description of him as the "last Adam" (1 Cor 15:45), so, in view of Mary's inverted parallel to Eve—who would not keep her Lord's word—first drawn by Irenaeus of Lyons (*Against Heresies* 3.22.4; 5.19.1), she is called the New Eve; and what is more, largely due to the influence of medieval commentators on the *Song of Songs*, she is said to be uniquely the bride of the divine Bridegroom.

In the first selection, Keefe not only makes clear that Mariology lies at the heart of his own approach, he contends that it must occupy a central place in any intellectually vigorous Catholic theology. The second is meant as a further illustration of the same point, but the essay from which it is taken goes on to develop at some length the Mariological dimension of the Eucharist. The order of human life, Keefe argues, whether it be life simply as created, as restored, or finally as transformed, has of its nature a nuptial structure, that is, a structure whose appropriate sign is marriage. Thus, the people of Israel, who thought of themselves as having been called to be a force for restoration, but from whom was born the source of life's transformation, are frequently described in the Hebrew scriptures with bridal imagery. True of the order founded on the Old Covenant, it is certainly true of the New. And the order of life ushered in by the New Covenant is both present and at work in the Eucharist, in this analogous way: as the very flesh of Mary became the flesh of Jesus, so, too, does the offering of the Church become his body and blood, to which she then is joined. Keefe, in the third selection, uses this covenantal understanding of the Eucharist to explain the theological significance of masculinity in Holy Orders.

Mary and the New Creation

If it be kept in mind that the covenanted freedom of the people of God is a marital freedom and that this freedom is no other than the imaging of God which is inseparable from their creation as a people, it is difficult to avoid the conclusion that the marital relation which Paul saw to be grounded in the relation of Christ to the Church is given its primary expression in the "*Fiat mihi*" by which Mary uttered forth the beauty and splendor of the New Creation in the free affirmation of that Creation's mediatorial destiny. As the Second Eve, by her free appropriation of her own created reality, that of the *Theotokos*, Mary reverses the refusal of her antetype, and does so in a correspondence to the Second Adam which is the inception of a radically new relation of the Lord of history to the world of men and of Uncreated to Created Wisdom. In this New Creation, this New Covenant, the immaculate Woman of this New Genesis utters and makes concrete the plenitude which is hers as the Daughter of Zion, the final bearer of the hope of Israel. As unfallen, immaculate, integral, she fulfills totally the mediatorial role of her people: a role at once virginal and maternal, Daughter of Zion, Mother of God, Bride of Yahweh. What would for fallen femininity be an impossible splintering of existence is found integrated in her integrity; she is at once the little child of Proverbs 8:30, joyful in the creative presence of her Lord, and the *Mater Dolorosa* at the foot of the Cross, whose soul a sword has pierced. The fragmented elements of fallen femininity, mutually exclusive in their disintegration, find in her their unfallen and eschatological unity, the unity which is the splendor of the Good Creation, once refused by Eve, now realized in the New Covenant of God's definitive presence to His people, the One Flesh

From Donald J. Keefe, S.J., "Mary as Created Wisdom: The Splendor of the New Creation", *The Thomist* 47, no. 3 (July 1983): 395–420. The article was based on a paper presented at the meeting of the Institute for Theological Encounter with Science and Technology (ITEST) held in Columbus, Ohio, in January 1982.

of Mary's conception of Our Lord. This relation, the created bi-polarity of the New Adam and the New Eve, constitutes the New Covenant by which God is mediated to and present in our human-ity; it is at the same time and under the same aspect the single, the unique relation of God to that creation which, through the New Covenant, is now redeemed.

This relation is of course Trinitarian: the Father's sending of the Son to give the Spirit, and its sole mediation, the *sine qua non* of the mission of the Son and the outpouring of the Spirit, is the Incarnation of the Son through the motherhood of her by whose "*Fiat*" the Uncreated and the Created Wisdom are united in a society which is at once the definitive (and, because integral, also primordial and eschatological) presence of God in the world and the equally definitive imaging of God. This imaging is bi-polar; its dialectic is that of Mary's consent, *plena gratia*, to the plenitude offered her by God, a plenitude which is at once her own creation as the immaculate Woman and the created immanence within her of the Man, the Son whose mission is also the Gift of the *Creator Spiritus* in whose outpouring creation is at once given and renewed.

The integrally free society of Mary and her Son, the New Adam and the New Eve, the New Covenant and the New Creation, is then that by which the Trinity has signed creation with God's own unity, truth, and goodness: qualities of being which can be appropriated only in worship, for they are not concepts but mysteries, to be received as gifts rather than grasped as properties of nature. This New Creation knows no "nature", no latent infrastructure which would not be gift, would not be signed with the Trinitarian image. If one wishes to make rational distinctions between nature and grace, it is then necessary to assign the totality of concrete finitude to grace, upon which postulate, itself no more than a corollary of the Christocentric and Trinitarian faith of the Church, the reality of nature becomes entirely abstract, unreal because uncreated—for only that is created which is created in Christ and sealed with the image of the Trinity.

To appreciate the Trinitarian imaging proper to the marital society which is the New Covenant, whether this be viewed most inclusively as the New Adam-New Eve polarity or as the Christ-Church cor-relation or that of the Incarnate Logos and Mary, it must be under-stood in all these instances that we have to do with the "one flesh" whose eschatological perfection is symbolized uniquely by marriage, rather than by one of the other polarities (father-daughter, mother-son, brother-sister, etc.) found in human sexuality, for of these sexual polarities, only marriage is a sacramental sign and a Trinitarian symbol. Therefore our avenue to any understanding of the *Imago Dei* is a sacramental one: this should not be astonishing, for sign, sacrament, symbol, and *imago* have a single ground, the actual presence of the eschatological Good Creation within the worship of the Church. This ground is Eucharistic, and as Ephesians assures us, it is also marital.

The Trinitarian structure of the marital symbol is evident enough: the total self-donation of two persons to each other is constitutive of each, as husband, as wife, and is productive of a third reality, the marriage bond itself, the marital society, the substantive love of each for each which cannot be undone, and whose self-subsistent character is evidenced by its irrevocability. This love, or covenant, cannot be identified with either of the covenanting parties; this, and its radical permanence as a relation, makes the marital covenant of husband and wife the Trinitarian image and sacrament par excellence. It is only within this context that the Trinity is in fact "imaged" even by the Incarnate Son, for He is Image as sent, as obedient to the Father in a sacrifice which has no other finality than that *sancta societas* which is fallen humanity's sole means of union, with God. The Christ cannot be approached except by the mediation of this society, which concretely is the New Covenant, and Mary finds her whole meaning within its mystery. It must be remembered that the reality of the New Covenant is eschatologically complete and achieved; it is not then a sacrament, but [is] that final creation to which the sacraments point and upon whose eschatological perfection they depend for their sign value. If this be forgotten, the New Covenant loses its newness, to become no more than a mere continuation of the old Covenant, one in which the Christ is not what Chalcedon taught, one in which his stature is no more than that of a prophet and in which there can be no question of a Mother of God, no question of a Church which would offer a Sacrifice transcending that of the temple.

Consequently, any theology which would speak of Mary's imaging of God must recognize that her whole reality must be dealt with as possessing that fullness of grace which lifts her above the sacramental order. That she is immaculately conceived, free of all taint of concupiscence and sin, is the commonplace of Catholic doctrine, but the implication of this doctrine for her worship of God, her imaging of God, is not much discussed—yet it is this worship alone in which her titles of Created Wisdom and Beauty are understandable. Her "*Fiat*" was her bodily reception, her conception, of the Christ, an act of integral freedom and so of worship upon which our own Eucharistic worship is totally dependent. As this conception was an act of eschatological freedom, the freedom of the *Theotokos*, it transcends that fallen freedom by which we, her children, worship her Son in the Eucharist, as it transcends that freedom by which the sacrament of matrimony is ministered. As Christ did not partake of the Eucharist at the Last Supper—for He *is* the Bread and the Wine—so also it would be incongruous to think of Mary as one of the exiled People of God to whom this manna is offered—for of all the daughters of Eve, she alone has known no exile.

Therefore, Mary's imaging of God is that which is proper to the eschatological New Creation, to the Covenant of the New Adam and the New Eve. It is in this Covenant that she is created; her whole reality is Covenantal, as is her Son's. As Paul Tillich might have said, they both manifest this reality under conditions of existence; as Rahner has said, with reference to the hypostatic union, the intuitive vision of God which is proper to Christ's integral humanity does not place him at some beatified remove from our fallen history, for He, like us, is *ensarkikos*, bound to the suffering and death of fallen humanity. So also for his mother, whose integrity and unfallenness and utter freedom only radicated her more deeply in the redemptive suffering of her Son. Her imaging of God, her worship of the Father through her Son in the Spirit which He gave her fully from the first moment of her existence, is the utterance of the splendor and beauty of the New Creation, but in the idiom of a fallen people, for it is addressed to them. In fact, it is by this covenantal presence of the eschatological Good Creation in fallen space and time that this fallenness is valorized and given sacramental (eschatological) significance, for it is of this Good Creation that the sacraments speak; it is this that they signify, and for this reason, the Eucharist, as the sacramental continuation of the New Covenant, underlies the other sacraments, as the New Covenant underlies the Eucharist.

Mary's Assumption is similarly to be understood with reference to her eschatological creation. The Assumption into the heavenly Kingdom of the Queen of Heaven is no mere sign of divine favor, no inference from a more or less sentimental love of the Son for his mother; it is the strict counterpart of her Immaculate Conception, of her substantial integrity. As in the Resurrection, which is the ontologically first moment of the fulfilled creation, Jesus is lifted up from the subjection to fallen space and time in such wise as to be present in that realm henceforth only in sign and sacrament, so Mary, the immaculate recipient of the fullness of His grace, was also removed, as integral with that fulfilled creation, from the corruption of the earth at her death. The Created Wisdom by which she is *Theotokos* and *Mater dolorosa* is that by which she is also *Regina coeli*, still the first beneficiary of her Son's mission from the Father, his obedience unto death. It is only when systematic theology begins to understand the necessity linking Mary's integrity with her Assumption that the latter can itself be used as a *point d'appui* for a further inquiry into a point of some difficulty, the meaning of the distance between our own death and our resurrection in Christ. Fallen human beings are not assumed into heaven upon their deaths so as to leave no body after them on this earth. Until the history of its salvation is complete, the earth shall bear some temporal and spatial relation to those whose mortal remains are mingled with its elements—a relation entirely lacking in the Risen Christ and in his mother. Given that upon their death (*mox* [thereupon], as wrote Benedict XII) the fallen dead are judged and enter upon their final destiny, nonetheless they do not rise until the last day. The meaning of this truth is not an easy thing to grasp: given the discontinuity between this world's history and whatever manner of duration is appropriate to the fallen dead, the continuity implicit in the postponement of their resurrection to the last day places a real link between even the justified dead and the dust to which they returned upon their deaths, and so to the time and space of the fallen world in which they no longer live, but to whose final redemption and recreation their own is indissolubly connected.

The kind of criticism of this Catholic doctrine which rests upon the physical sciences is obviously beside the point, but it is perhaps necessary to remark that the philosophically grounded objection, which would insist that a separated soul has lost the materiality which any waiting or duration after death would imply, also lacks an assured place upon which to stand. It is all too easy to read into the doctrine which describes death as the separation of soul and body some Aristotelian or quasi-Thomist metaphysic, a procedure no more justified here than in the case of the Tridentine doctrine on transubstantiation. A "separated soul" is a doctrinal, not a philosophical concept, despite the metaphysicians' struggles over it. If the doctrine is to be clarified, as distinct from the resolution of some metaphysical difficulty, the appropriate starting point is doctrinal: one proceeds from the "limit case" of an unassailable truth whose meaning is pertinent to the question at issue, and here Mary's Assumption is precisely in point, for it sets off, as Jesus' Resurrection does not (if only because He is divine as well as human), a concrete distinction between integral and fallen humanity, in the unique instance of Mary's death. It is quite clear that the matter is too difficult to be dealt with in this place; nonetheless, it is well to point out the advantages of Mariology for Catholic theology, in a time when, for perhaps the majority of contemporary Catholic thinkers, the doctrines concerning her are felt as a burden and an embarrassment rather than as the enormous resource which they actually are for systematic theology. Even those of us who do not share that embarrassment are too passive in our appropriation of the Marian dogmas, to the point that even for us they do amount to a burden—outposts to be defended, but from which no sorties need be feared. This is a garrison soldier's mentality, inappropriate to a theologian whose legitimate defensive function can be met only by an entire confidence in the truth of the mystery to whose intelligibility without limit he is committed.

A further illustration of the same point may be ventured: would not much of our confusion over the meaning of Mary's virginity "*ante, in et post partum*" be removed by the postulate that integral human sexuality is virginal as such? From this standpoint, physiological integrity need no more be associated with her childbearing than is freedom from the common cold associated with her Immaculate Conception, for integrity under conditions of a fallen world carries with it no immunity from physical trauma, and it is integrity which controls the meaning of her virginity. Thus viewed, virginity is simply an aspect of Mary's *Fiat*, of her total self-donation to God in the New Covenant. It is then the physical actuality of the exclusivity of her relation to her Son; by this, her femininity is fulfilled integrally, completely, beyond any possibility of increase or altereity. If one must speak of her marriage to Joseph, it should be made clear that this relation is marriage only by an extrinsic denomination, for it lacks the intrinsic symbolism or sacramental quality which the term marriage demands in its ordinary acceptation. As unfallen, integral, Mary is beyond any sacramental expression of her relation to God, for such an expression looks to and causes a personal completion or integration which was Mary's from her conception.

In fact, many of the difficulties which Catholic theologians encounter in meeting the questions posed to them by contemporary dissent from Catholic practice and doctrine may well be met by a firm reliance upon and confidence in the profound truth of those doctrines as the firm ground of much of what has gone unexamined in the traditional practices of Catholic life. A vigorous inquiry into the contemporary implication of such doctrines will find much more meaning in them than the contemporary diffidence has come to expect. How often, for instance, does one hear it argued that priestly celibacy is the strict implication of the priest's sacramental offering of Christ's marital sacrifice for his bridal Church, and that the abandonment of celibacy by those ordained to offer this sacrifice is also the abandonment of the *alter Christus* function by which it is offered? On the other hand, how often is the irrevocable union of Christ with his Church put in issue by talk of a "sinful Church", as if the alternative were a triumphalism contemptuous of history, and as though the Eucharistic Lord could be irrevocably related to the Church through a freedom less integral and a worship less adequate than that of the Woman who is the Church's antetype? Such talk, common enough since the [Second Vatican] Council, concedes more to the *Zeitgeist* than a careful examination of central Catholic doctrines can admit. Only a confident rejection of that dispirited mentality and a Spirit-led return to the doctrinal, moral, and liturgical tradition will permit Catholic theologians to perform their task. The Marian component of that task is indispensable.

Catholic theology may then be said to have paid too little attention to Mary's integral and eschatological stature; while the Fathers have recognized it since Justin Martyr, while the doctrinal tradition since Ephesus has made it increasingly explicit, and while the liturgical tradition has spoken of it unhesitatingly, Marian theology finds little interest outside of conferences and journals expressly devoted to that now esoteric topic. Particularly, the Vatican II reference to a "hierarchy of truths" is often taken to have a typical if not general reference

to the Marian doctrines; these, it is frequently asserted, have less rele-
vance to contemporary catechetical needs than do the central Trinitarian and Christological doctrines. Particularly, this is thought to be the
case with respect to the relatively recent definitions of the Immaculate
Conception and the Assumption. Doubtless there is little point in pur-
suing an inquiry into the precise sense in which this "hierarchy" is to
be understood, since it is quite clear that the Conciliar fathers themselves did not attain to any precision in this matter. The existence of
very brief kerygmatic and baptismal formulae of the faith in the earliest
layers of the New Testament tradition is itself testimony to an ecclesial
recognition that certain truths are of primary concern for the primitive
Church and that the list of these can be quite compact. It is much
less clear that the making of such a list is any longer a possibility; the
post-Conciliar attempts to discover a credal formula satisfactory to the
contemporary Church are of a dwindling interest today; such projects
as that which would re-institute the earlier Apostles' Creed in place of
the Nicene-Constantinopolitan Creed at the Mass are rather the products of liturgical conferences and commissions than the expression of
any need felt in the pews. Academic fashion has little to do with the
lex orandi; it owes much more as a rule to the charms of some such
anachronism as Schoonenberg's Christology than it does to a valid
insight into the *sensus fidelium* [the believers' intuitive judgment about
matters of faith]. The fear, not infrequently voiced, that the centuries
have piled up far too great a burden of doctrine and dogma to be
borne—as though every baptizand, every practicing Catholic, must
have to hand a ready recollection of Denzinger's† latest edition—has
its origin in a profound distrust of history as the medium of the Christian revelation, and in a consequent desire to be rid of its harvest, root
and branch. However, it is not necessary to share a Veuillot's ultra-
montanism to recognize with Newman that to be Catholic is to be
deep in history, a history which is not dispensable. The centuries of

---

*Abbreviated form of the expression *lex orandi, lex credendi*, "The law of praying is the law
of believing", meaning that the text of the Church's prayers are an expression of the mind of
the Church concerning the faith.

†In 1854, Heinrich Denzinger published a collection of Church creeds, conciliar canons and decrees, and selections from papal documents, in their original languages, arranged
chronologically in numbered sections. The forty-third edition was released in 2010 with over
fifty-one hundred sections of material.

the Church's worship are normative for what worship is. Manifestly, one does not require of the ordinary Catholic an articulate familiarity with all of the doctrinal achievements of two thousand years, but one does require—the Church requires—that such a Catholic accept that tradition for the seamless web it is, that he commit himself to that historical reality which is the teaching Church, with its past and its future. The essential simultaneity of the Marian and the ecclesiological doctrines is evidenced by their treatment in a single dogmatic constitution at Vatican II: ecclesiology and Mariology are indissociable, and any attempt to relegate the Marian doctrines to some peripheral Catholic interest immediately runs into major ecclesiological obstacles, obstacles which are not other than the sacramental presence in our fallen world of the eschatological perfection of the New Covenant. This sacramental worship is specific and essential to Catholicism, and any dilution of the eschatological stature of Our Lady immediately and necessarily puts in issue the ground of the Church's faith: the actual presence in space and time of the Eucharistic Lord in the worship of the Church. It is in Mary's act of eschatological and integral freedom, her consent to be the Mother of God, that this Covenant is given: here and here alone the eternal and the created Wisdom meet; here the freedom of the Creator and of the Good Creation are agreed; here the most High is pleased to take to Himself our fallen flesh. It is by Mary's *Fiat*, where alone the created beauty and wisdom and freedom of our redeemed humanity find adequate and full expression, that He became "one flesh" with us forever, and the promises of the Old Testament are fulfilled, in the Covenant by which He has fixed his tabernacle in his chosen people, irrevocably. But if any of the Marian doctrines are doubted or denied, then the Church is not the Church; if any of them are neglected or disdained, so also is the splendor of the Church.

The Marian doctrines are therefore not only not negotiable, not dispensable to the Christian faith: their exploration is an essential task of theology, and any systematic theology which would ignore these doctrines, or fail to integrate them, particularly those most recent promulgations of Mary's eschatological perfection, is doomed to lapse into that kind of "identity system" which von Balthasar properly condemned in Barth's dogmatics, which is latent in Tillich's systematic theology, and which is all too easy to extrapolate from any theology which would prefer, for its principle of explanation, some immanent dynamism, human or cosmic, whose relation to the grace of the New Creation is at best and finally uninteresting. The Marian doctrines enter theology at the level of method, for the conversion process which the Christian faith demands of any prior anthropology, cosmology, sociology, politics, or other humane discipline in order that it become a theology is that by which such a discipline loses its immanent necessity to become Christocentric. Christ, the new center of existence by which autonomous rationality is freed from its immanence to become a quest for wisdom, is the mediation of the truth of God, but He is this mediation as the *Christus integer*, the New Covenant, the concrete event of the unity, *una caro* [one flesh], of created and Uncreated Wisdom. It is this New Being, to use Tillich's phrase, which is the concern of theology; if it is simply identified with the Son of Man, his presence among us must be understood to be unmediated, unreal, inhuman, and unintelligible, except insofar as He is reduced by a "Christology from below" to merely human and non-redemptive dimensions. It is only by Mary's perfect freedom that one may understand that God's presence among men is not inhuman and despotic, an arbitrary exercise of *potentia absoluta*. It is one of the tragedies of Catholic theology that Scotus' Augustinian insight into the Christ-Mary correlation should have so little interested his contemporaries and followers, so that the Scotism of the fourteenth and fifteenth centuries should now provide such a paradigm for the poverty of the theological minimalism which governed the decline of medieval theology and the emergence of the anti-sacramentalism of the Reform, as it now governs the regnant American Catholic theological scholarship.

That much deplored axiom of Marian piety, *numquam satis de Maria* ["There is never enough concerning Mary"], therefore, has sounder foundations than much of what passes for theological sophistication in our schools today. In the six centuries of theological doldrums in which the spirit of Ockham has dominated theological speculation by conforming its subject matter to the immanent structures of autonomous reason, Marian piety, nearly bereft of scholarly sustenance, has fed on another food, the One Flesh of the Eucharist, the New Covenant which cannot be undone, even by our neglect. It is faith in this Whole Christ which is Catholic, and the *quaerens* which ever seeks the *altitudo* of that mystery cannot see it by any other light than that which Mary bore for the world's salvation.

A Eucharistic Mariology

The significance of Mary's motherhood of God for Eucharistic doctrine was pointed out more than fifteen centuries ago by Cyril of Alexandria vis-à-vis Nestorius' rejection of the legitimacy of the liturgical attribution to her of the title *Theotokos* or Mother of God. Cyril recognized that if Mary is not truly the "mother of God", it can only be because Jesus, her Son, is not God, and therefore his Eucharistic flesh, as merely human, cannot be as John the Evangelist named it, the "bread of life", [or] what Ignatius Martyr called "the medicine of immortality". Only God can bestow life.

Clearly there is no novelty in a contemporary assertion of the indispensability of the Marian doctrines to Eucharistic theology. Within the tradition of the Church, Mary was early recognized to be the "second Eve". The patristic meditation dwelt largely upon the contrast between her obedience and the disobedience of Eve, recognizing in Mary's "*Fiat mihi*" the antitype of Eve's disobedience and sin. The comparably negative correlation between Jesus and the first Adam is of course established by Paul, who recognized in the Christ's redemptive obedience on the Cross the antitype of the first Adam's disobedience. The Fathers were also intent upon seeing in the blood and water drawn from the side of the Crucified the ecclesial fulfillment of the taking of Eve from the side of Adam.

That there was a patristic reluctance to accept the nuptial implication of the "second Eve" title given Mary is understandable: that implication savored of incest.

However, a moment's reflection will dismiss the objection, for we know that in Mary's sinless integrity, untouched by Original Sin, the disparate roles of a fragmented and fallen femininity are at one: it is the faith of the Church that Mary is at once virgin and mother, daughter

From the version in Keefe's electronic files of an essay published as "The Relation of Nuptial Symbolism to Eucharistic Realism", *The Pacific Journal of Theology*, series 2, no. 21 (1999): 88–119.

and bride. The One Flesh symbolism inherent in her virginal conception of her Son makes of Mary's "*Fiat*" the antetype of all Catholic
worship. It is in the same sinless freedom of the worship of her Lord
that, in and by that worship, the sacramental Church celebrates, as
the second Eve, the Eucharistic immanence within her of Christ her
Lord. Mary's conception of her Lord and the transubstantiation of
the Church's offering fall under the same plenary Gift of the Spirit
by the Son. They are indissociable: both are celebrations of the One
Flesh of the second Adam and the second Eve.

There has been an academic discussion, now some decades old, concerning which of Our Lady's titles is foundational for the others. Without trying to resolve the question, it may be said that within the patristic
tradition, and from the second century, stemming from Justin and Irenaeus, she has shared with the Church the title of the second Eve.

The scriptural foundation for the patristic ascription of the title of
second Adam to the Christ and of second Eve to the Church is evidently the Pauline understanding of Jesus as the new Adam, found in
Rom. 5:12–21; in 1 Cor. 15:21–22, 45–49; in Eph. 1:10; and especially
in Eph. 5:21–33, with its explicit reference to the union of Christ and
the Church on the pattern of the creation account in Genesis 2:24:
"and they become one flesh."

The patristic recognition of Mary as the second Eve is mainly the product of a meditation upon the role of Mary's obedience to the angelic
Annunciation of her unique role in the redemption of the world, contrasted with the role of Eve's sinful disobedience in the fall, recited in
Gen. 3. Irenaeus led the way in this development of doctrine, which
found its first dogmatic expression at the Council of Ephesus in 431,
where Mary was proclaimed the *Theotokos*, the Mother of God. In 1854,
in the bull *Ineffabilis Deus*, Pope Pius IX defined her Immaculate Conception, her unqualified sinlessness from the first moment of her existence. Just short of a century later, in 1950, in the Apostolic Constitution
Munificentissimus Deus, Pope Pius XII solemnly proclaimed her bodily
Assumption into Heaven.

The unity of this development of doctrine is simple enough. It rests
upon the Pauline reference in Eph. 5:31 of Christ and the Church to
the "one flesh" of Gen. 2:24, with its implication that wherever the
new Adam, the Head, may be, there also is the new Eve, for their
union is irrevocable: "what God has joined, let not man put asunder."

The Church has concluded, from the utter freedom of this nuptial union, to Mary's sinlessness. Had she been like the other daughters of Eve, a sinner, her consent to be the Mother of God would, by her sinfulness, have been less than free. The Son of God could not then have been covenantally present in the world by her conception of Him for, without her free assent to his conception, His presence in history would have been and would remain an imposition upon her, the result of coercion, to the extent that her conception of her Lord would have been unfree and in some degree made servile by her servitude to sin.

Further, the consequent servile passivity, at best, of the created order to the immanence of God would reinvoke all the dualisms latent in the pessimism of the pagan cosmological myths, wherein it is recited that the gods made men slaves that they might be free, wherein evil and material finitude coincide, so that redemption from evil is understood to be [a delivery, not] from sin, but from the anguish inseparable from concrete human existence in time. The danger is not slight. Such dualism has already been observed in much of the current theology of original sin and the fall and is inherent in the historical criticism of current exegesis, insofar as this is dominated by the Enlightenment's historical determinism.

It is only by taking seriously, not as a metaphor but as a profoundly metaphysical truth, the free and covenantal unity in "one flesh" of the second Adam and the second Eve, whether achieved in Our Lady's conception of her Son or in the Church's Eucharistic worship, that the true importance of the Marian tradition becomes clearly evident, together with the indispensability of the nuptial imagery by which it is intelligible. The second Eve's motherhood of God cannot but be the antetype of the One Flesh of the New Covenant, instituted by the One Sacrifice of the second Adam, who is her Son. Her nuptial role is then utterly foundational, even primordial, for the second Eve is by definition the Bride of the second Adam. With this doctrinal and liturgical foundation, the *fides quaerens intellectum* that is Catholic theology cannot but see as indissociable the theology of Mary and of the Church, of the Incarnation and of the Mass. The nuptial symbolism of the One Flesh controls them all, for the foundation of all theology is Eucharistic.

The Covenantal Meaning of Gender

The most fundamental and the most archaic liturgical symbols are sexual; all western philosophy has its remote origin in the pagan reading of that symbolism as it was found in the Dionysian-Orphic religious tradition of the Greek world. Inasmuch as Christianity consists in conversion from paganism, so the meaning of its symbols is also the product of a conversion from the historical pessimism which those symbols invoke, evoke, and express in their pagan guise and which pervades the classic tradition of Greek philosophy.

The meaning of sexual symbols is of course the quality of their correlation or polarity; the spontaneous evaluation or interpretation of this polarity, because it reflects the most fundamental experience of the human condition, is an utterly basic characterization of existence, of the reality which is human and historical. This interpretation of sexual symbols connotes and in fact constitutes and reinforces, however liminally and inchoately, a judgement or decision passed upon the goodness or not of history itself. As Eliade has shown, this evaluation, insofar as uttered in the symbols of the pagan liturgy, is negative: the preservation of the cosmos requires a liturgical flight from history, and in fact all pagan morality is resumed in an unreflective obedience to this cosmological precept, which as cosmological proscribes as profane all exercise of free personal responsibility in history.

The flight from history is always a flight from woman, for the suffering consciousness which spurs that flight knows no more radical liturgical symbol of its frustration and anxiety than the paradoxical, irreconcilable, and yet irreducible polarity of the masculine and the feminine. The alternating Platonic and Aristotelian philosophical analyses

From Donald J. Keefe, S.J., "Gender, History, and Liturgy in the Catholic Church", *Review for Religious* 46, no. 6 (November–December 1987): 866–88; available online as part of the Saint Louis Universities digital collection. The article was originally delivered as a paper at the Thirty-Second Meeting of the Anglican-Roman Catholic Consultation in the United States (ARC-US), Jamaica, N.Y., December 7–10, 1986.

or rationalizations of the cosmogonic pagan liturgical symbols of the *hieros gamos* ("sacred marriage") are at bottom no more than alternative expressions of this flight: the feminine, once viewed as incompatible with the masculine because qualitatively irreducible to masculinity, must either (1) be opposed to the masculine in an irreconcilable standoff which is the very structure of the pagan experience of history as irrational, ambiguous, absurd, and unhappy, or (2) be suppressed by the masculine in the name of an abstract rationality whose ideal and nonhistorical criteriology for the true and the real forecloses all personal exercise of historical responsibility by damning whatever is radically new and free for its nonconformity to timeless paradigms. This irreducibility of personal responsibility to the impersonal ideal is precisely its unpredictability, its irreducibility to the mythic past, and the disorder, randomness, and unintelligibility which consequently mark it.

To these options, classic in Greek philosophy, as typified by Plato, on the one hand, and his stubbornly contrary student Aristotle, on the other, gnosticism has added a third, well known to the pagan liturgical tradition if less so to its classic philosophical rationalizations.

This third option is the merger of the historically polarized feminine and masculine symbols into a primordial androgynous One or Humanity. This merger is achieved by the reduction of this cosmic dichotomy to an ineffable, precosmic, or primordial identity as seen from the viewpoint of eternity, an identity which is thereupon identified as the Alpha and the Omega of cosmic space and time, at once the primordial source from which this cosmos is fallen as well as its eschatological redemption from all its inherent injustice of differentiation and qualitative distinction—which is to say, from all inequality—by the ideal, a priori, and monist nullification of the significance of all historical particularity.

The pagan "ontological hunger" for the ineffable ideal unity of being can find no sustenance in history, only a continual frustration. This frustration can be denied à la Aristotle, "transcended" after the manner of Hegel, or overcome by a Marxist political praxis, but always and inevitably this is done only at the price of denying or transcending or overcoming the historical free responsibility of concrete human beings. Over and over again, from Plato to Engels to the present-day liberation praxis, marriage provides the test case for this historicist and cosmological suppression of historical particularity. This is simply because marriage provides the clearest instance of irrational, idiosyncratic, and obstinate perdurance in the positive valuation of the unique personal particularity of individuals. The free decision to marry, which even in its pagan format establishes and insists upon a special, indeed a unique, relation of privacy between these two particular human beings, a relation which as exclusive is incapable of rational justification and so must be accounted unwarranted and absurd, is a decision that at once establishes, underwrites, and insists upon that which from the view of the pagan liturgy is always and everywhere wrong, the perennial "injustice" ascribed since Anaximander to unique personal high-profile significant historicity, and therefore to any intimation of a responsible personal dignity able and in fact destined to affirm itself against all historical erosion and relativization.

The nonhistorical or cosmological morality of paganisms old and new is a function of a nonhistorical freedom, a freedom that is experienced as impinged upon, diminished, and denied by every discrete historical structure and event, by every confident concrete reality which is encountered in space and time. The pagan liturgy, as did later the pagan rationality, existed and yet exists to nullify the oppressive and burdensome significance of all of these, to reduce them to triviality and insignificance, to relativize them all in the name of an eternal return to the cosmogonic moment of truth before it fell into the vagaries of matter and in that fallenness became corrupt, disunified, and thus ambivalent, its formal simplicity contradicted by the irrationally random multiplicities of cosmic time and space.

The pagan morality, in which responsibility is so viewed, cannot but look upon marriage as the paradigmatic symbol of our cosmic fallenness into the supposedly chaotic differentiation and multiplicity from which humanity must be redeemed. The nuptial masculine-feminine polarity is then the radical symbol of what is wrong with the world: to affirm the value, the irreducibility, of that polarity is to act in a manner unresponsive to the pagan liturgical symbolism, and therefore to act immorally. The pagan marital liturgy has always struggled with this ambiguity, which is inseparable from the pagan experience of marriage.

The Christian conversion which underwrites the sacramental and historical celebration of marriage transforms the masculine-feminine symbolism from a static structure of oppression, of cosmogonic fallenness, into the constitutive event of free historicity, the marital covenant which in the book of Genesis is the radical pattern of the good creation. In that covenant, husband and wife each encounter in each other's concrete free historicity a unique and irreplaceable dignity which is indeed qualitatively and irreducibly different from their own, and yet which in this mutual freedom of marital love is encountered precisely as good: that is, as responsive, responsible, complementary, and indispensable to their own reality, for only in and by this marital covenant is human dignity recognized, discovered, and appropriated; only in this covenantal event does the free responsibility of a man evoke the free responsibility of a woman; only here does the free nuptial responsibility of a woman evoke the free nuptial responsibility of a man. In this mutuality, each affirms not self but a qualitatively irreducible other in a moment of selflessness by which the irreducibly unique masculine or feminine self is realized, received, made actual in the covenantal self-forgetful freedom that is love. This is the concrete paradigm of human existence as historical rather than as cosmological; it is not idea, not structure, but the free event of our imaging, covenantally, the Triune God.

This discovery is liturgical; it entails a free conversion, a free entry into a free and irrevocable society, one which at once is freely realized in history and yet transcends history as its formal principle, as the freedom by which the variety and mutability of temporality becomes meaningful, significant, historical. The heretofore random and incalculable character of this now free historicity is encountered as transformed and exorcised, no longer demonic but the very goodness of a world whose truth is at one with its historicity, at one with its nuptiality.

Within this liturgical community, the truth of the human condition, because freely given and appropriated freely in history, can no longer be imprisoned within the narrow and immanent necessities of a categorical or mathematical rationality. This is perhaps the most general statement of the "good news" which the Christian receives in faith: that the entirety of reality and of truth is free, incapable of enclosure in any conceptuality. Historical rationality is in consequence of this faith to be exercised in the continual appropriation of mystery, not in the nullification of the new as a thing unintelligible until reduced to the potentialities of the past.

This gift of free historical truth is the revelation and the covenant; its receptive appropriation and affirmation is the worship of the Lord of history and implies a conversion and liberation from all the inexorable determinisms which pure rationality in its demythologization, whether cosmological or anthropological, of the primitive pagan liturgy cannot but construct. Calvin cogently observed that the mind is a factory of idols; left to its own "devices", it is rather a forger of chains. Nor is this paradox; the irrevocability of the covenantal commitment, whose freedom is immune to all relativization by the circumstance and fatality of a fallen world, rests upon nothing but the providential, covenantal, and redemptive dominion of God over our history which is his creation. This dominion is the mission of the Lord of history, of the Word made flesh, by whose One Sacrifice for his people, his bridal Church, the covenant is actual. Marriage thus viewed is nothing other than the liturgical appropriation of this historical Wisdom, this covenantal Providence, which is to say, of the covenant itself, the very form of history, that by which history is good. Sacramental marriage is therefore the very sign and effective or constitutive symbol of the good creation whose goodness is the historical truth and freedom of the New Covenant, given and received in the worship of the Lord of history, and only there.

Marriage as the sacramental sign of the New Covenant thus flatly contradicts the pagan pessimism, the pagan liturgy, the pagan view of the world, whether ancient or contemporary. Sartre somewhere observes that hell is other people: the pagan liturgy knew this before any sophisticate ever thought of existentialism. The pagan liturgy requires in and by all of its multitudinous symbolic forms that the covenantal freedom which Christian marriage affirms and appropriates be continually suppressed in favor of the faceless anonymous mimeticism of the we-saying community. Only in that community's conformist flight from free and personal responsibility is society seen to be secure from all the hazards, incalculable because unpredictable, and from all the risks and terrors of an uncovenanted free history—and paganism knows no other history, for the pagan gods, whether primitive, gnostic, or secular, have no historical reality and cannot be worshipped in covenantal freedom.

The flight which all pagan worship requires from the chaos indissociable from the randomness and incalculability which the supposed arbitrariness of free personal responsibility is thought to connote is therefore also a flight from personal responsibility in and for history; it is by that fact a flight as well from historical significance and from personal significance, and so is an a priori refusal of the covenantal dignity and responsibility which sacramental marriage attributes to all historical existence.

As all paganism finds history finally irredeemable, so also is found to be the man-woman relation, the universal symbol of that pagan melancholic consciousness, of its despair and its servitude to idols of its own manufacture. Wherever found, paganism is characterized by and finds indispensable to cosmic security the denial of the dignity, the significance of one's concrete existence as this unique and quite irreplaceable man or woman, who can love and can be loved only because and as unique, as historically significant because incapable of assimilation to or by any other.

In the Platonic and Neoplatonic philosophical tradition which has so deeply colored the patristic theology, this pessimism with regard to individual personal existence finds expression as misogyny, a distrust and fear of spontaneous feminine resistance to all the rational, masculine, ideal formalities, whose security is their character as absolute, as unrelated to any non-ideal, non-rational, non-masculine reality; the logic of this pagan heritage prevented Origen and Augustine from seeing in the tri-relationality of the marital covenant any image of the Triune God....

When the medieval Christian theologies began to exploit systematically this pagan wisdom, this melancholy historical consciousness, it became apparent that there the structure of reality, of existence in space and time, is experienced as given over to rational necessity, whether the necessity be stated in the binary logic of mathematics which for the followers of Augustine as of Plato provides the rationality of physical phenomena, or in the immanent structure of a material noumenal essence locked into the ideal necessary reasons discovered in the discursive analysis of its own intrinsic causality. These alternatives still dominate the contemporary theological discussion; insofar as unconverted to a free because covenantal rationality, modern theologians still seek for the necessary reasons underlying the reservation of orders to men, or seek in the resources of a contemporary phenomenology the rationalist criteria for judging that liturgical practice.

Such efforts are beside the point; within any theological community the liturgical symbolism which utters its consensus judges and cannot be judged; wherever such symbolism is encountered, it represents within a community of worship the most fundamental understanding of the actual human condition, and to submit its truth to any supposedly higher criterion of truth is to enter upon the appropriation of that higher truth and, therefore, upon conversion to another and superior religious symbolism.

This, as I believe, is the point at which we now stand, as we have indeed stood since the Reformation. The only real issue [before] us is whether the Mass is the One Sacrifice of Christ, represented sacramentally and really by a bishop or a priest under a bishop's authority, acting *in persona Christi*—for in no other *persona* can the One Sacrifice be offered. So offered, it is the dynamic unity of history, the Event which joins the Old Covenant to the New, which links the Jesus of history and the Christ of faith; this sacrifice, this nexus, this free historical actuality of the good creation, is the nuptial union of the second Adam and the second Eve, the One Flesh of the "holy society by which we belong to God".

Within the Roman Catholic tradition, that society is marital; it is at one with the Sacrifice of the Eucharistic celebration, in which the Bridegroom gives himself totally to and for his bridal Church in the freedom of his mission from the Father, and receives from his immaculate Bride that which is indispensable to the New Covenant, all that she, in her created and covenantal and immaculately free dignity, has to give: the nuptial Body of which he, by her self-giving, her "sacrifice of praise", is the nuptial Head.

In this marital union, the Head is represented sacramentally by the bishop or by the priest who assists him; only thus does the one acting in the person of Christ represent the Body, the Church, the Bride. That this representation is not to be subsumed to sociopolitical categories concerned finally with the quantitative distribution of power should be self-evident; the priestly representation of the Head is marital and covenantal, one which not only cannot exclude but in fact invokes the personally and irreducibly distinct representation of the Church by the laity, a representation which as covenantal, as responsibly responsive to that of the Head, cannot be servile or submissive; at the same time, it is irreducible to that of the Head, and so cannot be supposed to imply the capacity of the Body to represent the Head: this would be to identify irreducibly distinct authorities.

We have seen that this episcopal responsibility, as covenantal, at once affirms and requires the liturgical significance of masculinity and femininity in the free covenantal mutuality which we have here briefly examined. To say only this much is to leave much unresolved; most particularly in this present context it leaves unexamined the nature of the authority of women in the Church. That their authority in the Church is analogous to their authority in marriage is axiomatic; their authority is then that of the Body, which is distinct from but not less than that of the Head.

Even when the theological ground is thus cleared for the examination of the meaning of this feminine authority, by an insistence that the covenant is the criterion of all Church authority, it remains extraordinarily difficult to free one's inquiry of the overburden of the cosmological and monist image of authority as power. When so misunderstood, the bishop's authority immediately becomes unqualified, and any limits upon it are quantitative, the result of a mere political and therefore arbitrary distribution of power. The impression is then inescapable that the entirety of ecclesial authority is realized in a quasi-monarchic and despotic episcopacy, whose power insofar as it is reserved to the bishops is denied to and oppressive of the laity: to underwrite such a situation with marital and covenantal imagery then becomes derisive. But the cosmological imagination provides no more than a parody and a caricature of reality; it cannot serve a theological purpose, and our reliance upon it has in fact stultified the entire contemporary discussion of the place of women in the Church and equally has blocked an adequate theological understanding of episcopal authority in the Church.

Someone[1] has observed that it has not pleased God to make his people safe by dialectic, which we may understand to mean, by theology. The basis of our freedom, our responsibility, and our concretely historical existence is liturgical and Eucharistic: it is this that sustains the freedom of Church and society, the dignity of men and women, and all authority in the Church. There is no other recourse; to seek one nonetheless is precisely to abandon the questioning which is theology, and which is integral to the faith. Theology must continue to seek and continually to discover in the Eucharist the firm foundation which no dialectic can provide, and without which sustenance it must degenerate into an ideology finally contemptuous of history.

---

[1] In the copy of the article kept in his electronic files, Keefe identified the line as coming from St. Ambrose, *De Fide* 1.5.42: "Sed non in dialectica complacuit Deo salvum facere populum suum."

10

THE SACRAMENTAL ORDER
OF THE MORAL LIFE

In 1993, Pope John Paul II issued *Veritatis splendor*, one of the most significant of his encyclical letters. Its subject is Catholic moral teaching, and yet what strikes the reader at the outset is its stated audience. For going back to Pope John XXIII's *Mater et Magistra*, the practice had been to address letters dealing with ethical questions, since they are human questions, not only to the Catholic faithful but "to all men and women of good will". Yet *Veritatis splendor* addressed neither all humanity, nor all the faithful, nor even all the clergy, but exclusively the bishops of the Catholic Church. It was a letter from the premier teacher to his fellow teachers, the members of the episcopal magisterium. And its concern was radical. Within the Church herself, and among the ranks of her own theologians, Catholic teaching was facing resistance. What was more, it was "no longer a matter of limited and occasional dissent, but of an overall and systematic calling into question of traditional moral doctrine" (*Veritatis splendor*, 4).

There could be little doubt that the "dissent" to which the pope referred centered on Pope Paul VI's letter *Humanae vitae* and its condemnation of contraception twenty-five years before. It may also be that the charge by its critics that in basing its teaching on the natural law—which had been a principal category of Catholic moral teaching for nearly a thousand years—*Humanae vitae* had chosen to argue from reason, accounts for why John Paul structured his own letter as a commentary on Scripture; though Paul VI had been careful to specify that his teaching was "founded on the natural law, enriched and illuminated by divine revelation" (*Humanae vitae*, 4).

If it was common among moral theologians to criticize *Humanae vitae* for having relied upon a natural law argument, nevertheless it was precisely on the basis of the natural law that many concluded its teaching was not authoritative, not binding, or simply false. Then as now, the natural law was widely taken by moral theologians to be an inherently secular category, and the bishops as a whole, and the bishop of Rome in particular, were thought to provide no greater insight into its content than any other persons of experience and reflection. After all, it was said, the natural law is the law of human nature, meaning human reason, and its precepts are the formulation of reason. That is why it not only pertains to all humanity, but its precepts, at least in principle, can be agreed upon by any individual or group, in any place or time. The natural law has need of no special revelation, and so the custodians of revelation, the bishops, have no special authority concerning it.

What really was at issue, then, was the distance that separated two very different understandings of the natural law. The view that predominated in the university and seminary classrooms of Europe had been developed in the midst of the devastation brought on by World War II, with its attendant moral crises and cultural upheavals and social fragmentation. Deep-seated divisions, including religious, were a luxury of the past; ecumenism, always a desideratum, was now a necessity. And Catholic theologians saw ecumenical potential in the natural law. Their Protestant colleagues spoke of the believer being guided moment by moment in the lived, concrete situation by the inspiring presence of the Holy Spirit. The natural law provided a distinctively Catholic parallel, for it, too, spoke of the individual being guided in the concrete situation—by the operation of reason, specifically practical reason, reason as concerned with action. Further, with its appeal to reason and its focus on the dignity of the person, the natural law offered ground for collaboration with non-Christians, even atheists, bridging political divides in a common effort to build a social union that avoided the reductive, collectivist ideologies of the right and left.

So far as these theologians were concerned, however, it was not the doctrine of the natural law of one or two or three centuries prior that could be of any help. That doctrine was a mockery of what was to be found in Aquinas, having no sense of the historicity of morality—meaning the importance of circumstance to moral action—but rather treating morality as it if were nothing more than the deduction of necessary conclusions from unchanging principles, based on an abstract notion of human nature, even to the point of regarding the brute structure of the body to be normative for a person's behavior. In every respect, this past approach subordinated the free person to an unfree, impersonal facticity.

For these writers—Louis Janssens in Belgium, Peter Knaeur in Germany, Josef Fuchs also from Germany but teaching in Rome, and others—the moral agent was first and foremost a decision-maker. Since morality is a matter of promoting one's own humanity and the humanity of others, in each situation one's primary responsibility is to determine which, among all the considered possibilities, is the act that is most likely to advance, or at the very least avoid injuring, the human values involved: values such as well-being, friendship, knowledge, and, most basic of all, life. The difficulty is that more often than not, these values conflict. The value of telling the truth might in this particular instance put at risk the well-being of someone fleeing persecution. Hence the importance of prudence, a virtue that played a prominent role in the thought of Aquinas where it referred to the quality that shapes the perception and judgment required to apply general principles to a specific state of affairs. In this new approach, however, the function of prudence was to guide the process of weighing values and disvalues that precedes a determinate act. The fundamental question for Aquinas was always, "What should I do, given that I may never directly harm a human good?" Here the question became, "What action, on balance, is going to achieve the greatest proportion of human value to disvalue? Because that is what I should do."

The method was called proportionalism, and to the minds of its proponents it was the most realistic way to address moral problems. It was the most objective, because it based decisions on what was actually encountered and not on some purist ideal. Like the tradition, it gave special authority to one's conscience, which the tradition had referred to as the proximate or immediate norm of morality. But then it went far beyond the tradition, giving defining authority to conscience. Human goods like health and knowledge and life may be values, but they become *moral* goods, objects of duty, when conscience, which is prudence in action, determines that these are the values, here and now, that one is obliged to protect. It is one's decision that makes an action binding. The approach was the most realistic, too, because among the considerations that were to enter into one's proportional calculus was the practicality of an act. In a perfect world, one could be called upon to endure all manner of hardship rather than injure a human value. But ours is a broken world, and we are broken agents within it. Hence, it is the proper operation of one's conscience to issue a dictate that acknowledges one's very real limitations. In one instance or another, one might very well imagine having chosen different, perhaps more laudable, conduct; there may often be reason for regret, Fuchs wrote. But that is different from a feeling of repentance. Repentance is appropriate only when the person deliberately violates what conscience has determined is the correct course of action, including in view of what is personally, emotionally feasible for the individual acting. Morality has its standards, but one can hardly expect heroics.

A further consideration for writers like the German theologian Bernard Häring was that true unrighteousness, and so mortal sinfulness, has to be regarded as a core orientation of the person, the result of a "fundamental option", something running much deeper than conscious, surface choices. The roots of the moral life extend into a region not easily apprehended by the agent himself; certainly no external action will ordinarily be the occasion, or even the expression, of what is essentially a self-defining aversion from God.

For the proportionalist, then, there can be no such thing as a prescriptive norm that is formulated apart from a particular situation; and so no such thing as a universally binding norm, that is, a rule governing human action everywhere and always. What is universal in an injunction like "Do not murder" is the acknowledged value of human life. So far as its content goes, what it actually is saying is "Do not kill unjustly", meaning, one may never kill without justification, without the weighing of values and disvalues. One might specify a norm to the point that it might seem no unbiased calculation could possibly justify it—say, the torturing of children. Still, no conclusion can be simply presupposed, and so none can provide the basis for an absolute, a priori prohibition. What follows as a matter of course is that there is no such thing as an act that is always wrong because it is wrong in itself. Pope Paul VI's claim to the contrary in section fourteen of *Humanae vitae*, where he spoke of actions that are "intrinsically disgraceful" (*intrinsece inhonestum*), drew fierce criticism. Nevertheless, John Paul II not only repeated the claim in *Veritatis splendor*, he maintained that in a tradition extending back to the letters of Saint Paul, the Church has taught that there are actions that, speaking even more bluntly, are "intrinsically evil" (*intrinsece malum*) and, therefore, can never be performed, no matter what the reason (*Veritatis splendor*, 80–81).

The emphasis in proportionalism on one's moral assessment of possible choices was not meant to foster individualism; it was always understood that the person both exists in a particular cultural setting and is a product of that setting. The result, however, was to remove even further the possibility of any critical vantage point from which behavior could be evaluated. Every society, for example, has established some form of marriage, of settled, public, sexual union, thereby recognizing—and encouraging its members to recognize—the value of social stability, of complementary social roles, of offspring, etc. Perhaps there is an ideal pattern of marriage that best promotes these human values. But for the proportionalist, what is morally relevant is the fact that the particular form (or forms) of marriage practiced in a given society is the product of that society's effort, in its own way and under its own circumstances, to develop human value. Whether it be monogamy, polygamy, or polyandry, each is an equally valid pattern of marriage, and there is no legitimate basis upon which one form might in any concrete sense be said to be "superior" to another. By extension, there can be no ranking of how societies regard the sexes, assign sexual roles, rear their children, etc. Social and cultural practices are different, not better or worse. The irony is that in the hands of the proportionalists, the idea of a natural law and so of common moral ground, which had begun as a call to moral consensus, ended as an argument for reducing morality to cultural relativism and, so, for being reconciled to the absence of consensus.

It was ironic, too, that while scorning the version of the natural law to be found in the so-called manual tradition of Catholic theology (referring to the textbooks most often used in seminary training) with its putatively abstract conception of nature, many of the proportionalists nevertheless accepted one of the characteristic premises of that tradition in the two centuries or more before Vatican II, namely, that the life of grace is superadded to the human condition. Our nature, it was said, has its own order, serving as a substratum for the supernatural. So, again, if there is such a thing as an ideal pattern of marriage—and if there is, its structure would be inferred from reflection upon experience—that pattern obtains with or without the divine offer of grace and with or without our ordination to Christ. All morality is human morality. That is why faith, as central as it is to the Christian life, pertains only to one's intentionality, accounting for the "why" of a believer's action but not the "what". For just as there is no such thing as a morality unique to Christians, so Christian faith offers no unique insight into the content of morality. But how, then, do you avoid the question: What remains of moral theology?

It was Plato in *Gorgias* 483e who coined the phrase "law of nature", placing it in the mouth of Callicles when he challenges Socrates' assertion that it is more disgraceful to commit an injustice than to suffer injustice. It was an expression tinged with sarcasm, uniting as it does two conflicting ideas. Nature is the world as given. Law (*nomos*) meant custom or convention, the fabrication of humans. In the polis, says Callicles, the majority look to frame conventions that will restrain the action of their betters, who, as better, will always try to dominate them—and this according to nature's convention. For it is the law of nature, Callicles declares, governing both animals and all people and attested to by the gods, that the stronger rule the weaker; echoing here, nearly forty years later, the very words that had been spoken by the Athenians before they laid waste to the island of Melos.

When Saint Paul in Romans 2:14 spoke of law and nature, he may have been speaking of how Gentile Christians, although not having the law of Moses by nature, meaning birth, like their Jewish Christian brethren, yet fulfilled the precepts of the law; or he may have been saying that these Gentile Christians fulfilled the law by nature because the law was written on their hearts. In either case, the law he spoke of was the divinely revealed law; and by "nature" he meant one's native identity, which for the believer, Jew and Gentile, now reborn in Christ, means life filled by the Spirit of Christ (Rom 7:6). His remark, however, was taken by early Christian writers as validating the notion of a law of nature, although four hundred years after the *Gorgias*, the idea of natural law that most had in mind came from Roman Stoicism via the eclectic work of Cicero, whose thought went considerably beyond the injunction to follow the animals (though one would still find that definition as late as the Roman jurist, Ulpian, d. 228). True law, Cicero maintained, is right reason in conformity with nature, that is, with the order of the real. Its precepts and prohibitions are obeyed by the virtuous and ignored by the perverse; yet it is a single rule issued by one, divine author, known by all, eternal, unchanging, universal. It does not vary from city to city, from Rome to Athens, nor can the statute of any city supersede its authority. To disobey this law is in fact to flee oneself because it is to reject one's human nature (*Republic* 3.33; *Laws* 1.24–25). And an example of this flight from self would be the aggression lauded by Callicles.

Read, then, through the lens of Stoicism, Saint Paul was seen as teaching that what the people of Israel had received from Moses, the Gentiles knew through reason; further, that this law of reason, the natural law, is the means whereby God directs each person in every generation to himself. Natural law, in other words, became a theological concept. As early as the second century, we find Justin Martyr writing in the language of Greek Stoicism that the human mind operates through a given share in what he terms the "spermatic word" (*logos spermatikos*), meaning the intellectual seed, scattered through humanity, by the light of which we are able, some more clearly than others, to perceive what is true. But Christians love and worship the Word himself, the Truth, of which each knowing mind is a kind of imitation, who became man in order to heal us of our suffering and whom the believer imitates by participation in him, through grace (*Second Apology* 13).

Aquinas opens his discussion of natural law in the *Summa theologiae* (1–2, q. 91, a. 2) by describing it as a participation in God's eternal law and describing the light of reason, whereby we know and apply the principles of morality, as an impression on us of the divine light, quoting the line from Psalm 4:6: "Lift up the light of your countenance upon us, O Lord!" Our share in that light diminished following the alienation of sin, but it remained, as did the corresponding inclination, the prompting, of our nature to the full range of ends (Aquinas calls them *bona*, "goods") in which human flourishing consists, chief among them being dedication to God. And continuous, too, before sin and after, was God's revelation of how our flourishing would ultimately be perfected—by his dedication to us (*Summa theologiae*, 2–2, q. 2, a. 7). For Aquinas, the law of our nature, the law of Moses, and the law of Christ are part of a single, still-unfolding, providential plan effected by divine action and human choice.

Competing with reason are the biases and desires that erupted after sin (of which the proportionalists are so keenly aware and which is how Aquinas accounts for the contradiction between Cicero and Callicles), rising at times to become the norm of an entire community.

Even apart from the pull of egoism, however, an inequity now exists between human minds, so that not everyone actually knows what in principle anyone should know about the moral good. There are those who are simply better able to think fully and accurately about the meaning of an action. Hence Aquinas speaks of the wise, who occupy the place of moral instructors (*Summa theologiae* 1–2, q. 100, a. 1). Some of the precepts that Aquinas considers to be most important require this fuller thinking, principal among them being the precept of marriage's indissolubility. It is a dictate of reason, he argues, that follows from the good of offspring and the human inclination to form a permanent bond in friendship (*Summa contra gentiles* 3.124). One cannot help but think, though, that other considerations fuller or deeper than these are required, if only because in point of fact, no other community ever concluded to the indissolubility of this union but the Christian.

From the outset of *Veritatis splendor*, Pope John Paul makes clear his intention that the natural law once more be understood as belonging to the history of the covenant, citing in the letter's opening lines the same verse from Psalm 4 as Aquinas. Of even greater moment, he underscores the point that our nature was the foundation of human morality even before the covenant, meaning before the promise that followed upon sin. The standard of moral action, he states, is our nature as it has been "from the beginning" (*Veritatis splendor* 22). The phrase is taken from Matthew 19:8. The occasion was the effort by some Pharisees to draw Jesus into the rabbinical debate over the circumstances under which the law allows a husband to dismiss his wife and marry another. His answer was to quote the first book of the law, Genesis. God made humanity male and female, and for this reason he declared that a man is to leave his father and mother, cling to his wife, and become with her one flesh. "What", Jesus concluded, "therefore God has joined together, let no man put asunder." When the Pharisees asked why the law would speak of certificates of divorce (Deut 24:1–3) if no divorce should be permitted, he replied that this was a concession Moses made in view of human obduracy; "but from the beginning it was not so."

The meaning of the person had not changed, the meaning of a man and woman uniting in marriage had not changed. The perception of that meaning, the comprehension of the searchings in our nature, the readiness to make a gift of oneself when what was sought has been found, these things had changed because of sin; thus the incompleteness of what Moses could teach on the plains of Moab. But, John Paul writes, "Christ is the 'Beginning'" (*Veritatis splendor* 53). He is the root meaning of our nature, whose life is the perfection of our nature, the life to which each of us is called. The only teaching he can possibly give is the teaching that is true to his identity: for one to leave one's spouse and marry another is to commit adultery (cf. Mk 10:11–12; 1 Cor 7:10–11). It is by virtue of the light of faith, having the eyes of faith, that the indissolubility of marriage belongs to practical reason as its own conclusion rather than as a directive having no other basis than external authority. In the same way, it is with the eyes of faith that reason sees the intrinsic connection between the self-transcendence of the person and life, and that the final purpose of life is its transformation in Christ. For John Paul, the body itself, as a personal reality, is expressive of the person. He talks of the body's "spousal meaning" (*Veritatis splendor* 15), referring to how marriage uniquely displays the capacity of the human person to speak a word and create an enduring union that can be the source of another life; but more, how the body in its sexual difference, male and female, signifies the dynamic union of the incarnate Christ, drawing humanity to be one body with him (Eph 5:31–32).

These, of course, were points that Pope John Paul had been making since the famous Wednesday audiences he delivered between 1979 and 1984, which he regarded as simply a development of the argument proposed by Pope Paul VI in *Humanae vitae*. Pope Paul, too, had maintained that the dynamism of our nature toward life, and so toward fulfillment in Christ, is reflected in the body's sexual distinction. Which is why the criticism that his teaching was erroneously "biologistic" or "physicalistic", deriving moral precepts from a purely material description, was so mistaken. Finally, to say that intention plays a pivotal role in morality, so that no one can be culpably immoral who seeks to do what he considers to be morally right, although true as far as it goes, is nevertheless not to have said enough. There is the act itself, having its own structure, its own meaning. And there is even further distraction from the act when the intention of the agent is focused on the results of an act or the values it will effect. Such a "teleological" approach, John Paul writes, stressing the agent's end (Greek *telos*) or reason for acting, such as utilitarianism, whose regulative principle is that one should always act to produce the greatest amount of happiness for the greatest number of people, or consequentialism, to use the term coined by Elizabeth Anscombe in her famous article "Modern Moral Philosophy" (1958), where the standard is the achievement of the best consequences, misplaces the moral norm. It cannot be the subject's intention, the consequences that are projected to result from an act, or the values preferred by an individual or the behavior that predominates in a community—the data of empirical science. Life is the one norm of human action; life as it was, and is, in "the Beginning" (*Veritatis splendor* 112).

For Keefe, the appearance of *Veritatis splendor* was absolutely groundbreaking. For the first time the moral norm, because human, was said to be Christological and, because Christological, to be Eucharistic. Christ is the immanent principle of life and of history—of time, that is, that is more than time, endowed with the unity of history in virtue of its being handed over by the Son as a gift to the Father. To be human is to be a living sign of the dynamism of this offering, received by the Father, effected in Christ; and the event that constitutes the leading edge of this ongoing dynamism, of offering made and offering received, is the Eucharist. There is, then, no more vitally human activity than that of participation in the Eucharistic liturgy. It is, for Keefe, the source and summit of the moral life. And as the Eucharist constitutes the gift and the fruit of the gift by the Son who has bound himself unqualifiedly to human life and to the human condition, so the one norm adequate to our sacramental nature is an equivalently absolute commitment to life and life's goods.

All of this was developed at length by Keefe in a commentary that he finished in January 1995. Too long to appear in any journal unedited, an abbreviated version, in Italian, came out the next year as two separate articles, "La *Veritatis splendor* e il fondamento eucaristico della morale" in *Rivista di Teologia Morale* 110 (1996), pages 209–20, and "La legge naturale da ripensare alla luce della *"Veritatis splendor"* in *Rivista di Teologia Morale* 111 (1996), pages 391–402. What follows is excerpted from his original, unpublished essay, entitled *"Veritatis Splendor* and the Eucharistic Foundation of Morality".

Nature: The Sacramental Norm of Morality

It is commonly recognized that the recent encyclical of Pope John Paul II on Catholic morality and moral theology, *Veritatis Splendor*, is a reaffirmation of the natural law, the traditional norm of Catholic moral doctrine. From this point onward, little agreement exists. The reasons are many and complex.

Those who may be expected to uphold the doctrine of *Veritatis Splendor*, i.e., the moralists who defend the natural law tradition, are divided among themselves on the crucial point of the source or foundation of the natural law itself, which is to say, they do not agree on the meaning and reality of human nature. This internecine disagreement is too various and too complex to permit summary; it has at any rate become increasingly arcane.

Regardless of their disagreement over the meaning of nature, and thus over the foundation of the natural law, most traditional moralists have difficulty in accounting for the privileged insight into the natural law morality which the Catholic Magisterium asserts, since in any of its disputed interpretations, "nature" appears to have no particular relation to historical Catholicism, and this by reason of its very universality.

The upshot is that many avowedly Catholic moralists now rely upon the universality of human nature and of natural law, whether as empirical, ideal, or metaphysical, to deny or question the teaching authority of the Church in matters of morals; to this theoretical dissent they summon the further authority of church historians who would put in issue the factual existence of any magisterial proclamation *de fide* of moral doctrine. This dissenting stance at once frees their theological speculation of the need to account for—and to—a Catholic moral Magisterium, whether in theory or in practice. Some of these theologians assign the ordinary Magisterium no more authority than

From Donald J. Keefe, S.J., "*Veritatis Splendor* and the Eucharistic Foundation of Morality", unpublished essay.

attaches to any more or less probable theological opinion; others suppose the magisterial function to be dependent for its content upon the consensus of the theological academy and, thus, to be subject to an academic veto.

In the absence of any agreement as to the foundation of natural law, which is to say, any agreement on the intelligible content, the meaning, of the "nature" upon which the Catholic natural law tradition relies, the moral consensus which travels as the natural law tradition exists today rather as a moral praxis and a doctrinal consensus than as a rational synthesis in the sense of a broadly accepted ethical theory or moral theology. The evident disarray among the defenders of the natural law can only diminish their ability to uphold the salient moral affirmations of the Church's teaching authority, namely, (1) the inherent moral significance of historical human acts, and (2) the existence of concretely historical negative moral norms of universal application. It is particularly the teaching authority of the Church which has affirmed these truths, and the deprecation of that authority is particularly associated with the deprecation of these affirmations.

The consequence is that those moralists who attack the natural law have all too easy a task. Over the past two decades and more in which the natural law tradition has been effectively challenged within the Catholic theological academy, its opponents first achieved respectability, and then dominance. Insofar as they accept the notion of human nature as the ground of morality, they suppose its content to be that which the positive sciences reveal to be universally given in human societies. This dependence upon pragmatic criteria for the "natural" evacuates human nature of any permanent moral significance, any intrinsic dignity which might be profaned. It is easy enough to show that the Ten Commandments are honored largely in the breach. The decade-old dispute over "naturalness" in sexuality is illustrative of the theological uses of nature *qua* empirical; another illustration immediately at hand is the now common notion that a sacramental marriage, *ratum et consummatum*, may evanesce, may die and cease to exist in the sense that a subsequent marriage is valid: the underlying assumption is that our human condition *qua* "natural" simply does not warrant the supposition that we have the moral capacity to utter ourselves irrevocably in history. The implication, little pursued by the dissenting moralists, is that since we have no word to give, no inner truth to utter, neither do we have any dignity which might be affronted;

certainly, positive research into the human condition is hard put to defend the inherent dignity of the human person.

The triumph of such dissent to the Catholic tradition, and particularly to the historical objectivity of the Catholic tradition of sacramental realism, is reflected in the now commonplace moral relativism which afflicts the Catholic Church and, increasingly, the rest of the world. For, if only by default, the Church has come to represent the single serious defender of the moral culture which once civilized the Western world and which, as debilitated, is now failing to civilize the postmodern world. . . .

The regnant turn to moral relativism is the major target of *Veritatis Splendor*'s condemnation of the dissociation of truth from freedom, for by that dissociation moral relativism lives. However, it is worthy of note that the encyclical's restatement of the natural law tradition against its opponents does not take up or resume or resolve the debate over nature, now of thirty years' standing, whether as internecine or as between the natural law moralists and their opponents, the proportionalists, consequentialists, and situationalists.

More explicitly, *Veritatis Splendor* simply transcends the contemporary scholastic debate between the relativists in their several guises and the defenders of the natural law tradition. The dissenting moral theology has been put out of court by this document, and this for reasons which undermine as well much of the theology (not the doctrine) which has been summoned to the explanation, and lately to the defense, of the natural law tradition.

John Paul II has made obsolete the moral speculation, pro and con, over "nature" by insisting upon a historical-sacramental view of the "natural" foundation for Catholic morality which the moral theologians, whether orthodox or dissenting, have for practical purposes ignored. The pope treats "nature" neither as the product of a metaphysical analysis nor as an empirical datum nor as a timeless ideal. "Human nature" in *Veritatis Splendor* is the primordially good creation, the free nuptial unity of man and woman which "in the beginning" is deathless, integral, and unfallen, which fell in Adam, which is redeemed in Christ, and which, in union with him as the second Adam, the Head, is raised to the right hand of the Father.

This forthrightly historical, theological, and sacramental understanding of human nature, together with the theological *munus* consequent upon it, has deprived the dissenting moral theologians of their common subject matter, which is, at bottom, a nonhistorical and nontheological view of what nature is and, inevitably, a non-theological and abstract understanding of morality. All that debate over nonsacramental "nature", whether as empirically given, as ideally conceived, or as the subject of metaphysical analysis in the non-historical terms of form-matter, substance-accident by the Thomist schools, is now irrelevant. If the Catholic inquiry into the foundation and the legitimacy of the Catholic moral tradition of natural law is to be resumed, it must now bear upon the reality of human nature as restated by the pope, that is, as assimilated to the sacramental realism of the Church's worship, now understood as normative for the intelligibility of the human *telos* and so for the inherent moral significance of human existence in history. Moral theology and sacramental theology now have the same subject: the sacramental objectivity of human existence in history, in Christ.

This papal doctrine is a return to the morality of the Old Testament and the New. It inculcates a covenantal morality, normed by the Covenant itself: radically, the One Flesh of Christ and his Church.

It is or should be evident that only the integrally good human nature can ground morality. In our fallen brokenness, that is, in our fallen unfreedom, the integrity belonging to our nature is not manifest, nor can it be made so by taking thought, by diligent inquiry into the pragmatics of the human condition, [or] by any of those soteriological devices for social control which human cleverness may contrive. All of these approaches to establishing a criteriology for moral existence conclude by dismissing its very possibility, for they one and all presuppose a necessary world in which historical freedom and the exercise of personal responsibility [are] unintelligible and so [are] reduced to simple randomness and irrationality.

In brief, such methods of ethical inquiry merely normalize the fallenness of the good creation into sin and death. In so doing, they each must reconstitute the ancient problematic of the pagan soteriology, in which the enigmatic tension between our personal and our communal existence finds its resolution only in an unconditioned flight from personal existence, and so in a flight from the exercise of personal responsibility in history. Only thus, by the programmatic abolition of every historical expression of the unique human person, is personal suffering to be exorcised.

Nonetheless, despite the universality of the suffering personal consciousness of the self, original sin did not undo the good creation; the integrity of that creation, i.e., its wholeness or holiness, is objectively given in the world. This is the Catholic faith, the presupposition of Catholic morality. The integrity of human nature, which is the object of the divine creation by the Father's sending of the Son to give the *Spiritus Creator*, is restored in each of us by baptism, is strengthened by Confirmation, is sustained by Communion, is affirmed in Marriage, is restored in Reconciliation/Penance, is healed in Anointing, and in Orders is enabled to approach the Holy of Holies to offer *in persona Christi* the One Sacrifice by which we are redeemed and by whose Eucharistic immanence our history is freely, nuptially, ordered to salvation, to the Kingdom of God.

This historical nature is nuptially ordered from its creation in Christ "in the beginning"; its free historical and public expression is the unity of the One Flesh of Christ and his Church, imaged in the marriage covenant. This is the ground of morality as Catholic, as historical, as free. One cannot too strongly insist that the natural law is fulfilled in the free exercise of our covenantal responsibility, which is always a nuptially ordered responsibility within a nuptially ordered history of salvation. This nuptial order of history is the *ex opere operato* effect of the Eucharistic immanence of Christ our Lord, who transcends history, exercising his Lordship over it, precisely and solely by that immanence within it—*per modum substantiae* as St. Thomas said—in the sense that as risen, and as nonetheless historically and salvifically present in and to the world in the Eucharistic sacrifice, Christ is the Lord of history through an Event not subject to the temporal and spatial limitations of fallen time and space. Rather, he transcends and intrinsically unifies the spatial and temporal fragmentation of the "world", making its unity to be free, the covenantal history of salvation. This salvation is appropriated personally in a free, personal re-entry into personal responsibility, a responsibility effectively exercised and sustained in and by the signs and symbols of the Church's sacramental worship....

Moral theology has to do with creation and existence in Christ and must develop an anthropology which rests upon that postulate. The Pauline tradition has provided the vocabulary for this existence, this passage from fallenness to fulfillment *in Christo*; we can only suggest its exploitation here.

Basic to that existence in Christ is the Pauline and Johannine doctrine of creation in Christ. A dehistoricizing exegesis of John 1:14 has nearly removed this doctrine from the Catholic consciousness by

referring the "in the beginning was the Word" of the Johannine Prologue to a nonhistorical moment and a nonhuman Word. But this
reading is merely a Neoplatonizing, Thomist eisegesis; the hymn in
the Prologue, like the comparably ancient hymn in Phil. 2:5–12, is a
liturgical, not a Thomist statement.

Our humanity, freely created to be free in Christ, is fallen from that
integral freedom from "the beginning": there is no moment in our
temporal universe and no point in its spatial extension that is not fallen.
The historical condition of universal fallenness, which is equivalent
to the subjection of the universe to servitude, suffering, and death (cf.
Rom. 7:14—8:25) is in the New Testament commonly termed "flesh"
(*sarx*). The sole remedy for this fallenness, that by which it is redeemed,
is the reintegration of the fragmentation and futility of the "flesh" into
the One Flesh of the New Covenant, instituted on the Cross. Paul,
followed by the entire Augustinian tradition, has identified the New
Covenant with the nuptial relation of Christ the Head and his Body,
the Church, which is their free union in One Flesh (*sárka mían*, Eph.
5:23–32; cf. Eph. 2:15–16, *kainòn ánthropon ... en henì sómati*). But
the reintegration and redemption of *sarx* by its incorporation into the
Body which is the bridal Church, and thus into the union of Christ
the Head with the Church, his Body and his glory in One Flesh, is
given through the outpouring of the Holy Spirit by which the Church
is constituted as the sacrament of the Kingdom of God and by which
all those for whom Christ died are freed to enter into her sacramental
reality by baptism, and so into her full Eucharistic communion.

To enter into the Church and, through her Eucharistic worship, into
full union with the risen Christ is to live in the Spirit, the source of all
life in the Church and the principle of our filial relation in Christ to the
Father. But this historical existence *in Christo, in ecclesia*, this *mia sarx*,
looks to fulfillment in the Kingdom of God: that is, it looks to a fullness
which in history is manifest only obscurely, however objectively, in the
sacramental signs of the Church's worship. For in fallen history, Christ's
glory, the Church, is veiled, as Christ himself, the Glory of the Father,
was veiled on the Cross and is veiled in the Eucharist.

As the One Flesh of the Eucharistic sacrifice is the fulfillment, the
recreation in sacrament, of our *sarx*, so the *mia sarx* of the historical
union of Christ and his Church is fulfilled in the full gift of the *Spiritus Creator*, the *pneuma* or eternal life which we possess only in the

Resurrection of the flesh. Christ, our Head, is by his Resurrection made to be a "life-giving spirit" (1 Cor. 15:45); this term connotes not immateriality but his final triumph, as Head, over sin and death. His triumph is also the triumph of his Church—where the Head is, so also is the Body. This is the significance of Our Lady's Assumption, for as also the second Eve, she is the antetype of the Church.

Thus the remedy for our fallenness is historical: it finds expression in the free unity of *sarx, mia sarx, pneuma*. It is the tragedy of much of contemporary moral theology that the historicity of our fallenness, of our "flesh", is ignored, rationalized out of existence, in such wise as to make *sarx* itself to be "nature" and thus to be the criterion of our humanity, of our morality, whether *sarx* be understood empirically, as open to statistical analysis, or ideally, as a concept defining the human condition as such, or "metaphysically", in terms of necessary intrinsic causes. These devices can only consider our fallenness as in dissociation from all that could make it meaningful: its redemption in Christ, its eternal destiny. Similarly, they must make morality nonhistorical: a mere conformity to some unfree pattern of existence, which can know nothing of personal responsibility.

It is only in their free and redemptive association, in their free covenantal unity, that *sarx, mia sarx,* and *pneuma* provide the free and moral intelligibility of historical existence in Christ. This free association is given only in the worship of the Church, in which our *sarx* is baptized into the *mia sarx* of Christ and the Church, and by that baptismal entry into the Church's Eucharistic worship we receive the "medicine of immortality", "that we should not die".

This is the criterion of human existence in salvation history. There is no other free, responsible existence than this, which is in Christ. To seek a moral ground elsewhere is to enter once again into one or another of those rationalizing and dehistoricizing programs for the abolition of man, of whose disastrous consequences this century has seen so much, yet which Catholic scholarship seems ever willing once again to endorse.

It must never be lost sight of that the New Covenant by which we are redeemed, the one flesh of Christ and his Church, is a historical reality only as Eucharistically represented, as redemptively transcending, *in sacramento*, the brokenness of the fallen spatio-temporality of our universe. Were it not thus Eucharistically represented, it would recede ever more into the past, to become ever more inaccessible, ever more merely a fading memory, obscured by the conditioning of a time unredeemed and consequently opaque to the risen Christ, finally forgotten. The Cross of Christ could not then be salvific except as merely eschatological. It would have no historical efficacy because it would lack all historical mediation.

But that supposition would eliminate history as intrinsically intelligible. It would suppose time itself to be demonic, antagonistic to man, standing between us and our salvation. That pessimism with respect to historical existence implies the dualist and finally pagan world of personal irresponsibility. All evil is there accounted for as the fatal implication of temporality itself, and all salvation must be by way of a flight from history, rather than as mediated by history. The theological dehistoricization of the natural law is only a modality of this flight.

Both *sarx* and *mia sarx*, that is, flesh in need of redemption and the One Flesh by which we are redeemed, are then historical, in the free relation by which our redemption is free. But their unity is as yet incomplete. It looks to that eternal life which is the full gift of the Spirit, poured out upon the Church by Christ's One Sacrifice.

The sacramental understanding of human nature, taught in John Paul's *Veritatis Splendor*, has never been given any serious consideration by the Catholic moral-theological community, and of course it has been ignored entirely by the non-Catholic moralists who reject Catholic sacramental realism a priori, simply as a matter of theological method. However, the Catholic neglect, insofar as moral theology is concerned, of the very sustenance of historical existence in Christ is now concluded. Henceforth moral theology *qua* Catholic coincides with sacramental theology. Morality as freely responsible historical existence must now be seen to be liturgical existence, Eucharistic existence. In the concrete, morality is covenantal existence in Christ—existence as baptized, as nuptially ordered, as Eucharistically sustained, and therefore as free, as historical, for only the free is historical, is moral. . . .

The basic postulate of *Veritatis Splendor* is that as historical we are freed by Christ and are free in Christ, whose presence to us is Eucharistic simply. The universality which attaches to the moral law is precisely its Catholicity, its sacramentality, its salvific historicity—in sum, its covenantal quality; for the Covenant, the good creation, and the

Eucharistic *Una Caro* are the same, the single terminus of the Father's sending of the Son to give the Spirit.

Over the centuries since the death of St. Thomas, traditional Catholic moral theology had come to accept a highly rationalistic and non-historical view of the natural law and so of morality itself. In the hands of theologians who claim the authority of St. Thomas, the notion of natural law has been "naturalized", worked out in terms of intrinsic logical/metaphysical necessity, whether as the rational implication of timeless moral principles or the rational implication of abstract human nature understood as the resultant of necessary intrinsic causes: matter-form, substance-accident. In such analyses, "natural law" has lost its immediate application to history, not by reason of the moral doctrine of St. Thomas himself but rather by reason of the rationalist exploitation of those inadequately converted remnants of Aristotelianism which haunt the metaphysical analysis that is also his bequest to the Thomistic schools of moral theology. At bottom, it is the nonhistorical and deterministic metaphysical analyses left over from an inadequate conversion of Aristotelianism which have reduced the Thomistic understanding of human nature to the product of its intrinsic and necessary causes. These deterministic matter-form, substance-accident analyses of material substance underlie the difficulties in which Catholic moral theology is now enmired.

Nonetheless, the moral tradition which intends to rely upon St. Thomas, in its discussion of *phronesis*—meaning moral prudence, the particular virtue of the practical judgment, the virtue by which the universally valid moral norm is applied to the concrete act—has not much adverted to what St. Thomas thought obvious, the Christological foundation of that virtue, of that moral judgment and moral existence. It is further obvious that for him, as for the tradition of which he is the reliable mediator, our access to that moral foundation, the risen Christ, is sacramental and finally Eucharistic. But this is little noticed.

It is in consequence of this forgetfulness that avowed followers of St. Thomas have found themselves forced by their own logic to reduce morality to conformity. Whether applied to nature understood simply as the moral law or understood as the metaphysical cause of our acts as substance to accident, this moral rationalism cannot avoid an identification of morality with obedience to nature as the cause of morality, whether taken to be a necessity of thought in such wise that sin is finally irrational, a mistake and not a moral fault—for no realm of free, moral responsibility remains to a nature thus conceived—or taken to be an intrinsically necessary cause of intrinsically necessitated conduct.

The unsatisfactory devices which over four centuries were excogitated by Jesuit and Dominican theologians to defeat this internecine Thomist riddle are the subject of the famous debate *de auxiliis*.[1] It is long since time to admit that the problem these theologians faced was the product of a dehistoricization of the moral life, that it had no historical existence, that thus it has no theological solution, and that its dehistoricizing presuppositions should now be dropped. Moral freedom is *ex nihilo* and so can have no prior necessity; it is irreducible to "necessary reasons". The historical exercise of divine omnipotence is the Father's sending of the Son to give the Spirit. This has nothing to do with the nonhistorical dilemma of abstract divine omnipotence versus abstract human freedom with which that dispute was concerned. We live in a covenantal creation, not in the adversarial relation to God which that baroque Thomistic rationalism supposed.

A single illustration of the necessity for the reform of moral theology on sacramental grounds should suffice. When it is supposed that such a deed as we have addressed, say that of "the termination of a pregnancy", has in the first place no verifiable intrinsic moral intelligibility, no public moral significance for good or evil of its own, and when it is further supposed that only the impossible identification of such a putatively meaningless act with the abstract definition of killing the innocent could justify its condemnation as a kind of murder, then clearly one must look outside the act itself—to its consequences and its circumstances—if one is to judge its moral standing.

It is precisely this squaring, by *phronesis*, of the concrete deed with the abstract moral norm which, from the Thomistic viewpoint of Karl

---

[1] The reference here is to the, at times acrimonious, dispute between the followers of two Spanish theologians, the Dominican Thomist, Domingo Báñez (d. 1604), and the Jesuit, Luis de Molina (d. 1600) over the difference between sufficient and efficacious grace. The latter, the so-called Molinists, argued that as matter of fact there is no difference—if one's will consents to the offer of grace and converts, then the grace is said to be efficacious; otherwise its offer must be said to have been sufficient for conversion, but not effective. The former maintained that they really are two distinct graces. Sufficient grace provides the impetus to conversion, which, admittedly, the will is free to refuse. However, as Augustine taught, God is able to persuade a will no matter how resistant; and this further, ultimately persuasive grace is called efficacious.

Rahner and his followers, lacks inherent justification. The abyss which the dehistoricizing matter-form, substance-act analysis of a rationalized Thomism established between the intrinsic meaninglessness imposed upon the concrete historical event in its moral uniqueness and the abstract-because-universal moral norm cannot be bridged by autonomous reason, even by the use of the practical or prudential reason, for there cannot be a logical or rational link between a concrete event which, because historical, is said to be a priori intrinsically unintelligible or meaningless and a moral criterion which, insofar as intelligible, is a priori abstract and nonhistorical.

In sum, the Thomist commonplace that one understands only by abstracting specific forms from the concrete things and events of historical experience, and thus that one knows such things only by subsuming them to such an abstract definition, to such an abstract criterion of truth, can have no place in Catholic morality. For really all that the proportionalist, consequentialist, or situationalist ethician is affirming is the epistemological impossibility of knowing a historical reality otherwise than by arbitrarily assigning it membership in an abstract class. This is the separation of truth from freedom which *Veritatis Splendor* condemns; it is far older than the contemporary moral "teleologism".

Fortunately, it is now no longer necessary to enter into a discussion of the speculative issues which have divided the defenders of the natural-law moral tradition. Those questions, like the dissenting, relativizing rationalizations of the human telos that are condemned in *Veritatis Splendor*, presuppose the nonhistorical, ideal, or abstract meaning of nature, whether as comprising eternal moral principles or as "second substance". For such abstract issues cannot arise within the concretely historical and liturgical context posited by the sacramental and historical objectivity of human nature which is henceforth foundational for moral theology.

Still less is it necessary to enter into debate with the moralists and ethicians who advocate a consequentialist, proportionalist, or situationalist approach to moral questions, for these dissenting theologies also are governed by similarly abstract and nonhistorical postulates. It is not surprising that they dismiss the historical Catholic moral tradition in favor of a relativistic morality. Their presuppositions permit nothing else.

John Paul II has converted moral theology from the futile pursuit of such nonhistorical inquiries to the radically theological examination of the moral freedom of historical, sacramental existence in Christ. Existence in Christ is intrinsically and substantially graced and, so graced, is thereby intrinsically significant, and significant precisely of salvation. This intrinsic significance, this nuptially ordered free unity or integrity, pervades our personal existence as such; it is our very dignity, inseparable from our creation to the image and likeness of God. Elsewhere, *per longum et latum*, the pope has insisted upon the nuptiality of that image; it is as nuptially ordered that our historical existence images the Triune God. The primordiality of that image has been the subject of John Paul II's exhortation from the beginning of his pontificate.

In sum, the doctrine set out in *Veritatis Splendor* makes quite irrelevant the contemporary disagreements among moralists, whether they are the merely internecine disputes between divergent approaches on the part of the moral theologians who defend the Church's interpretation of the natural law or the flat dissent to that natural law tradition on the part of moralists such as Bernard Häring. Henceforth, moral theology insofar as Catholic stands firmly upon a sacramental and Eucharistic foundation, and any discussion of natural law which does not rest upon that foundation is simply out of court insofar as the Catholic project in moral theology is concerned.

The effect of Thomism's methodological disinterest in the concreteness of historical existence is illustrated by the difficulty that Thomist theologians—defenders of Church teaching and dissenters alike—have in accounting for the most morally significant fact of our common humanity, its radical division into two sexes. The sexual determination by which historical masculinity is at once irreducibly different from and intrinsically ordered to femininity, and vice versa, is for Thomism systematically insignificant, unintelligible in the sense of incapable of being given a coherent account; thus it is of negligible metaphysical moment, comparable to such accidental and nugatory matters as color, weight, or height. Should sexuality be given metaphysical significance within the Thomistic act-potency analyses of substance, the division of humanity into two substances, male and female, is logically inescapable. The alternative and pagan view of the human condition, by which the sexual differentiation is without intrinsic significance, is defended by theologians rather more today than in the past, however unpersuasive it remains in practice.

In any event, within Catholicism, sexual differentiation and the marital union which freely integrates it have always been matter for liturgical celebration, which fact controls the metaphysical significance of sexuality for the purposes of Catholic moral theology. Yet more profoundly, the New Covenant is marital, as is its Eucharistic representation in history. Where this is forgotten or neglected, the awareness has been lost that covenantal morality is nuptially ordered and sacramentally sustained existence in Christ. The history of moral theology sadly details that loss.

The Autonomy of Conscience

It is obvious that each moral act is unique, an incommunicable exercise of personal responsibility, and thus that each moral act is highly idiosyncratic, irreducible to any abstract moral category or set of such moral categories. In a word, human conduct is mysterious, laden with a significance for good or evil which is manifest only to God. For ourselves, who live in enigma and obscurity, the positive or salvific significance of our actions is and can only be veiled: more precisely, its historical expression is sacramental. Thus, it is by the efficacy of the Church's worship that we freely appropriate the integral goodness of creation and, so, our human dignity, our historical significance, our eternal destiny. In sum, in that worship we appropriate our true humanity in consequence of the *Spiritus Creator* poured out upon the Church. This humanity is created in Christ, freely fallen in the first Adam, redeemed in the second Adam, raised in its Head to the right hand of the Father. There is no other humanity than this, of which the risen Christ is the Head. And there is no other freedom, [or] other morality, than that which we enter upon by [worshipping] in the Church which is his Body.

Therefore the Catholic moral-doctrinal tradition, which is radically Eucharistic, has insisted that moral deeds are in this sense historical: they are personally significant of a personal salvation and so are unique, unrepeatable, and irreducible to abstractions. Catholic morality is a free, personal conformity to Christ, not a flight from history to moral irresponsibility by way of an impersonal conformity to nonhistorical criteria of the moral and the good, for there are no such criteria. We are saved neither by our submergence into an impersonal nonhistorical mass of irresponsibly servile we-sayers, nor by assuming a solitary personal eminence and arrogating to ourselves the divine authority to make reality in our own image in the manner of Nietzsche's *Übermensch*. Our morality is historical and, therefore, is at once free and covenantal. It is only by our freedom, or moral imaging of the Triune God, that we, in our multiplicity, are freely one, a nuptially ordered covenantal community of personally responsible men and women. This community is not empirical and not ideal. It is sacramentally signed and radically is Eucharistic, the One Flesh of Christ and his Church.

When the concrete historical human act committed by a given person in the here and the now is recognized to be thus unique in its morally significant historical concreteness, its moral significance is clearly inherent or intrinsic to it in such wise as to be the appropriation or the rejection of the historical (because sacramentally objective) truth of human existence as salvific, as Eucharistically normed. It is manifest that the moral significance of the concrete human act, so understood as historical and sacramental, cannot be measured by its conformity to a nonhistorical criterion or to an abstract command or prohibition, for the density of its liturgically normed historical significance as salvific or damnific forbids every abstraction of the human act from history.

Yet at the same time, as subsumed to and normed by the symbols of the Church's sacramental worship, our actions have the historical universal significance that is their sacramentality. Morality then possesses the universality, not of some abstract criterion, but of the concrete Catholic liturgical symbols, which transcend, in the Eucharistic Lord, all space and all time, not as an idea or law or nature abstracted from the historical dynamics of the world, but as sacramentally immanent in history.

This must be understood, for the rationalizing and therefore relativist attack upon the natural law moral tradition is inescapably an attack upon sacramental realism. To be exact, it is a rationalistic disintegration of the free unity of sacramental history. Augustine's "*In Vetero, Novum latet; in Novo, Veterum patet*" ["In the Old (Testament) the New lies hidden; in the New the Old is revealed"][2] did no more than summarize the patristic tradition of the East as well as of the West.

---

[2] St. Augustine, *Questions on the Heptateuch* 2.73.

Yet this free unity of the Old and New Testaments cannot be shown to be a rational necessity. The New Testament is more than a logical deduction from the Old, and its focusing of the Old Testament upon the Christ is clearly not forced by a merely analytical reading of the Old Testament.

To worship personally in the Church is personally to enter into, to appropriate, this historical, sacramentally mediated salvation, whose universality is that of history itself, history as salvific. This worship is free appropriation of the free, moral universality of covenantal existence, of covenantal morality....

It is of course a commonplace that each of us has an autonomous moral conscience, an innate personal intuition of our own moral condition, as formed by our own assumption or avoidance of moral responsibility. The pope is eloquent upon the sovereignty of this conscience, from which all moral responsibility proceeds. This is not to be read, however, as a papal warranting of the rationalized autonomy of the individual conscience *qua* moral atom: for John Paul II, the individual conscience rests upon an inherent truth, not upon a moral freedom understood as transcendent to all responsibility other than to the self, as indifferent to a truth transcending that autonomy. Only when the conscience is understood as *Veritatis Splendor* understands it, as the intuitive or infused percept of moral truth, does the individual conscience ground moral life....

The methodology of the situationalist bars the existence in history of such a universal category, of such a moral species, as, for example, "adultery". In order to arrive at the logical universality of such a category, it is taken for granted that one must abstract it from the particularities and the dynamics of history and that, in doing so, one must also accept the consequent impossibility of its return to historical concreteness, which is to say, the impossibility of its rationally justifiable application to any concrete and particular historical deed.

As there are only nominal men, but no assuredly real ones in history, so also there are only nominal acts of adultery. Morality, like everything else in this relativist universe, is by extrinsic attribution merely: like the starry universe, it has no metaphysical standing.

Thus, as we encounter animals which more or less approximate the abstract form or definition (the "second substance") of, e.g., man, so also we encounter deeds which more or less approximate the abstract formality, the criteriological definition, of adultery. But in the end, there is no real conformity between the encountered man and the abstract definition, any more than there is between the encountered violation of a marriage and the abstract definition of adultery. Thus argues the relativizing moral dissent and, within the universe of discourse framed by its own postulates, no adequate reply to it is possible.

Although, like the rest of us, the proportionalist or situationalist admits the existence of evil in the world, unlike most of us, he is not persuaded that any given action can be known with certainty to be morally evil. When a man sleeps with a married woman not his wife, the relativizing moral theologian must scrutinize that deed in all its bewildering concatenation of circumstances, consequences, and motives before he may assess it in moral terms, and the more detailed his findings, the more hazardous the moral assessment in view. Any truly diligent inquiry into the morality of a given extrinsically normed deed can only defeat its own end: the data are finally unmanageable.

The relativist "new morality" thinks also to find support for its relativism in our inability to judge our neighbor. At the outset, any Catholic moralist knows that judging the personal moral condition of the perpetrator of such a deed is in fact simply forbidden us by Christ himself. The New Testament notoriously condemns the presumption of personal moral transcendence implicit in our judging the moral state of our neighbor. There is no moral device comparable to a criminal jury or to one's personal conscience with regard to one's own moral state by which we may pass upon the moral guilt or innocence of another person. Even the confessional waits upon the resolution of that issue by the individual concerned: the priest does not initiate the sacrament of penance, and his absolution is entirely conditioned by the penitent's sincerity.

The prohibition of our judging our neighbor hardly stands on relativist grounds, but the relativist nonetheless relies upon it to support his argument. If in fact one cannot synthesize the welter of empirical data, if one cannot reduce the complexus of circumstances and situations surrounding the particular act into an intelligible unity whose rational analysis could justify a definitive moral judgment upon it—as many, following Karl Rahner, now agree—we seem to be left with only the inner state of the alleged perpetrator upon which to base such a judgment. But apart from its comparable empirical unavailability to persuasive analysis, the reality of such an intra-personal ground has already been denied by the relativist, who cannot admit an inner moral state as criteriological without abandoning the extrinsicism which grounds his relativism.

Unable alike rationally to integrate the ambiguities which mark historical existence and to pass upon the conscience of the neighbor as moral agent, the relativizing moralist has by his recourse to an extrinsic moral norm melded these quite dissimilar incapacities—the former fictive, the latter real—into one.

In their merger, these twin postulates—the supposed ambiguity of history and the real inscrutability of the neighbor's conscience—underlie the relativist versions of Catholic morality which the pope has summarized and condemned as teleologism. In fact, their merger forces the practical abandonment of the Catholic sense of personal sin. When the person is accepted, quite properly, as morally inscrutable, and when his deeds are held, quite improperly, to be equally and inextricably immersed in the inscrutability of his historical person, there is no alternative; historical existence is intrinsically meaningless, and morality, now submitted to external criteria, becomes itself merely extrinsic. If it is to be common and not simply individualistic, morality must then be public, which is to say, political: subservience rather than free personal responsibility; which goes some way toward explaining why one hears more now of "social sin" than personal. . . .

Conscience as personal knowledge of the moral law, and personal assessment of one's own conduct in light of that knowledge, has become impossible with the denial of intrinsic moral significance to any concrete exercise of personal responsibility.

For, once this denial of intrinsic moral significance to human acts is in place, the only possible moral scrutiny which remains is that which is provided by whoever possesses "authority". Authority is now absolute, having barred all freedom, all personal dignity, from history. It has only a quantitative expression: it identifies with power, with a coercive *force majeure*, which replaces the moral criterion. The nomenklatura becomes the public conscience, the public will, and its propaganda, the "magisterium" of the idolatrous state, will prescribe the public decencies. . . .

Within the public arena or open forum, the problem of determining the moral quality of a personal free act always finds some manner of practical resolution, although the resolution found is not always one that is consonant with a free society. For example, in the case of the grosser public violations of the public decencies which are criminalized, whether as felonies or as misdemeanors, the gulf between the indictment and conviction or acquittal has traditionally been bridged in this country and in other common law jurisdictions by that curious survival, the common-law jury of one's peers.

The justification for such juries, as well as their practical usefulness, rests upon the existence of a free, responsible, and traditional public consensus upon the content of the public decencies, a consensus now increasingly difficult to verify and, where verified, increasingly difficult to defend. For that defense of the public decencies, traditionally "before the bar of reason", now confronts a "bar" whose "reason" is the autonomous rationality of the Enlightenment, which is willing to affirm as true only what is verified according to the canons of necessity, whether logical or practical. Increasingly, any concrete legislative determination of the public decencies (in the sense of the minimal moral demands of public life in a given free society) is constitutionally challenged on grounds of lacking a necessary connection with an established public policy. Such proof, such reduction of the moral common good to necessary reasons, is of course impossible: morality is the order of freedom, not necessity. One cannot, for example, show a necessary connection between pornography and crime. To show such a necessity would be to exculpate the offender....

Moral-Sacramental Theology

The sacramental emphasis of *Veritatis Splendor* is the consequence of the fallen historicity of our imaging of God. The integral freedom and nuptial unity of humanity was lost in the fall and is objectively available in history for our free appropriation only in the worship of the Church. To enter into this worship is to enter into the single history of the world, the history of salvation, which is so by its Eucharistic order.

Morality is then historicity. One is moral or immoral by the historical appropriation or refusal of historicity, under the Christian postulate that there is only one historicity, that of salvation in Christ, whose order is nuptial, covenantal, the order of the One Flesh of Christ and his Church. In brief, all our free acts, the "human acts" of classical moral theology, have either a sacramental or an antisacramental, demonic significance. There is no neutral ground, no nonhistorical realm of activity. We are unable to be morally insignificant. We are created in the image of God, and our whole purpose is to fulfill that image, which is public, not private. To paraphrase the fighter Joe Louis, we can run, but we can't hide.

It must follow that all moral prohibitions are liturgical. They proscribe the profanation of the inherent sacramental significance of human existence in history, that of the imaging of God.

This profanation can be active, meaning self-induced. We speak in that case of personal sin, whose gravity is measured by the depth of its lie, of its destruction. For sin is destructive *ex opere operato*; as morality is the liturgical appropriation of being, so sinfulness is its refusal, the personal appropriation of *nihil*. This choice is effective. Only in freedom can we appropriate our own reality, and if we turn from it, that choice cannot but be honored....

Our humanity can also be profaned passively, as when it receives the destructive and annihilating impact of an idolatrous symbolism, which can only deny the truth of the good creation, whose goodness is its nuptially ordered humanity, expressed in its nuptial symbolism. All profanation of the good creation is anti-nuptial; as this is the single order of free significance, of moral existence, so it is the single object of the idolatrous counter-symbolism....

Consequently the Church's moral exhortation should place particular emphasis, as does *Veritatis Splendor*, upon the Eucharistic grounding of all moral life and upon marriage, which transforms society by imparting to it its own free order, and most assuredly upon [the sacrament of] penance (reconciliation), by which we are enabled to return to the nuptial fidelity in which morality consists and which by sin we have broken.

Finally it should be stressed that the Church's understanding of moral freedom as nuptially ordered bars any suppression of the moral freedom of others in the name of morality, as though we lived in a zero-sum world in which one person's possession of freedom—and of the dignity, responsibility, and authority which are at one with it—were with a logical inevitability the diminution of the freedom of everyone else. Catholic freedom is covenantal, for freedom is moral only as covenantally, nuptially, ordered, as typically exercised in that turning away from self for the good of the spouse which is the very index of nuptial freedom and of nuptial morality—there is no other.... And covenantal freedom is Trinitarian: it is possessed in its fullness in the exercise of its marital symbolism, wherein the man, the woman, and the covenant they constitute by their free commitment to each other have each the full authority of the marriage, but have it in distinct ways, analogous to the distinct manners in which the Persons of the Trinity possess each the substantial fullness of the One Divinity.

Humanity, in its historical and sacramental existence, which is to say, in its use of freedom, is thus freely triune. This is the meaning of historical freedom, as it is of the dignity, responsibility, and authority which are intertwined with freedom.

This Catholic understanding of human beings as nuptially signed with the dignity of images of the Triune God from the moment of creation simply eliminates the ancient pagan dilemma of the human one and the human many. It is no longer possible to suppose that human unity, goodness, beauty, and truth are found in their fullness only in the lonely individual, who is then forced to compromise and give up some of this fullness if he would live in society. Neither can the fullness of our human reality be assigned simply to the community, in such wise that any person exercising personal authority as a member of society thereby is in rebellion. All that is the political puzzlement of paganism, the product of an identification of government with stasis, a permanent stand-off between authority and rebellion. It has nothing to do with Christianity.

Such considerations may seem to be remote from *Veritatis Splendor*, but the implications of that restatement of Catholic morality are inescapably political. They bear immediately upon the free society we form by our moral deeds. It is evident enough that at the end of this century, something is seriously wrong with the Western culture. Its secular symbols do not work, and never have. They have fed on a free moral consensus which they cannot sustain and which finally their own symbolism must be seen to contradict.

It is only when the civil institutions which frame and articulate our public existence are well understood to be secondary, to be the product of our freedom rather than the source of it, that we are free in the sense of needing no one's permission to assert and to maintain our full dignity, responsibility, authority, and freedom. Thus civil and legal institutions of this secondary kind, which are of the sort called constitutional, are predicated upon the existence in historical society of an authority and dignity greater than their own. They stand under the judgment which in the Anglo-American world is called the rule of law—which is to say, under an understanding of our rights and obligations which is constitutive for the freedom of our public community. [More, this rule of law stands under a still greater authority.]

This greater authority is of course God, but not God in general, not God as a sort of least-common-denominator divinity. It is only when God is freely present in history in the events of history that his authority is exercised historically and has historical consequences. In short, it is only the worship of the God of the Covenant that can underlie the rule of law which governs a free society, for only in that worship is freedom understood to be covenantal and history to be salvific....

Whenever we are deprived of our dignity, whenever our exercise of free responsibility for the future is without moral meaning or value of its own, insignificant until someone else shall have passed upon it, this occurs by our failure to make our own the Eucharistic ground of our dignity, our freedom, our moral responsibility. We are created in the nuptial image of God, the Eucharistic One Flesh, the truth of every marriage, and of every man and woman from their first moment of life. The message of *Veritatis Splendor* is perennial in the Church, ancient, and yet ever new. In the fallen history which, in Christ, continues to be the history of salvation, this message is never heard too late. Yet it is very late, for we must also take with a complete seriousness another perennial conviction of the Catholic faith: that we live in the last days.

DEATH AS WORSHIP

If death is not itself the greatest of mysteries, it is at least the moment in which, for each of us, all other mystery is included and concluded, for there the mystery of grace and the mystery of iniquity meet in the intersection which is the cross, the paradigm of Christian worship. It is the cross of Christ, the summation of his earthly life, which gives meaning to our own ending, as it is the resurrection from death which demands that we see our own dying as Christ saw his, as the deed by which each of us gives himself over to the hands of the Father in a total act of worship. And by this worship which is our death, our fallen humanity enters fully into the redemptive mission of the Son: As this mission is inseparable from the death of the Christ, so we cannot share in the new creation over which the risen Christ is Lord unless we share in the mission which culminates in the cross.

Briefly, the worship which is life in Christ requires that we die in Christ.

This dying should not be glossed over, as though for Christians death were merely a departure to a better world. Such an attitude trivializes humanity, making illusion of all the grief and suffering which death works in our lives and in the lives of those we love. Such a denial of the reality of death makes little of Christ's death for us, reducing it to some gnostic conjuring trick. When Paul, marveling at the redemption worked by Christ, cries out, "Death, where is thy sting?" he is speaking of the release from the burden of sin, that release which

This article, published in *Theology Digest* 21, no. 4 (Winter 1973): 334–41 (the text given here), was originally the last in a series of talks delivered by Keefe at Kenrick Seminary, St. Louis, Missouri, spring 1973. It was reprinted in *Studies in Formative Spirituality* 2, no. 2 (May 1981): 167–77 (with minor differences) and was also reprinted in Michael J. Taylor, S.J., ed., *The Sacraments: Readings in Contemporary Sacramental Theology* (Staten Island, N.Y.: Alba House, 1981).

is worked by the death of Christ; he is not at all to be read as implying that death is a negligible thing, little to be regarded or thought upon. From the First Epistle to the Thessalonians, in Romans, and in the Second Epistle to the Corinthians, to the Pastoral Epistles, Paul's theology is a continual pondering on that existence in Christ which dies with him that it may rise with him. We have no business denying the loss and the bitterness of death, for in dying we share in the reality of the death of Christ, and we are too near to the scene and the liturgy of Good Friday to think that death a little or an easy thing. Christ's sacrifice makes our own death meaningful and makes it possible for our death to be also our worship, our sacrifice; by no means does his cross remove our own: the opposite is true, for by entering into his death, our own dying has the value of worship, the worship of the cross.

In consequence, then, of the death of Christ, our life is given a focus, to become most powerful, most itself, at the point of its extinction in the negation and darkness of death. Here is more than paradox; it is the flat nonsense, at which the Sadducees mocked, and the Greeks on the Areopagus, with a disdain as articulate in their day as it remains in our own. For no more than could Jesus, no more than could his Apostle, can we give convincing reasons, convincing, that is, to the unbeliever, for finding a positive significance in our dying; the faith that finds in death more and other than the final absurdity is too basic to have any argumentation underlying it. It rests upon the Resurrection of Our Lord. If he is not risen, Saint Paul has told us, our faith is in vain. As his Resurrection is not the annulment of his death on the Cross but rather its validation, so our rising in him is not the nullification, the reduction to insignificance, of our own dying.

The Pilgrim Church

So then our death has value and meaning; so the Church of the martyrs has ever taught: Precious in the eyes of the Lord is the death of his saints, for in this do they most truly image him in whose image they are made. Such imaging of God is the very meaning of worship, and in seeking out this meaning we must remember that we do not know how to worship as we ought; there is no model of worship which we can construct by human inquiry and talent, by a misplaced reliance upon our own judgment of what is properly owing to God. That kind of worship is the domestication of God which Kierkegaard condemned in the last century, which Bonhoeffer has pilloried nearly in our own time, and which in the Book of the Apocalypse is castigated in unforgettable language as neither hot nor cold, a tepidity which nauseates the Christ who died for us. Rather, it is the self-donation of the martyr, the witness of the faith whose ultimate affirmation is his explicit entry into the death of Christ, that is the test-case of Christian worship, of Christian life. In our own day, this truth has been some little neglected by a new idiom, which prefers to speak, not of the Church militant, but rather of the pilgrim Church. This language, established in the Second Vatican Council, is intended to stress the viatory character of the Church and of the Church's institutions, an emphasis all too necessary for a generation which had come to suppose that the Latin language was constitutive for the Catholic faith. The viatory or pilgrim Church is not, however, in any tension with the Church militant: These understandings of the Church are both necessary, and neither need suppress the other. The pilgrim Church is the Church of martyrs for so long as her children shall wander in this desert which their sin has made of the world. In our own day, the notion of pilgrimage is devalued; we have heard too much of pilgrimages to this shrine or that to take seriously the hardships of the journey, and so the word conjures up a vision of pious jollity in a sedate and comfortable style. Applied to the Church, it can invoke precisely the mentality, too much at ease in our Father's house, which we have seen excoriated in the Apocalypse. To such a mentality, quite familiar to all of us, the equation of worship with death, the equation of Christian witness with martyrdom, comes as something of a shock. To the extent that we are shocked, we have forgotten that our journey toward the Kingdom is not through a green and pleasant land, but through a wilderness, even a howling wilderness, whose chaos and bitterness are as much within us as they are outside us; the desert is our very own, for we have made it out of the world which God made good.

This desert is so much our own that we can become accustomed to its climate; we can begin to find it possible to find here a full and pleasant life and can learn to silence the conscience which tells us that such an ambition is fraudulent, that we have here no lasting city,

that this night our lives may be required of us, who have made ourselves so comfortable. These are the temptations of affluence, of a
people who are not reminded by every feature of a harsh and painful
existence that we are a fallen race, which shall find no rest until it rests
in the City of God. It is hard for us, the rich, to remember who we
are; the poor know their world for what it is and can find in their own
destitution the apt symbol of the human condition. For we are all poor
in that strict sense of being totally unable to help ourselves or those we
love; we cannot, by taking thought, remove our death or theirs, and
in the face of that full stop to our reality, all the blandishments of this
world are ashes.

The Search for Significance

The fact of death is then that which summons us to recognize the
desert for what it is; the only question which then remains is that of
who we are, who must die. Does death reduce us to insignificance,
as every paganism has thought? Does it place on one single level of
futility the life-history of every human being who has ever existed?
Does it cancel out the dignity of each of us, so that it is a matter of
indifference what we do or think or say? Some philosophers, even
some theologians of despair, have thought as much, but those whom
men have held to be the wisest and the best have always refused the
full implications of such nihilisms; the poets, the seers, the prophets
have known better. On such hopes this dying race has been nourished
for millennia before Christ; deprived of all assurance, men have never
ceased to hope, in the very face of death. They have buried their
dead with care and some approximation to reverence; such graves,
such burial sites, are almost the first index of the humanity of their
occupants, and this valuation of the dead is nearly the first indica-
tion of some kind of cultus, some sort of worship, among the earliest human beings. Death and worship are given together very early
in human pre-history, and they remain together, for all the ability of
men to prove their own insignificance.

We may affirm with some confidence then that it is death which
calls us to worship, and this in a complex reaction: we are provoked by
it to consider the possibility of our futility and, generally, to reject this

possibility, for all its surface plausibility, as finally untrue; secondly, we are driven by death to consider the human need for something like redemption, for death simply should not be, yet it is. And this turns us to God, the author of life, in a quest for that value, that worth, which is at once ours and not ours, which is lost and yet belongs to us. This quest is worship, the seeking for the vindication of the worth of our humanity at the hands of God, who is its author. This worship is inseparable from the value of our individual lives: Apart from the faith which fuels this quest, there is nothing in any of us which is worth being loved and nothing capable of love. Nor without that faith is there anything in our world which is not blighted utterly. All positive valuation of it, in terms of truth and goodness and beauty, is reduced to illusion: supportable perhaps for a little time by those who can afford such luxuries, but without meaning in the end. For the poor man, the desert in which he wanders is absolute, apart from faith, and his destitution is without end, for without faith his world is loveless, valueless.

It is fortunate for us who are affluent and consequently forgetful of reality that we are all summoned to it, at least once in our lives, and more often, as our love for others may draw us closer to the poverty of our humanity. Death, ours or that of someone we love, is a destitution difficult to camouflage. If it is the death of someone whose life is intertwined with our own, so that the loss in some sense shakes our own foundations, we must either cease upon this dying to love the dead, or love them in a faith which then becomes more clear and explicit for being the correlate of love.

Those human bonds, forged of our baser metal, whether of family, of neighborhood, of race or nation, cannot resist the acid test of death. By it they are either brought to nothingness or are transmuted into the agape, the love of which Paul wrote in 1 Corinthians 13. This transmutation of our all-too-human loves into the stuff that outlasts time and death is at the same time our baptism, our entry into the redemptive death of Christ and, thus, into the Church which is his body. That body is risen and is still with us, and our worship is the celebration of this truth, this reality which we are given in the pledge of the Eucharist, the sustaining manna in this desert through which we live, in which we are to share in the salvific work of Christ. It is in the circumstances of death that our dependence upon this risen

life is brought home to us most clearly; this is obvious enough, and
the familiar deathbed conversion accounts are eloquent testimony that
then at least we are forced to acknowledge who we are and how total
is our dependence.

But even so, the proportion of instances in which one has an oppor-
tunity for such reflection is small, given the enormous range of human
history and pre-history; even in our own century, the indiscriminate
carnage of two major wars and half a hundred minor ones has littered
the earth with tens of millions whose death looks remarkably unlike
prayer; what have these to do with the thanksgiving which is Christian
worship? What has the love of God to do with the slaughter of the
battle of the Somme in 1916, with the shambles at Caporetto or Loos
or the Argonne? The story of the Angel of Mons stales somewhat at
Verdun, where somewhere between a million and a half and three
million men lost their lives over a year and a half—and these are only
the battle casualties, in which notions of self-sacrifice and courage can
lend some semblance of meaning to death. But what of such plagues as
swept over Europe in the late Middle Ages, destroying whole towns,
and wiping out a third of the entire population of Christendom? What
of the mindless lottery that leaves some fifty thousand dead on our
highways every year?—And so on, and so on. Death, on the aver-
age, has little concern for the niceties, with preparation and penitence:
Now, as ever, we know not the day nor the hour. How then can death
be worship? How, apart from pious imaginings, can it mean anything
at all, even in the life of a saint? Augustine died in bed at seventy-five;
Robert Southwell was drawn and quartered some years short of thirty:
How can their deaths be compared in the single notion of worship?
Some answer must be made if it is death as such which is worship and
not simply the life, long or short, which preceded it.

Quite clearly, no human person's death, taken in itself, is a matter
of any particular importance, as the individual himself is not. Nature
intends what is permanent, so the Philosopher said, and individuals,
being highly impermanent, have no significance which touches any
cosmic concern. Life goes on whether or not we share in it, and the
teeming millions who are here today will be gone tomorrow without detriment to a world which indeed needs people, but not, so it
appears, any particular people; all of us are eminently replaceable.
But so to look upon the human situation is in fact to hate it; it is to

wish the annulment of the human, to want to reduce the individual man to a thing, neither just nor sinner, but a mere cog in a vast and implacable machine.

Sin and Servitude

We have seen that the redemptive work of Christ has revealed the falsity of such a nihilism; we are each significant and freed from cosmic necessities, free for the heights of sanctity as for the depths of malice by the freedom of the Spirit: by this Spirit, we are freed to love each other or to hate each other, and this freedom was purchased at a great price. It is not possible, in this brief compass, to deal with the primal tragedy of the Fall of man: it is enough to say here that in the primordial moment of the creation of men in their freedom, a creation possible only by the presence of the Christ in his creation, the gift of freedom was refused, and the creation fell with the men upon whom it is focused to an unfree level of what we have called cosmic servitude; men became subject to the physical laws of the material universe instead of being free in that universe, and these cosmic laws are fundamentally inimical to life: The wage of sin is death.

The original sin of the refusal of freedom was not the undoing of creation, but it made the presence of Christ, in the world which is created in him, to be re-creative of the fallen world, rather than simply creative of it. We have no justification for entering into speculation of what an unfallen world would have been like; what we do know is that the world is created in Christ and that this is also the creation of man in freedom. This freedom has been refused, but not wholly, for it is still offered by the presence of Christ in the world of men—but the offer by Christ of the Spirit which he was sent by the Father to give is also his redemptive life and, more especially, his redemptive death. By that death, his humanity is freed of this cosmos: death has no more power over him, and since it is in him that we are created continually, so also death has no final power over us. This is true, as Karl Barth has recently insisted, as Origen insisted eighteen centuries ago, whether we like it or not; to be at all is to be in Christ; the damned are no less dependent upon the Christ than the elect. Whatever our relation to God, whether it be that of a pilgrim in search of the Kingdom, that of the saint who has attained it, or the damned who has rejected it, we have that relation in Christ, without whom we are nothing at all. This relationship of ourselves to God is fundamentally our creation in Christ, a creation which is radically complete in the presence of Christ in our world: that is, in his life, his Passion, his death, and in the eucharistic worship of the Church, by which he is present, in his risen humanity, to the end of the world, for he has not left us orphans. He is risen, and still with us.

Death and Eucharist

It is the intimate relation between the worship which is the Eucharist and the worship which is our death that we must begin to understand. Perhaps the best model or exemplar of what this relation is may be derived from the notion of the inseparability of Christ's presence in this world and his mission or "sending" by the Father, a notion which pervades the Epistle to the Hebrews. Christ's presence here, his reality, is to do the will of the Father; for this he was sent into the world. This is the meaning of his humanity, and consequently it is the meaning of all humanity, and it is this meaning, this humanity, this obedience to the will of the Father, which we celebrate in the worship, the eucharistic worship of the Church. That obedience led Christ to a criminal's death on a cross; in that death, he affirmed his own reality, his divinity and his humanity, to be that of the Son of God who is also the Son of Man, the First Adam and the Last, the Alpha and the Omega. In his Resurrection, that affirmation, made in the abandonment and the bitterness of his last hours, was vindicated, and the Fall, which had hidden and brought to death the humanity which is created in him and which he handed over totally to the Father in his death, is overcome in his Resurrection by the Father as the final meaning, the full accomplishment, of his sending of the Son to do his will. It was necessary, as Saint Luke records, that the Christ should die; if not, the mission of the Son by the Father, which is the full creation of the world and of humanity, is not fulfilled, and it must be fulfilled.

But it is not fulfilled by any overpowering by the omnipotence of God of our humanity, of our freedom; for our obedience must be in freedom, or it is not obedience, and our creation in the freedom of Christ, the freedom of the Sons of God, would be impossible. Further, the very purpose of the mission of the Son, which is to give the spirit of sonship, of obedience, of freedom, of life, would not be accomplished, but it is accomplished by the divine omnipotence which is not competitive with our freedom but precisely is creative of it.

This Holy Spirit, by which we say "Abba, Father" is the gift to us of our humanity, our freedom, our sonship, our obedience: by this gift we are created, by it we live. And finally, by this gift we are enabled to understand the revelation of Christ; a hearing ear is given us, and we come to see who we are, what it is to be human, what it is to be free, and what is the worship which is the meaning of our life. Our freedom is understood, dimly, hesitantly, as in a glass darkly, to consist in that lifting up of our minds and hearts to God by which, over few years or many, we are unchained from our necessities to the point that in the encounter with the last necessity of death we are free indeed. And this is gift; it is not earned, not by an Augustine, not by a Southwell, not by any of the myriad millions who have inhabited the earth, not by any of the sons of Adam or the daughters of Eve. Nor is the gift to this one or that; it is to the Church. It is the creation of the body of Christ and of the history in which that body grows to the full maturity of the Christ, its head. This growth is hidden; we cannot judge or pass upon it. Rather, in it, our use of the gift is judged. This growth is universal; as Christ died for all men, so all men die in him. But this growth is not automatic, as some incautious ecumenists would suppose and as the several advocates of theories of predestination have believed, for it is worship, personal and free; it can be refused. Our human inability to judge the worship of others, to pass upon their sanctity, does not mean that there is no judgment; as we are created in Christ, so we are judged by him. This judgment is as much a part of his obedience to the Father as any other aspect of his mission. We, who can have no peace until we rest in him, can refuse that rest. His judgment is respectful of our choice, for it is left to each of us to reply on our own responsibility to the only important question, "What think you of Christ?" As we answer, so we are.

For those who die in the distraction of disease or war or the work of the world, who die suddenly in whatever way, death is still the ultimate dispossession of all the baggage which constitutes our poverty while masking it and which all too often has played no part in our worship, so that it impedes rather than enriches our freedom. We are dispossessed as well of all the burden of age, illness, and the like; we stand, in short, outside the cosmic necessities which prevent all of us now from saying decisively, definitively, personally, and with a total assurance, precisely who we are. This standing outside the cosmos is the meaning of death. We are separated, not from bodiliness as such, but from the body which binds us to this fallen world. And in the freedom thus given us in death, we utter ourselves to God.

In that utterance, we know ourselves even as we are known. A life has prepared for this moment, whether the life be long or short, but the preparation is not the utterance, for only in death is one substantially accountable for oneself beyond all possibility of error, with a total clarity of decision which is decisive utterly. This decision is the moment of mystery: Only Christianity has dared assert so enormous a human freedom and dignity before the majesty of God. The decision is either a total unconditioned love of God in Christ or a total aversion; no hesitation or compromise is possible. If our decision is worship, then our vision of the Christ seated at the right hand of the Father is our purgatory and our beatitude; if, as with Milton's fallen angel, we refuse that worship, we stand condemned before the Son of man, whose judgment of us is precisely the truth we have uttered of ourselves: as we know him, so we have him.

With these considerations, my treatment of this theme is ended; it is not of course complete, for the meaning of death raises questions which not even a lifetime of study can measure. What I have said, I have of course said as a private theologian, speaking responsibly, I trust, but with no more authority than attaches to the reasoning I have employed—which in a brief sketch cannot but be scanty. In concluding, let me read a few lines from the First Epistle to the Corinthians, which you have all heard many times, and which it is well to hear again:

If there is no resurrection of the dead, then Christ has not been raised; if Christ has not been raised, then our preaching is in vain and your faith is in vain. We are even found to be misrepresenting God, because we testified of God that he raised Christ, whom he did not raise if it is true that the dead are not raised. For if the dead are not raised, then Christ has not been raised. If Christ has not been raised, your faith is futile and you are still in your sins. Then those also who have fallen asleep in Christ have perished. If for this life only we have hoped in Christ, we are of all men most to be pitied.

But in fact Christ has been raised from the dead, the first fruits of those who have fallen asleep. For as by a man came death, by a man has come also the resurrection of the dead. For as in Adam all die, so also in Christ shall all be made alive. But each in his own order: Christ the first fruits, then at his coming those who belong to Christ. Then comes the end, when he delivers the kingdom to God the Father after destroying every rule and every authority and power. For he must reign until he has put all his enemies under his feet. The last enemy to be destroyed is death.

The eucharistic complement of this passage in 1 Corinthians is taken from the sixth chapter of the Gospel according to John:

I am the bread of life; he who comes to me shall never hunger, and he who believes in me shall never thirst. But I said to you that you have seen me and yet do not believe. All that the Father gives me will come to me; and him who comes to me I will not cast out. For I have come down from heaven, not to do my own will, but the will of him who sent me; and this is the will of him who sent me, that I should lose nothing of all that he has given me, but raise it up at the last day. For this is the will of my Father, that every one who sees the Son and believes in him should have eternal life; and I will raise him up at the last day.

Taken together, these lines from Paul and from the Johannine Gospel provide some basis for the assertion that our life and our death are inseparable from our eucharistic worship in the Church, and that only by entering into the mystery of his death can we enter into the fullness of his life.

GENERAL INDEX

SCRIPTURE INDEX